DISCOURSE ANALYSIS OF BIBLICAL LITERATURE

THE SOCIETY OF BIBLICAL LITERATURE
SEMEIA STUDIES
Edward L. Greenstein, Editor

DISCOURSE ANALYSIS OF BIBLICAL LITERATURE
What It Is and What It Offers

edited by
Walter R. Bodine

Scholars Press
Atlanta, Georgia

DISCOURSE ANALYSIS OF BIBLICAL LITERATURE

Library of Congress Cataloging in Publication Data

Discourse analysis of biblical literature : what it is and what it offers / edited by Walter R. Bodine.
p. cm. — (The Society of Biblical Literature Semeia studies)
Essays delivered orally at the 1988 annual meeting of the Society of Biblical Literature to the Linguistics and Biblical Hebrew unit.
Includes bibliographical references and indexes.
ISBN 0-7885-0010-4 (alk. paper). — ISBN 0-7885-0011-2 (pbk. : alk. paper)
1. Bible. O. T. —Language, style—Congresses. 2. Hebrew language—Discourse analysis—Congresses. I. Bodine, Walter Ray. II. Society of Biblical Literature. Meeting (1988) III. Series: Semeia studies.
BS1184.D57 1994
220.6'6—dc20 94-27542
CIP

Printed in the United States of America
on acid-free paper

Table of Contents

C. Grammar

PREFACE

In committing themselves to the study of texts, linguists have taken a long stride in a literary direction. As discourse analysts bring the tools of linguistic analysis to bear on stretches of material larger than the sentence, they come into close contact with the artistry of literature. In the last third of this century, scholars of the Hebrew Bible are gravitating in the same direction. Perhaps even more consciously, they are studying their texts as literature. Cross-pollination between these two groups is now in order. The present volume is intended to help that happen. It originates with biblical scholars and is addressed to our colleagues. Its purpose is to introduce to them the developing field of linguistics known as discourse analysis.

In addition to students of the Hebrew Bible, those who study ancient Near Eastern literatures, the New Testament, and early Jewish writings should find the following essays immediately relevant. Students of literatures from other times and areas should also be able to benefit because of the pervasive emphasis on methodology.

All of the essays included here were delivered orally at the 1988 annual meeting of the Society of Biblical Literature to the Linguistics and Biblical Hebrew unit. They have been revised in 1992 for publication with the exception of the chapter by Tova Meltzer, who was unable to carry out revision because of her move to China.

An introduction explores the potential value of the work of discourse linguists for those who study the Hebrew Bible.

The two essays that examine texts from a discourse perspective illustrate such study in the case of a longer stretch of text and a short section. Robert Longacre, emeritus professor at the University of Texas at Arlington, distinguishes the genre of instruction from other discourse genres and discusses the role of the Hebrew verb at the discourse level in Exod 25:1–30:10. David Carr, of the Methodist Theological School in Ohio, investigates the purpose of Isa 40:1–11 and its relation to the rest of Second Isaiah.

The following three essays examine and elaborate several current approaches to discourse analysis. Randall Buth, of the United Bible Societies, basing himself on a function approach, shows how several discourse phenomena can illumine aspects of Hebrew and Aramaic syntax. Kirk Lowery, of Pécel, Hungary, explores several approaches to discourse analysis in order to argue for the priority of a grammatical approach and to set forth a proposal for a discourse grammar of Biblical Hebrew. Tova Meltzer, now of the Institute for the History of Ancient Civilizations in Changchun, shows how intimately bound together are our perceptions of style and text.

The concluding two essays illustrate a discourse approach to syntactic phenomena of Biblical Hebrew. Cynthia Miller, of North Carolina State University, examines the syntax of direct and indirect speech and suggests a new analysis of the function of לאמר. Douglas Gropp, of the Catholic University of America, shows the necessity of a discourse model for refining the traditional characterizations of the Hebrew infinitive construct with two prefixed prepositions.

The bibliography and the indexing of authors included in the bibliography were prepared by Lowery during a busy time of moving his family from Austria to Hungary.

Several people deserve thanks for their part in helping this volume along its way to publication. Robert Culley and Edward Greenstein have been important people in the process. Professor Culley attended the Society of Biblical Literature sessions of the 1988 annual meeting when these papers were delivered orally and encouraged me to submit them for publication. Professor Greenstein has been a catalyst to the SBL unit and to this volume, both since their respective inceptions. His editorial work has considerably enhanced every essay that follows. I thank Julie Atwood, Belinda Breitling, John DeAcutis, and Jmel Wilson for volunteer typing help. Finally, I must mention Robert Longacre's encouragement to me in my work, both in the preparation of this collection and in my exploration of linguistics generally. For his pioneering work in the field that is the focus of this publication, all of us who aspire to a better grasp of the dynamics of discourse are in his debt.

Walter Bodine

ABBREVIATIONS

AAL	*Afroasiatic Linguistics*
AB	Anchor Bible
AnBib	Analecta Biblica
AOAT	Alter Orient und Altes Testament
ATD	Das Alte Testament Deutsch
BALLC	*Bulletin of the Association for Literary and Linguistic Computing*
BETL	Bibliotheca ephemeridum theologicarum lovaniensium
BEvT	Beiträge zur evangelischen Theologie
Bib	*Biblica*
BiOr	*Bibliotheca Orientalis*
BJRL	*Bulletin of the John Rylands Library*, Library of Manchester
BK	*Bibel und Kirche*
BN	*Biblische Notizen*
BT	*Bible Translator*
BZ	*Biblische Zeitschrift*
BZAW	Beiheft zur *ZAW*
ConBOT	Coniectanea Biblica, Old Testament Series
ConNT	Coniectanea neotestamentica
CTR	*Criswell Theological Review*
GKC	*Gesenius' Hebrew Grammar*, ed. E. Kautzsch, trans. A. E. Cowley (1910)
HS	*Hebrew Studies*
HSS	Harvard Semitic Studies
IB	*Interpreter's Bible*
IJSL	*International Journal of the Sociology of Language*
Int	*Interpretation*
JAAR	*Journal of the American Academy of Religion*
JANES	*Journal of the Ancient Near Eastern Society*
JBL	*Journal of Biblical Literature*
JL	*Journal of Linguistics*
JLS	*Journal of Literary Semantics*
JNES	*Journal of Near Eastern Studies*
JP	*Journal of Pragmatics*
JSOT	*Journal for the Study of the Old Testament*
JSOTSup	*JSOT* Supplement
LB	*Linguistica Biblica*

LBer	*Linguistische Berichte*
NTr	*Notes on Translation*
OBO	Orbis biblicus et orientalis
OPTAT	Occasional Papers in Translation and Textlinguistics
Or	*Orientalia*
OTL	Old Testament Library
OTS	*Oudtestamentische Studiën*
PTMS	Pittsburgh Theological Monograph Series
RivB	*Rivista biblica*
SBLMS	Society of Biblical Literature Monograph Series
SBLSP	Society of Biblical Literature Seminar Papers
SILPL	Summer Institute of Linguistics Publications in Linguistics
TZ	*Theologische Zeitschrift*
UF	*Ugarit-Forschungen*
VT	*Vetus Testamentum*
VTSup	*VT* Supplement
WBC	Word Biblical Commentary
ZAW	*Zeitschrift für die alttestamentliche Wissenschaft*

INTRODUCTION

DISCOURSE ANALYSIS OF BIBLICAL LITERATURE: WHAT IT IS AND WHAT IT OFFERS

Walter R. Bodine

ABSTRACT

Discourse analysis is a relative newcomer to general linguistics. The focus of the field is on blocks of material that are larger than the sentence. In North America until the latter half of this century, the purview of linguists was limited to the sentence. Now that this limitation has been relaxed, linguists are asking questions that are distinctively theirs of larger stretches of spoken and written material. While European linguists were never bound to the sentence, they are now on the forefront of developing theory and methodology of discourse analysis, or, as they call it, text linguistics (also written textlinguistics).

While a holistic approach to texts has always characterized literary criticism, the same has not been true for biblical scholarship throughout most of the modern period. In Hebrew Bible studies the earliest dominant methodologies tended in the opposite direction, toward breaking texts down into their smallest parts. There is now a growing interest among Hebrew Bible scholars in the shape of their literature as it stands. The work of linguists generally and of discourse analysts in particular offers new ways of examining the Hebrew text.

The Rise of Discourse Analysis

Within the field of general linguistics, discourse analysis is a relatively new discipline. It may be surprising to biblical scholars to know that from the beginning of modern, general linguistics until fairly recently, linguists have regarded the sentence as the largest unit for linguistic analysis. This was implicit in the work of de Saussure,[1] which is often regarded as the starting point of modern, general linguistics. It was quite clear in Bloomfield, the paradigmatic North American descriptive linguist, who wrote that "each sentence is an independent linguistic form, not included by virtue of any grammatical construction in any larger linguistic form" (170). Even with the fundamental new departures of the Chomskyan revolution (inaugurated by Chomsky, 1957 and set upon a broad base in Chomsky, 1965), the sentence as the largest unit of analysis was not changed.[2]

A shift among linguists to analysis of units beyond the sentence has not taken place without a struggle. It is significant that as early as 1964 Katz and Fodor, in their interaction with Chomsky and in their effort to construct a theory that would deal adequately with semantics, found it necessary to address the question of the nature of discourse. Their position was that a discourse can be regarded ultimately as a single sentence (Katz & Fodor: 490–91). This view has been defended more recently by Dascal and Margalit in an attempt to deny the need of text grammars and argue for the adequacy of sentence grammars when they include a pragmatic component.[3] More persuasive has been the view of a discourse, or a text,[4] as a sequence of sentences.[5] Yet the

---

[1] Cf. his discussion of whether the sentence belongs to language (*langue*) or speaking (*parole*) and, consequently, whether it can be considered the concrete unit of language. No larger potential units are mentioned (de Saussure: 106–24).

[2] Enkvist has written that ". . . of all grammars, the generative-transformational ones have been the most sentence-centered. S was their input symbol, and the sentence was their ceiling; in their classic forms, they were incapable of describing anything above and beyond the sentence" (260).

This has been true in Chomsky from the earliest phase: ". . . I will consider a language to be a set (finite or infinite) of sentences . . ." (1957:13), through the so-called, and in many ways definitive, Standard Theory: "A fully adequate grammar must assign to each of an infinite range of sentences a structural description indicating how this sentence is understood by the ideal speaker-hearer" (1965:4–5), up to his theory of Government and Binding: "The basic elements we consider are sentences . . ."; "The language is the set of sentences that are described by the grammar" (1980:143, 220).

[3] Cf. in response to this view Szabó:435–36, de Beaugrande:119–22, and Ballmer: 183–84.

[4] "Text" and "discourse" will be used interchangeably here, though they are sometimes distinguished. What has been called "discourse analysis" in the United States has more often been known as "text linguistics" in Europe. A discourse, or a text, will refer in this article to any set of sentences which are so

preferable position would seem to be that a discourse is an autonomous entity.[6] In discourse there is a linguistic entity that is greater than any distilled, logical summary sentence and also greater than only the sequence of sentences that make up the discourse.[7] Given its existence, this entity is subject to analysis in its own right.

The recognition of discourse as a linguistic entity calling for analysis has come about among linguists primarily within the last three decades.[8] In 1968 Gleason could write, "Discourse analysis is really just getting underway" (41). In the same year Harweg produced the "first large-scale inquiry into text organization" entitled *Pronomina und Textkonstitution,* in which he investigated the mechanism of "substitution" as that which gives cohesion to a text (de Beaugrande and Dressler: 22).[9]

Actually, North American linguists working in Bible translation had recognized the need for an understanding of context beyond the sentence as early as the late fifties. Loriot had written an article on the paragraph structure of Shipibo, a language of Peru, in 1958. Although it was not published until 1970, at the time it stimulated other translators who were working on South American Indian languages.[10] In 1964 Pike called for discourse analysis within the tagmemic model (classically elaborated in Pike, 1967), and Gleason urged a discourse ap-

---

related that the interpretation of some of their elements is dependent on that of others. A brief discussion of the nature of texts may be found in Brown and Yule:5–12, 190–204 and in de Beaugrande and Dressler:1–13.

5 A selection of linguists taking such a position may be found in Ballmer:167. De Beaugrande and Dressler see this view as a result of efforts to extend the transformational model to texts (23).

6 The acknowledgement of even sequential relations among sentences already indicates the need for a linguistic study of discourse as such. Contrary to Dascal and Margalit (200, n. 7), a pragmatic component in a sentence grammar will not account for these dimensions. If one analyzes relationships among sentences, by definition the scope of analysis has already been expanded beyond the sentence. The admission of pragmatics for this purpose is an acknowledgment of the reality of discourse dimensions.

7 Representative bibliography is given in de Beaugrande:114. De Beaugrande himself makes a strong case for the point in this article.

8 Harris attempted to move in this direction earlier (1952a, 1952b). That his lead was not soon followed up, although his early probes in the use of transformations were, reflects the direction American linguistics was to take shortly thereafter.

9 My exposure to Harweg is through de Beaugrande and Dressler.

10 I owe information on the early influence of Loriot's research to Longacre, 1979:248.

proach to a language of New Guinea (1964). Longacre began his study of discourse working with several colleagues on Totonac in 1965 (Reid et al.). He followed this with workshops for translators in several countries and has written extensively in the field.

There has emerged, since these beginnings, a formidable bibliography with several journals and monograph series devoted to the analysis of discourse.[11] Yet the theoretical underpinnings are still being established, especially by the work of Europeans.

Van Dijk has developed a highly formal theory, which focuses on semantics and pragmatics and attempts a sort of transformational approach to text grammar, drawing on cognitive psychology. His demonstration of what he calls a "macrostructure," conveying meaning at the level of the text as a whole, in itself constitutes a strong argument for the necessity of text linguistics (1972, 1977).

Petöfi has departed decisively from the transformational model and taken formal logic as his starting point. At the same time, he attempts to interact seriously with the hearer's reception and understanding of texts and has, in the process, elaborated an increasingly complex theory with many components (1971, 1983).

De Beaugrande has set a promising new course by calling for a theory in which the science of texts is treated as a component of a larger theory of human cognition and communication. His emphasis is on theory design, which in the past had simply been assumed to be acceptable, with the result that attention has been focused on experimentation to prove or disprove hypotheses. De Beaugrande calls, rather, for a research program with design values to be pursued on a graduated scale and criteria that might yield a profile for any theory to be considered. Linguists would thereby be protected from the "autodeterminism" and "autoverification" that de Beaugrande has shown to be characteristic, in particular, of the standard theory of generative-transformational grammar. Even more important, genuine interdisciplinary progress would be facilitated between text linguistics and the many related disciplines that have already been acknowledged as essential by many text linguists.[12]

---

[11] E.g., *Discourse Processes, Text,* Paper in Textlinguistics, Research in Text Theory.

[12] On the interdisciplinary nature of text linguistics, cf. Szabó:436. The necessity of interaction with other disciplines is implicit in the acknowledgment that text linguistics concerns "the whole of the speech communication" (Gindin:110).

In fairness it should be said that the limitation of investigation to the sentence has been characteristic primarily of American linguists. It has not been the case generally in the Functionalism of the Prague circle, in the involved theory of Hjelmslev of Copenhagen (often called Glossematics), or in the British school of Firth. While none of these schools specifically emphasized text linguistics, in most cases their theory was amenable to the analysis of the larger context. This focus has become more prominent in the functional studies of Dik and in the systemics of Halliday.[13]

The Development of Hebrew Bible Studies

Historically, cross-disciplinary relationships in biblical studies have been closer to literary criticism than to general linguistics.[14] Scholars of literature have always dealt with entire texts.[15] To the extent that biblical studies have drawn on the work of literary critics, their interest has thereby been drawn to complete texts within the corpus of the Bible. This has, in fact, been one of the acknowledged influences of the renewed interest among biblical scholars in literary criticism. They have been brought into interaction with the text as it has been transmitted and to whole books as such.[16]

Yet for critical biblical scholars this has not been an easy transition.[17] From its onset in the modern West, the primary thrust of

---

[13] Halliday and Hasan 1976 is highly regarded among students of discourse.

[14] There was an earlier period in this century in which it was fashionable to read the Hebrew Bible as literature. The current, similar emphasis has been underway for over two decades. The interaction of Hebrew Bible scholars with general linguistics, on the other hand, is still barely beginning.

[15] Szabó draws the distinction between text linguistics, a general theory of texts, and stylistics and literary theory, which describe particular properties of specific texts (437).

[16] These two issues are not identical; they involve the history of transmission and the history of composition. Yet they impinge on, and even intertwine with, one another, as Talmon has shown (1975, with references to other major articles of his that make the same point).

James Muilenburg's 1968 presidential address to the Society of Biblical Literature is usually identified as the inauguration of rhetorical criticism of the Hebrew Bible. The kinds of interest which were developing at that time and to which he gave such apt expression have fed into both rhetorical criticism and literary criticism, which, often, can scarcely be differentiated.

[17] Robertson has spoken of the shift from reading the Bible in view of modern, historical/critical criteria to reading it as literature as a change of such proportions

biblical criticism has been toward detailed analysis (in the sense of breaking something down into its component parts). In Hebrew Bible studies the critical methodology to gain ascendancy first was source criticism.[18] Through the application of this methodology, unified documents gave way to sources that were disparate in time and place of origin. Even the acknowledgement of final redactors did not provide significant attention to the text in its present shape.[19]

The development of form criticism did constitute a move toward certain kinds of literary study, and Gunkel was committed to search for literary forms that were conventional in the ancient Near East; yet form criticism did not reverse the analytical trend. Rather, in the early phases of form critical research, the tendency was to isolate and explain smaller units and generally to equate earlier with shorter.[20]

This analytical tendency, with its primarily historical interest, pervaded Hebrew Bible studies until the early latter half of the present century. At that time literary criticism and other approaches emerged, calling scholars back to a renewed engagement with the Hebrew Bible in its present shape.[21] This new perspective has been fostered, though in each case for distinctive reasons and with distinctive objectives, by literary criticism, rhetorical criticism (closely related to literary criticism), structural analysis, and the theologically

---

as to warrant being called a paradigm change, comparable to the change that occurred when Newtonian physics was replaced by Einstein's theory of special relativity (4–5). Fokkelman's reflections on the resistance he experienced from other biblical scholars while pursuing his early work in Genesis are indicative (1991:vii–ix).

[18] While my present focus will be on the Hebrew Bible, a good deal of what will be said could apply to New Testament studies as well.

[19] It is true, for example, that von Rad spoke highly of the theological and literary skill of the Yahwist (50–74); but this is not a representative emphasis. It is difficult to find extensive discussion and especially literary appreciation of the work of final redactors among source critics until the time when literary critical studies had begun to make their renewed impact. There are some exceptions, but I believe this is a fair generalization.

[20] "This explains the extreme brevity and small compass of the ancient compositions. . . . Therefore the units in ancient times, both spoken and sung, are much shorter than the written ones with which we are more familiar today" (Gunkel: 62).

[21] One likely reason for the rapid increase in new methodologies has been frustration with the loss of holistic dimensions of the text that was produced by earlier approaches.

oriented work of Childs and others, often called "canonical criticism." The same is now true in the developing interaction of biblical studies with general linguistics, in particular with that branch of linguistics under consideration here.[22]

The Value of Discourse Analysis for Studies in Hebrew Bible

At this point the theme of my introduction can be brought into sharper focus. Discourse analysis is a relative newcomer to general linguistics. Although it is not new in principle to literary criticism, it is also surprisingly new to Hebrew Bible studies. Since scholars of the Hebrew Bible have not usually pursued their research with an eye to the text as it stands, at least until fairly recently, discourse analysis holds the promise of new perspectives.

Yet the question cannot be left at that. Even if my grievously oversimplified history of modern scholarship of the Hebrew Bible be granted, at least for the sake of discussion, a deeper challenge must be faced. Apart from the newness of discourse analysis within linguistics as a whole, what is the compelling claim of linguistics itself to a hearing from Hebrew Bible scholars? In particular, what can discourse analysis, as a field of linguistics that deals with texts, offer to us that is distinctive? Given the effort that is required to gain competence in such a field, even with adequate aids (which have just begun to appear, with virtually none oriented to biblical scholars), why go to such trouble?

New Lines of Linguistics

I believe that the effort should be made, at least by some, and will devote the balance of my remarks to trying to make that case. Because general linguistics has its own history, with only limited contact with biblical studies, we can expect that its young relation, discourse analysis, will offer us new insights. New kinds of questions give fresh insights into familiar data and uncover layers of information not hitherto noticed. For example, Grimes discusses the following categories of

---

22 Edward Greenstein has called my attention to the interesting parallel development between modern linguistics and biblical studies in which both have begun by trying to isolate and study minimal units of meaning only to move on more recently to seek the meaning of larger, even the largest, units amenable to disciplined interpretation (personal communication).

information that can be revealed through the linguistic study of a discourse: events, participants, setting, background, collateral, and performatives. By collateral he means the range of possibilities that might occur. These are usually revealed by the negatives, questions, and future indications within a text; and they influence the way events will later be presented (70–71). By performatives he means utterances the expression of which is also their doing, e.g., "I dare you," "I pronounce you man and wife," etc. (71–72).

I grant that the first four of these six are not new areas of inquiry, at least not at first blush. What introductory literature text does not teach the student to explore events, participants, setting, and background? Yet a closer look at even the first of these may prove helpful. In a lucid article published in 1979 Hopper proposes as a linguistic universal of narrative discourse a distinction between events on the main story line (which he calls "foreground") and supporting material (his "background").[23] This distinction may be indicated through tense-aspect morphology of the verb, word order, particles, or the use of active and passive voice (216–38). Whereas foregrounded events occur in the narrative in the same order as in the real world, backgrounded events do not. In background the sequentiality constraint is lifted so that events may occur at any point along the time axis, or not be located on the time axis at all (214–15). In foregrounded clauses the subject tends to be highly presuppositional, i.e., it does not introduce new information, which appears, rather, in the predicate. In backgrounded clauses, on the other hand, there is greater freedom for topic change; and new information is introduced more freely in the subject (215). By the same token, in backgrounded clauses it is frequently something other then the verb that is asserted (the subject, an instrumental adverb, the verb tense, or the direct object [220]).

Closely related to these patterns is the tendency for verbs that carry the main story line, those of the foregrounded clauses, to be punctual, in contrast to the use of durative/stative/iterative types of verbs in backgrounded clauses. Hopper illustrates from French and Russian (215–19). With the application of this sort of insight to the Hebrew verb (Longacre, 1981, 1982, 1989a, 1989b, 1992), together with the historical development now being clarified by the comparative

[23]Parts of Hopper's treatment have been revised in Ehrlich.

study of the verb in Northwest Semitic,[24] we are closer to a solution to what has been labeled "the enigma of the Hebrew verbal system" (McFall).

While it could be maintained, over against the article by Hopper, that students of literature have long distinguished between main and background events, I doubt that all of the devices for this distinction, which Hopper has discussed, have been recognized as such. In any case, let me press the point further. Jones and Jones, in their study of Mesoamerican languages, have gone beyond the two levels of foreground and background to elucidate six levels of significance in discourse information. These are peak, pivotal events, backbone events, ordinary events, significant background, and ordinary background. While these levels are not defined rigorously, since they must be established more precisely for each given language, and while languages vary in how many levels they distinguish, the authors illustrate language-specific devices that are used to distinguish up to five of their six levels in four different languages.[25] For example, in Totonac peak is indicated by a variety of means (including wordiness, onomatopoeia, long and involved sentences, and embedding), backbone events by the preterite plus the word *tuncan* (usually immediately preceding the main verb), ordinary events by the preterite, significant background by any tense other than the preterite plus the suffix *-tza'*, and ordinary background by any tense other than the preterite (14, 19). This is illustrative of what discourse linguists are

[24]The seminal work was done by Moran. A distillation, with further research of his own, may be found in Rainey (1986). Three scholars' discussions of his presentation (Greenstein, Huehnergard, Zevit) and his response (Rainey, 1988) appeared two years later.

[25] Since they do not find all six levels distinguished in any language they examine, and among the languages which distinguish five, the blank is always at one of the event levels, it could be argued that only five levels are necessary and that the distinction between pivotal and backbone events should be dropped. Jones and Jones observe this distribution of data and even present such a possibility, but argue that it is only an "emic" distinction (22–23). I see no way to maintain a distinction between pivotal and backbone events when they are never both present together with ordinary events, even as an "etic" distinction. Significant/ordinary would seem sufficient for all of their samples. Still, for our purposes, five levels is impressive.

The "etic/emic" distinction refers to the difference between what a linguist or a careful non-native speaker would recognize (actual sounds—"etic") and what is significant to the native speaker apart from linguistic training ("emic").

discovering. Surely it is sufficient to indicate the need for some of us who study the Hebrew Bible or, for that matter, texts in any ancient language, to draw upon the understanding these linguists are acquiring.

Exposure to Other Languages

I want to emphasize what is to me one of the most cogent reasons for biblical scholars' drawing out the benefits of the work of linguists. It is the exposure they offer us to a wide spectrum of the world's languages and language families. For better or worse, there are different emphases in their work as linguists and ours as philologists.[26] While we may spend a lifetime on the literature of one ancient language or, if we are more broadly oriented, several, a linguist may range over all of the major language families of the world to explore the varied outworking of some specific language phenomenon. Even more advantageous is the seasoned judgment of linguists who have also worked as philologists in the sense of learning some language and its literature in depth.[27] There is such variety among languages and language families that wide exposure may alert one to possibilities that might never have been suggested from within one's language of specialization, but might apply, or might lead, to still other possibilities.[28]

Tasks That Require a Discourse Approach

To return to the specific field of discourse analysis, Longacre has written of some of the tasks that discourse analysis can accomplish, but sentence grammar cannot. They are the explication of definitivization and the use of deictics; pronominalization; the use of tense, aspect, mode, and voice; word order phenomena; the use of locative and temporal expressions; the use of adverbial clauses; sequence signals

---

[26] The difference between philology and linguistics has often been discussed. Cf. Bodine, 1987 and the references in note 1 of that article; Bodine, 1992: note 3 with further references; and, in addition: Barr, Birkeland, Bolling, Doty, Drijvers, Gleason, 1963, and Schmidt.

[27] Such a combination is difficult to find. For collections of essays dealing specifically with discourse in a variety of languages, see Dressler, Grimes, Jones, Klein-Andreu, Longacre, 1984, and Longacre and Woods.

[28] On this front I think there is probably little, if any, difference between literary critics, on the one hand, and biblical and ancient Near Eastern scholars, on the other, so that the former can gain as much as the latter by an exposure to the work of linguists.

and conjunctions; variation in reported speech; variation in the length of syntactic units; and what he calls "mystery" particles and affixes (1979). Glancing over this list, several of the areas represent problem spots in biblical Hebrew studies,[29] and all of the others could gain from fresh input.

Genre Studies

I must mention briefly the area of genre studies. This has been a major concern for students of the Hebrew Bible since the advent of form criticism, as mentioned above. The Greeks already discussed genre. Demetrius wrote of the distinction between narration, dialogue, and exposition.[30] Longacre has identified as discourse genres: the narrative, procedural, expository, and hortatory (1978); the predictive (1989:109–11); and the instructional (his essay in this volume). He has pointed out that types of discourse differ in their backbone, or most essential part; constituent structure; type of supportive material; choice of diction; and other features (1978:551). Only when the particular type of discourse is identified can analysis and comparison proceed soundly. In this task form criticism and discourse analysis can collaborate.

There is already a growing body of published research that offers examples of the benefits to be derived from bringing the tools of discourse analysis to bear on the Hebrew Bible. This work includes Baker (1979, 1980), Bergen, Clark, Clendenen (1987a, 1987b), Fox, Hardmeier (with interaction from Schweizer, 1979), Jensen, Longacre (1979, 1985, 1989a), Schickelberger, Schweizer (1981, 1983), and Wirklander. These published examples and the preceding remarks are intended to be only suggestive. All of the articles that follow in this collection can offer no more than an introduction to discourse analysis. The purpose of the volume is to encourage biblical scholars to join in welcoming into their circle this now established and rapidly growing field.[31]

---

[29] E.g., definitivization; tense, aspect, and mode; word order; sequence signals and conjunctions; variation in length of syntactic units.

[30] Cited in Louw:103.

[31] Those of a more inductive bent who wish to try their hand in the Hebrew text may, in addition to the leads they will follow up from the present volume, find a good starting point in the model of Longacre and Levinsohn. Other approaches which lend themselves to ready use in actual texts may be found in Larson;

Works Consulted

Ballmer, Thomas T.
1981 "Words, Sentences, Texts, and All That." *Text* 1:163–89.

Baker, David W.
1979 "Division Markers and the Structure of Leviticus 1-7." Pp. 9–15 in *Studia Biblica 1978. I. Papers on Old Testament and Related Themes.* Ed. E. E. Livingston. JSOTSup 11. Sheffield: University of Sheffield Press.
1980 "Diversity and Unity in the Literary Structure of Genesis." Pp. 189–205 in *Essays on the Patriarchal Narratives.* Ed. A. R. Millard and D. J. Wiseman. Leichester: InterVarsity.

Barr, James
1968 *Comparative Philology and the Text of the Old Testament.* Oxford: Clarendon Press.

Beaugrande, Robert de
1981 "Linguistic Theory and Metatheory for a Science of Texts." *Text* 1:113-61.

Beaugrande, Robert Alain de and Wolfgang U. Dressler
1981 *Introduction to Text Linguistics.* London: Longman.

Beekman, John
1970 "Propositions and Their Relations Within a Discourse." *NTr* 37:6–27.

Bergen, Robert D.
1990 "The Role of Genesis 22:1–19 in the Abraham Cycle: A Computer Assisted Textual Interpretation." *CTR* 40: 313–26.

Birkeland, Harris
1956 "Some Reflections on Semitic and Structural Linguistics." Pp. 44–51 in *For Roman Jakobson: Essays on the Occasion of His Sixtieth Birthday.* Ed. Morris Halle et al. The Hague: Mouton.

Bloomfield, Leonard
1933 *Language.* New York: Holt, Rinehart and Winston.

Bodine, Walter R.
1987 "Linguistics and Philology in the Study of Ancient Near Eastern Languages." Pp. 39-54 in *"Working with No Data": Semitic and Egyptian Studies Presented to Thomas O. Lambdin.* Ed. David M. Golomb. Winona Lake, IN: Eisenbrauns.
1992 "How Linguists Study Syntax." Pp. 89–107 in *Linguistics and Biblical Hebrew.* Ed. Walter R. Bodine. Winona Lake, IN: Eisenbrauns.

Bolling, George Melville
1929 "Linguistics and Philology." *Language* 5:27–32.

Hollenbach, 1969, 1975 (both of the articles by Hollenbach from a generative semantics point of view); Beekman, 1970; Callow, 1970, 1974; and Hale.

Brown, Gillian and George Yule
1983 *Discourse Analysis.* Cambridge Textbooks in Linguistics. Cambridge: Cambridge University Press.

Callow, Kathleen
1970 "More on Propositions and Their Relations Within a Discourse." *NTr* 37:23–27.
1974 *Discourse Considerations in Translating the Word of God.* Grand Rapids: Zondervan.

Chomsky, Noam
1957 *Syntactic Structures.* Janua Linguarum, Series Minor 4. The Hague: Mouton.
1965 *Aspects of the Theory of Syntax.* Cambridge: MIT Press
1980 *Rules and Representations.* New York: Columbia University Press.

Clark, David J.
1985 "Discourse Structure in Zechariah 7:1–8:23." *BTr* 36:328–35.

Clendenen, E. Ray
1987a "Discourse Strategies in Jeremiah 10:1–16." *JBL* 106:401–8.
1987b "The Structure of Malachi: A Textlinguistic Study." *CTL* 2:3–17.

Dascal, Marcelo and Avishai Margalit
1974 "A New 'Revolution' in Linguistics?—'Text-Grammars' vs. 'Sentence-Grammars'." *Theoretical Linguistics* 1:195–213.

Dijk, Teun A. van
1972 *Some Aspects of Text Grammars.* The Hague: Mouton.
1977 *Text and Context: Explorations in the Semantics and Pragmatics of Discourse.* Longman Linguistics Library 21. London: Longman.

Dik, Simon C.
1981 *Functional Grammar.* Publications in Language Sciences 7. Dordrecht: Foris.

Doty, William G.
1973 "Linguistics and Biblical Criticism." *JAAR* 4:114–21.

Dressler, Wolfgang U., ed.
1978 *Current Trends in Text Linguistics.* Research in Text Theory 2. Berlin: W. de Gruyter.

Drijvers, H. J. W.
1978 "History of Civilization and the Teaching of Dead Languages." Pp. 86–92 in *General Linguistics and the Teaching of Dead Hamito-Semitic Languages.* Ed. J. H. Hospers. Leiden: E. J. Brill.

Ehrlich, Susan
1987 "Aspect, Foregrounding and Point of View." *Text* 7:363–76.

Enkvist, Nils E.
1985 "Introduction: Stylistics, Text Linguistics, and Composition." *Text* 5:251–67.

Fokkelman, Jan P.
1991 *Narrative Art in Genesis: Specimens of Stylistic and Structural Analysis.* 2nd ed. The Biblical Seminar, 12. Sheffield: JSOT.

Fox, Andrew
1983 "Topic Continuity in Hebrew Narrative." Pp. 215–54 in *Topic Continuity in Discourse: A Quantitative Cross-Language Study.* Ed. T. Givón. Amsterdam: John Benjamins.

Gindin, Sergej I.
1982 "What Is a Text as a Basic Notion of Text Linguistics." Pp. 107–11 in *Text vs. Sentence. Continued.* Ed. Janos S. Petöfi. Papers in Text Linguistics 29. Hamburg: Helmut Buske.

Gleason, Henry A., Jr.
1963 "Some Contributions of Linguistics to Biblical Studies." *Hartford Quarterly* 4:47–56.

1964 "The Organization of Language: A Stratificational View." Pp. 75–95 in *Report of the Fifteenth Annual (First International) Round Table Meeting on Linguistics and Language Studies.* Ed. C. I. J. M. Stuart. Monograph Series on Languages and Linguistics 17. Washington: Georgetown University Press.

1968 "Contrastive Analysis in Discourse Structure." Pp. 39–63 in *Report of the Nineteenth Annual Round Table Meeting on Linguistics and Language Studies: Contrastive Linguistics and Its Pedagogical Implications.* Ed. James E. Alatis. Monograph Series on Languages and Linguistics 23. Washington: Georgetown University Press.

Greenstein, Edward L.
1988 "On the Prefixed Preterite in Biblical Hebrew." *HS* 29:7–17.

Grimes, Joseph E.
1971 "Kinds of Information in Discourse." *Kivung* 4:64–74.

Grimes, Joseph E., ed.
1978 *Papers on Discourse.* SILPL 51. Dallas: Summer Institute of Linguistics and University of Texas at Arlington Press.

Gunkel, Hermann
1928 "Fundamental Problems of Hebrew Literary History." Pp. 57–68 of *What Remains of the Old Testament and Other Essays.* Trans. A. K. Dallas. London: George Allen and Unwin.

Hale, Austin
1984 "A Discourse Pecking Order." Pp. 1–24 in Longacre, 1984.

Halliday, Michael A. K.
1985 *An Introduction to Functional Grammar.* London: Edward Arnold.

Halliday, Michael, and Ruqiya Hasan
1976 *Cohesion in English.* English Language Series 9. London: Longman.

1985 *Language, Context and Text: A Social-Semiotic Perspective.* Language and Learning 3. Geelong: Deakin University Press.

Hardmeier, Christof
1978 *Texttheorie und biblische Exegese: Zur rhetorischen Funktion der Trauermetaphorik in der Prophetie.* Beiträge zur evangelischen Theologie 79. München: Kaiser.

Harris, Zellig S.
1952a "Discourse Analysis." *Language* 28:1–30.
1952b "Discourse Analysis: A Sample Text." *Language* 28:474–94.

Hollenbach, Bruce
1969 "A Method for Displaying Semantic Structure." *NTr* 31:22–34.
1975 "Discourse Structure, Interpropositional Relations, and Translation." *NTr* 56:2–21.

Hopper, Paul J.
1979 "Aspect and Foregrounding in Discourse." Pp. 213–41 in *Discourse and Syntax.* Ed. Talmy Givón. Syntax and Semantics 12. New York: Academic.

Huehnergard, John
1988 "The Early Hebrew Prefix-Conjugations." *HS* 29:19–23.

Jensen, Han Jorgen Lundager
1981 "Reden, Zeit und Raum in Genesis 28:10–15: Textlinguistische und textsemiotische Exegese eines Fragments." *LB* 49:54–70.

Jones, Larry B. and Linda K. Jones
1979 "Multiple Levels of Information in Discourse." Pp. 3–27 in *Discourse Studies in Mesoamerican Languages, Vol. 1: Discussion.* Ed. Linda K. Jones. SILPL 58. Dallas: Summer Institute of Linguistics and University of Texas at Arlington Press.

Jones, Linda K., ed.
1979 *Discourse Studies in Mesoamerican Languages, Vol. 2: Texts.* SILPL 58. Dallas: Summer Institute of Lingistics and University of Texas at Arlington Press.

Katz, Jerrold J. and Jerry A. Fodor
1964 "The Structure of a Semantic Theory." Pp. 479–518 in *The Structure of Language: Readings in the Philosophy of Language.* Englewood Cliffs: Prentice-Hall.

Klein-Andreu, Flora, ed.
1983 *Discourse Perspectives on Syntax.* New York: Academic.

Larson, Mildred L.
1965 "A Method for Checking Discourse Structure in Bible Translation." *NTr* 17:1–25.

Longacre, Robert E.
1976 *An Anatomy of Speech Notions.* Lisse: Peter de Ridder.
1978 "Discourse Genre." Pp. 551–54 in *Proceedings of the Twelfth International Congress of Linguists.* Ed. Wolfgang U. Dressler and Wolfgang

Meid. Innsbruck: Institute für Sprachwissenschaft der Universität Innsbruck.

1979a "Why We Need a Vertical Revolution in Linguistics." Pp. 247–70 in *The Fifth LACUS Form 1978*. Ed. Wolfgange Wölek and Paul L. Garvin. Columbia: Hornbeam.

1979b "The Discourse Structure of the Flood Narrative." *JAAR* 47, Sup. B:89–133.

1981 "A Spectrum and Profile Approach to Discourse Analysis." *Text* 1:337-59.

1982 "Discourse Typology in Relation to Language Typology." Pp. 457–86 in *Text Processing: Text Analysis and Generation, Text Typology and Attribution*. Ed. Sture Allén. Stockholm: Almqvist & Wiksell.

1985 "Interpreting Biblical Stories." Pp. 169–85 in *Discourse and Literature: New Approaches to the Analysis of Literary Genres*. Ed. T. A. van Dijk. Critical Theory 3. Amsterdam: John Benjamins.

1989a *Joseph, a Story of Divine Providence: A Text Theoretical and Textlinguistic Analysis of Genesis 37 and 39–48*. Winona Lake, IN: Eisenbrauns.

1989b "Two Hypotheses Regarding Text Generation and Analysis." *Discourse Processes* 12:413–60.

1992 "Discourse Perspective on the Hebrew Verb: Affirmation and Restatement." Pp. 177–89 in *Linguistics and Biblical Hebrew*. Ed. Walter R. Bodine. Winona Lake, IN: Eisenbrauns.

Longacre, Robert E., ed.

1984 *Theory and Application in Processing Texts in Non-Indoeuropean Languages*. Papers in Textlinguistics 43. Hamburg: Helmut Buske.

Longacre, Robert and Stephen Levinsohn

1978 "Field Analysis of Discourse." Pp. 103–22 in *Current Trends in Textlinguistics*. Ed. Wolfgang U. Dressler. Research in Text Theory 2. Berlin: W. de Gruyter.

Longacre, Robert E. and Fran Woods, eds.

1976-7 *Discourse Grammar: Studies in Indigenous Languages of Colombia, Panama, and Ecuador, Parts 1-3*. SILPL 52. Dallas: Summer Institute of Linguistics and University of Texas at Arlington Press.

Loriot, James and Barbara Hollenbach

1970 "Shipibo Paragraph Structure." *Foundations of Language* 6:43–66.

Louw, Johannes P.

1973 "Discourse Analysis and the Greek New Testament." *BTr* 24:101–18.

McFall, Leslie

1982 *The Enigma of the Hebrew Verbal System: Solutions from Ewald to the Present Day*. Historic Texts and Interpreters in Biblical Scholarship. Sheffield: Almond.

Moran, William L.
1950 *A Syntactical Study of the Dialect of Byblos as Reflected in the Amarna Tablets.* Dissertation, Johns Hopkins University, Baltimore. Ann Arbor: University Microfilms.

Muilenburg, James
1969 "Form Criticism and Beyond." *JBL* 88:1–19.

Petöfi, János S.
1971 *Transformationsgrammatiken und eine kotextuelle Texttheorie.* Frankfurt: Athenäum.
1983 "Text, Signification, Models, and Correlates: Some Aspects of Text Comprehension and Text Interpretation." Pp. 266–98 in *Psycholinguistic Studies and Language Processing.* Ed. G. Rickheit and M. Bock. Berlin: W. de Gruyter.

Pike, Kenneth L.
1967 *Language in Relation to a Unified Theory of the Structure of Human Behavior.* 2nd ed. The Hague: Mouton.
1964 "Discourse Analysis and Tagmeme Matrices." *Oceanic Linguistics* 3:5–25.

Rad, Gerhard von
1966 "The Form-Critical Problem of the Hexateuch." Pp. 1–78 in *The Problem of the Hexateuch and Other Essays.* Trans. E. W. Trueman Dicken. New York: McGraw-Hill (original German ed., 1938).

Rainey, Anson F.
1986 "The Ancient Prefix Conjugation in the Light of Amarnah Canaanite." *HS* 27:4–19 .
1988 "Further Remarks on the Hebrew Verbal System." *HS* 29:35–42.

Reid, Aileen A. et al.
1968 *Totonac: From Clause to Discourse.* SILPL 17. Santa Ana: Summer Institute of Linguistics.

Robertson, David
1977 *The Old Testament and the Literary Critic.* Guides to Biblical Scholarship. Philadelphia: Fortress.

Saussure, Ferdinand de
1959 *Course in General Linguistics.* Ed. Charles Bally and Albert Sechehaye. Trans. with intro. and notes Wade Baskin. New York: McGraw-Hill (French original, 1915).

Schicklberger, Franz
1974 "Jonatans Heldentat: Textlinguistische Beobachtungen zu Sam. xiv 1-23a." *VT* 24:324–33.
1978 "Biblische Literarkritik und linguistische Texttheorie: Bemerkungen zu einer Textsyntax von hebräischen Erzähltexten." *TZ* 34:65–81.

Schmidt, Daryl

1984 "The Study of Hellenistic Greek Grammar in the Light of Contemporary Linguistics." *Perspectives in Religious Studies* 11: 27–38.

Schweizer, Harold

1979 "Texttheorie und Beelzebub: Die Impulse Christof Hardmeiers für die Methodik der Exegese." *BN* 9:26–44

1981 "Prädikationen und Leerstellen im 1. Gottesknechtslied (Jes 42,1–4)." *BZ* 26:251–58.

1983 "Determination, Textdeixis—Erläutert an Genesis xviii 23-33." *VT* 33:113–18.

Szabó, Zoltán

1979 "Stylistics Within the Interdisciplinary Framework of Text Linguistics. " Pp. 433–49 in *Text vs. Sentence: Basic Questions of Text Lingistics. Second Part.* Ed. János S. Petöfi. Papers in Textlinguistics 20, 2. Hamburg: Helmut Buske.

Talmon, Shemaryahu

1975 "The Textual Study of the Bible—A New Outlook. " Pp. 321–400 in *Qumran and the History of the Biblical Text.* Ed. Frank Moore Cross and Shemaryahu Talmon. Cambridge: Harvard University Press.

Wirklander, Bertil

1984 *Prophecy as Literature: A Text-linguistic and Rhetorical Approach to Isaiah 2–4.* ConBOT 22. Stockholm: Liber Tryck.

Zevit, Ziony

1988 "Talking Funny in Biblical Henglish and Solving a Problem of the YAQTÚL Past Tense." *HS* 29:25-33.

A. Texts

1

Building for the Worship of God Exodus 25:1–30:10

Robert E. Longacre

ABSTRACT

The Hebrew text of Exodus 25:1–30:10, i.e., the instructions for building the tabernacle in the wilderness, for making the clothing of the priests, and for instituting worship is examined. Contemporary textlinguistic methodology is brought to bear on these five and a half chapters, which are seen to constitute a unified discourse in their own right although they are embedded in the larger discourse context of Exodus. As an instructional discourse, these chapters are similar to but distinct from procedural discourse (e.g., the prescriptions for sacrifice in Leviticus) and predictive discourse—although in all three discourse types the *waw*-consecutive perfect (WQTL) forms the backbone structure. This instructional discourse, although replete with specifications, is not simply the textual equivalent of a set of blueprints; it shines with an inner glory, the prospect of God dwelling among His people and being their God. The texture of the discourse is analyzed so as to reveal this dual nature ("the spirit within the wheels"). To this end I employ macrosegmention ("gross chunking"), posit macrostructures as summary-control devices on various levels, set up a peculiar agency hierarchy (God–Moses–artisans/priests–artifacts), trace the cumulative progress of the discourse towards its peak (the active institution of worship), and mention a few microstructural details (how one sentence immediately relates to surrounding sentences).

0. A study of the discourse structure of Exodus 25:1–30:10, which contains instructions for building the Tabernacle, making clothing for the priests, ordaining them, and instituting the daily worship, can serve the following purposes: (1) afford perspective on a Biblical Hebrew (BH) discourse type other than narrative; (2) at the same time serve to distinguish instructional discourse from predictive and procedural, on the one hand, and hortatory and juridical, on the other; and (3) further clarify the role of the various forms of the Hebrew verb in connected discourse.

The set of assumptions that underlie not only this study but also my previous work on BH discourse includes: (A) Discourse structure cannot be understood without a classification into discourse types. (B) Each discourse type has a mainline structure that consists of Hebrew sentences whose main verb is of a specified form, along with other sentence structures whose main verbs (including verbless clauses) round out in various ways the structure of that type of discourse. (C) Other discourse characteristics, e.g., characteristic sentence length, typical paragraph structures, and systems of nominal/pronominal reference, will also differ from type to type. (D) Attention to the factors listed above will prove insightful into the overall meaning and conception of a text and lead to new exegetical insights.

1. Instructional Discourse as a Distinct Discourse Type

In Longacre (1989) I assume four broad discourse types for BH prose: Narrative, Predictive, Hortatory and Expository. These types are distinguished mainly by having different mainline structures. *Narrative discourse,* the story, takes the preterite (the so-called *waw*-consecutive with the imperfect) as its determining verb form. Clauses with this form (necessarily verb-initial) typically represent punctiliar sequential happenings with causal connections at least partially uniting the sequence. *Predictive discourse,* a story told in advance, (cf. 1 Sam 10:2–6), is the inverse of narration. Here the *waw*-consecutive with the perfect (in necessarily verb-initial clauses) represents punctiliar and sequential projected happenings with at least partial causal connection. *Hortatory discourse* has a mainline that consists of command forms, with imperative, cohortative, and jussive forms roughly sorting out according to person and according to affirmative-negative polarity. Hortatory discourse thus conceived of as interpersonal (not juridical) can be mitigated in certain ways or shifted into deferential court speech. *Expository discourse* is completely static and takes as its mainline verbless clauses and clauses with *hāyâ,* "be." If dynamic verbs occur, they are subservient as anecdotes or illustrative material. Thus, expository and narrative discourses are polar opposites in regard to the use of dynamic versus static constructions. *Predictive* discourse is distinguished from *procedural* discourse (Longacre, 1982) in that while the former has a slate of participants, much as in a story, and is still agent oriented, the latter is goal oriented and the procedures may be implemented by any qualified agent—for example, sacrificial procedures may be implemented by a priest. A predictive discourse is, in reality, simply a projected story; and, as observed above, the perfect and the imperfect flip grammatical functions between the two. Procedural discourse uses the *waw*-consecutive perfect (*WQTL*) in VSO clauses and the imperfect (*YQTL*) in NV clauses according to the encoding of major versus minor procedures.

Thus my previous work distinguished narrative, predictive, procedural, hortatory (with variants), and expository discourses for BH. Notwithstanding, my analysis of the flood narrative (Longacre 1979) dealt with a type of discourse, in speeches of God to Noah (Gen 6:13–21 and 7:1–4), which was characterized by sparse use of imperatives, liberal use of the *waw*-consecutive perfect, a certain amount of specification data (especially in nominal, i.e., verbless, clauses), a second person orientation (to Noah), and orientation of the speeches towards construction and implementation. While I spoke of these two stretches of reported speech as "instructional" (or even "instructional" paragraphs), I failed to see the full import of the data, viz., the desirability of positing an instructional discourse type distinct from both procedural and hortatory discourses.

All of which brings us back to the theme of this paper, "building for the worship of God," i.e., the analysis of the constructional discourse found in Exod 25:1–30:10 (and in some following parts of chapter 30).[1] The purpose of this paper is to delineate clearly instruction as a discourse type and to present in some detail the structure and discourse-effectiveness of this passage. The latter concern—the discourse-effectiveness of this passage—is of major importance. For although the surface texture is that of a set of rather detailed and involved instructions, the purpose of the construction, the institution of the regular worship of Yahweh at a central sanctuary—albeit a

[1] The original impetus for doing this analysis and writing this paper came from Nicolai Winter-Nielsen of the Danish Bible Institute of Copenhagen. He wrote the first draft of what we hoped to make a joint paper. Although the latter has not worked out, I acknowledge here my considerable debt to Mr. Winter-Nielsen for stimulating my interest in this part of the Hebrew Bible and for several initial insights regarding the structure of the passage.

tent—is presented as something glorious and fraught with deep religious meaning.

Before plunging, however, into the macrosegmentation and microsegmentation of the text before us, it is necessary to mention still another discourse type that is contextually interwoven with the instructions, viz., the juridical discourse. The juridical component is prominent enough in the entire Pentateuch (but especially prominent in Exodus, Leviticus and Deuteronomy) to merit entitling the whole "The Law." In regard to the text under consideration: (1) juridical material both precedes our text (Exod 20–23) and follows it (30:11–16, 31:12–17); (2) furthermore, as we shall see in the internal analysis of our text, juridical paragraphs embed here and there within the instructional passages.

2. Discourse Unity and Macrostructures

It seems plausible to treat all of Exod 25:1–30:10 as one unit. Although there are main sections marked off by 28:1–6, 29:1–9, and 29:38, yet the whole is introduced by one quotation formula in 25:1: "And Yahweh said to Moses. . . ." There are no further occurrences of such formulas of quotation until we reach 30:11. Here and in 30:17, 22, 34, and 31:1, 12 we again encounter "And Yahweh said to Moses. . . ." Although a single speech can be interrupted by reiterated formulas of quotation (as in Gen 9:1–17), which mark off main sections within it, it may be argued that a section uninterrupted by such reiterated formulas of quotation is even more evidently a unit.

What then of the materials in 30:11–31:17? The paragraphs, except for the last (31:12–17 on the Sabbath), seem to relate in a loose way to the main preceding discourse, while at the same time patterning somewhat like addenda to it. Thus, the first such paragraph—30:11–16—has to do with raising revenue to support the "service of the Tent of Meeting" (30:16); 30:17–21 has to do with the construction of the bronze laver and is juridical (as indeed are some sections in the main preceding discourse); 30:22–33 has to do with the compounding and use of the anointing oil; 30:34–38 has to do with the compounding and use of the incense for the Tent of Meeting; and 31:1–11 records Yahweh's instruction to Moses that Bezalel, Oholiab, and other craftsmen are equipped by God with the skills to carry out the work of construction and clothesmaking. In summary: following the main, unbroken discourse (25:1–30:10) there is then a string of six further discourses (words of Yahweh to Moses), only three of which are plainly constructional, while others treat of raising revenue, compounding of oil and incense, finding the skilled craftsman, and the Sabbath. These "tacked on" pieces not only are set off by reiterated formulas of quotation but are somewhat disparate in subject matter when compared to 25:1–30:10.

What then is the macrostructure of the larger continuous unit? Let us begin by assuming three macrostructures corresponding to the three main sections. In 25:1–27:21 the macrostructure is indicated in 25:8, 9, which I will summarily give as "Have them make me a sanctuary—according to the pattern I'm showing you—so that I may dwell among them." The three elements here are: (1) Moses is commanded to have the people build the sanctuary; (2) it must be done according to the revealed pattern; and (3) the purpose is so that God may dwell among his people. We can, on the basis of this macrostructure, anticipate a discourse having to do with the construction of a sanctuary with cultic objects, furniture, and utensils. We can also expect to encounter a text heavy with clauses and sentences that give specifications of materials, dimensions, and the like. We can further expect overt references to the ultimate purpose, that God may dwell among his people, to crop up from place to place.

For chapter 28 in its entirety we find a macrostructure which is given with a certain amount of repetition and paraphrase in 28:1–5. I summarize: "Have them make sacred garments for Aaron and his sons that they may be clad with dignity and honor in serving me as priests." Perhaps mediatorial role and representative function are involved in the very concept of priest; if this is not granted, we would need to add to the above macrostructure a further clause that captures a motif that runs through chapter 28: ". . . and in representing the people before me."

A macrostructure for 29:1–38 can be given as: "Consecrate and ordain Aaron and his sons to serve as priests before me—with the privileges attendant on their office."

Since I regard 29:38–46 as a separate major section and as the peak (cf. 3.5) of the whole discourse (with 29:1–37 as prepeak and consequently sharing some peak features), I could also state its macrostructure as: "Institute the regular worship of God in the morning and evening sacrifices; thus I will dwell among my people."

The making of the altar of incense is given in a postpeak section (30:1–10); its macrostructure may be succinctly given: "Make an incense altar for the priest to offer incense to me morning and night." This is similar to the macrostructure given for the peak section.

A somewhat succinct macrostructure of the whole can be posited as follows: *Make me a sanctuary according to the pattern I'm showing you so that I may dwell among my people. Make sacred garments for Aaron and his sons and ordain them to serve as priests before me. Institute the regular daily worship.* Here the following key concepts are included: the SANCTUARY, the PATTERN, God's DWELLING among his people, the SACRED GARMENTS, ORDINATION, PRIESTHOOD, and the daily WORSHIP. If our macrostructure is carefully construed, it should entail the contents of this discourse and the relative detail and elaboration of the parts. We will have resort again to the macrostructure below especially in reference to the ordering of various subsections within the text.

3. Macrosegmentation (gross chunking)

Here I consider the articulation of the text into its various "chunks" with attention to features of opening, as well as attention to such privileged chunks as the "inciting incident" (cf. narrative), peak (cumulative development), and postpeak—and how the macrostructure controls the order of presentation. Although some features of paragraph structure are discussed in this section, most such features are not discussed here. These latter concerns of *microsegmentation* are discussed to some degree in section 4, but a full constituent structure of the discourse is not included in this paper.

The main divisions of the text have been referred to above in the consideration of the macrostructures. It now remains to justify this division of the text in terms of formal features. Analytically, of course, the procedure has gone in the opposite direction, i.e., it is the discovery of the formal features to be described below which led to the assumption of semantic unity within the sections thus marked. Evidence that our text has four main divisions is seen in the distribution of imperatives, cleft sentences, and, to some degree, in the distribution of explicit second person singular references. For the main sections (not counting the postpeak), onset of a new section is marked more clearly than closure.

3.1. The imperative as discourse opener

The incidence of the imperative is restricted in the text under consideration. In this section I consider all occurrences of the imperative in the MT as it stands—and dispose of one such occurrence as a textual corruption.

In 25:2, 28:1, and 29:1b a second person singular imperative occurs in the onset of new sections (embedded discourses).

25:2: "SPEAK to the sons of Israel and they will bring me an offering. . . ." The whole has the structure of an indirect command, "Tell the sons of Israel to bring me an offering," with a YQTL form serving at once as purpose and indirect quotation. Moses as mediator of the covenant passes on to the people of Israel God's command to take an offering and build a sanctuary. The second person imperative, directed to Moses as mediator, is the pattern for the imperative in this text.

28:1: "As for you, CAUSE Aaron your brother and his sons to COME near to you from among the sons of Israel to serve me in the priesthood." The imperative is a second person singular hiphil. The mediatorial work of Moses in hearing God's command and turning the priesthood over to his brother and his brother's sons is emphasized by *wĕʾattâ* ("now as for you") and by the use of the causative verb, "Now, as for you, cause X to do Q." The section thus introduced has to do with the making of sacred garments for the priests.

29:1b: TAKE a young bullock and two rams without defect . . . [various kinds of unleavened bread are specified in the balance of the sentence in v. 2]. Here the imperative is again directed at Moses who is to ordain his brother Aaron and Aaron's sons to the priesthood. The point of the imperative is that Moses is to gather the animals and breads necessary for the complex of ordination sacrifices in which Moses will turn over his implicitly priestly function to an explicit and duly instituted priesthood.

Besides the above imperatives, which contribute to the articulation of major sections (embedded discourses, i.e., distinctive sections couched within longer sections), there also occur imperatives in 25:40, and in 28:42.

The double imperative in 25:40, "SEE and MAKE [everything] according to the pattern which you see on the mountain," reminds us that the imperative need not be limited to the initiation of a new embedded discourse as illustrated above. Here the double imperative occurs at the end of the instructions (an embedded discourse) for building the Ark of Testimony, the Table of the Presence, and the Menorah. It can be taken as a sort of urgent but parenthetical reminder to Moses of his mediatorial responsibilities. It is probable, however, that it is not simply parenthetical but signals closure (see below, 3.2), since features of opening and closure often show resemblance—as in an overt *inclusio*. I therefore consider 25:10–40 to constitute a unit (i.e., an "embedded" discourse) on the making of the Ark, the Table, and the Menorah—with the double imperative marking closure of the unit.

The imperative in 28:42 is of special interest: "MAKE linen underwear to cover the flesh of their nakedness. . . ." While every other garment of the priests is specified in the cleft structure in 28:4, the linen underwear is not specified. But the clothes specified in 28:4 were meant to be visible and to give the priest dignity and honor. The underwear is described here in a paragraph, the second half of which is clearly juridical, as a precaution against exposure of the priest's genitals in the course of his discharging his duties. Thus, the little section 28:42–43 is like an addendum to the major instructions given in chap. 28. Furthermore, 28:41 is clearly a cataphoric link to the next major section: "And you shall clothe them, Aaron and his sons with him, and you shall anoint them, and you shall ordain them that they may serve as priests to me."

In that the section 28:42–43 is not anticipated in 28:4 and is skipped over in the cataphoric linkage of 28:41, it can plausibly be construed as a (somewhat urgent) parenthesis. The use of the second person singular imperative 'MAKE' in 28:42 serves again to put the onus of responsibility on Moses to see that this "extra" instruction is carried out. In this respect the parenthetical section 28:42–43 is reminiscent of the structure of a major section.

I have yet, however, to consider the imperative in the MT of 25:19a. I refer here to the totality of verse 25:19: "And MAKE [*waʿăśeh*] a cherub on one end and a cherub on the other end; of one piece with the atonement cover, you (plural) shall make [*taʿăśû*] the cherubim on the two ends of it." Here, in 19a and 19b, we encounter textual variants involving other forms of *ʿāśâ*, "make." No such variants are witnessed for any other imperative found in this entire text. In contrast, both 19a and 19b have divergent readings witnessed to by both the Samaritan Pentateuch and the Septuagint translation—while in 19b the divergent reading is also witnessed to in the Syriac, in some Targums, and in some of the Hebrew manuscripts from the Cairo Geniza.

Let me line up the variants as follows:

	MT	Samaritan Pentateuch
19a	וַעֲשֵׂה	יֵעָשׂוּ
19b	תַּעֲשׂוּ	תַּעֲשֶׂה

In summary, the MT text has a 2m.sg. imperative in 19a, and a 2m.pl. YQTL form in 19b, while the Samaritan Pentatuech and the LXX witness to YQTL, 3m.pl. niphal in 19a and 2m.sg. YQTL (qal) in 19b. These variants can be plausibly explained as a confusion (interchange) of final *waw* and *he* in alternate lines of Hebrew text, plus a further problem involving *waw* and *yod* in the first consonant of the form in 19a. This gives a new translation for v. 19. I present here vv. 18 and 19 together to give adequate context:

> v. 18: And you shall make (WQTL) two cherubim of gold; from beaten work you shall make (YQTL) them at the two ends of the atonement cover.
>
> v. 19: They shall be made (YQTL, niphal) one cherub on this end and the other cherub on that end; from the atonement cover you (sg.) shall make (YQTL) the cherubim at the two ends of it.

Notice that the first mention of making the cherubim is in v. 18 in a paraphrastic sentence involving WQTL and YQTL forms of the verb "make." Verse 19 is specificatory and therefore has no initial *waw* conjunctival (cf. sec. 4.1 below). Verse 19 is also a paraphrastic sentence and has a niphal YQTL in 19b and a qal YQTL in 19b. The only thing that is unusual in the new reading and translation is the use of a YQTL form in specification (rather than just nominal clauses), but this need not be a great problem.[2]

3.2. The cleft sentence as discourse opener

A cleft sentence is found in the paragraph or sentence that initiates each main section (embedded discourse) of this instructional text.

---

[2] In narrative discourse, where WYQTL forms are mainline, not only are N-QTL forms found in the secondary line but also some QTL forms (perfects without a preposed noun phrase). While only a few such examples occur, nevertheless they do occur, and represent a crucial witness to the secondary role of the perfect per se, even without a preposed noun. It seems to me that instructional discourse is somewhat parallel, in that, while N-YQTL occurs in secondary roles and YQTL forms are usually found in purpose clauses, the occurrence of a YQTL form in specification is not implausible, although presumably rare.

Each cleft sentence has the structure "this/these Ø the X which you shall do,"[3] i.e.,

zeh/ʾēlleh Ø X *ʾăšer* + Vb

In 25:2 the cleft sentence immediately follows the sentence that contains the imperative: "And this is the offering which you will take from them . . ." (materials to use in implementing the instructions). In 28:4, the cleft sentence is several sentences removed from the sentence (28:1) that contains the imperative, but is still in the stage paragraph: "And these are the garments which you shall make . . ." (enumerations of the garments to be made). In 29:1 the cleft sentence is initial in its section, and the sentence with an imperative follows: "And this is the procedure (*haddābār*) which you are to implement." In 29:38 there is no initiatory imperative; rather the cleft sentence initiates the section: "And this Ø what you are to do [= offer] on the altar: two lambs one year old each day continually."

In three of the major sections (embedded discourses) both an imperative and a cleft sentence serve to signal onset of the section; in the fourth a cleft sentence occurs, but no imperative.

3.3. Explicit pronominal references

As we have already observed, the whole text has a structure, "You tell them to do X," which gets shortened to "You do X." This 2nd p.sg. functioning as the causer of 3rd pl. actions is especially noticeable in the stage paragraphs of the first two major sections. There is, in fact, a special agency hierarchy in this text: God–Moses–others (includes artisans and priests)–artifacts. There will be reason to refer to this hierarchy later.

In 25:1–9 we have the following "You (sg.) tell them to bring me an offering." "You (pl., i.e., Moses and other leaders) are to receive their offerings." "They shall make me a sanctuary." "According to all I'm showing you (sg.) they shall make." This gets subsequently shortened to WQTL forms in 2 sg. "And you shall make" with only occasional resort to WQTL forms in 3 pl.

Likewise, in 28:1–5 we see a similar development in the second section:

> "And you (*wĕʾattâ*) bring to you Aaron your brother and his sons. . . ."
>
> "And you shall make holy clothes for Aaron your brother."

---

[3] Here Ø symbolizes a null verb in a nominal clause.

"And you (*wĕ'attâ*) shall speak to all that are wisehearted. . . . And they shall make holy garments . . ." [verse 4 has only "They shall make . . ." forms]. V. 5: "And they (*wĕhēm*) shall use gold and blue, purple and scarlet yarn and fine linen."

This passage is of special interest because of the 2nd person pronoun (*'attâ*) in vv. 1 and 3, and of the 3 pl. (*hēm*) in v. 5—thus making quite explicit the "you . . . they" relationship of the agency hierarchy on which the whole text is built.

Overt *wĕ'attâ,* "and you," also occurs in the last instruction paragraph of the first main section, where in 27:20 it initiates the paragraph which closes that section.

3.4. Construction of a crucial item as parallel to the inciting incident in narrative

In reference again to the first two major sections, I note that each has as its first item to be constructed a crucial item that entails the rest of the construction. In the first section (25:1–22) it is the Ark of the Testimony and its atonement cover that provide initial excitement. In section 2 (chap. 28) it is the ephod and its breastplate of judgment that provide the initial excitement. I do not find such a feature in the third major section—where there is rather a steady crescendo building up from the bullock of the sin offering, through the ram of the fellowship offering, through the ordination lamb to the eating of the ordination lamb. Nor do I find such a feature in peak or in postpeak.

The two paragraphs 25:10–16 and 25:17–22 together constitute a short embedded discourse on a low level of embedding. There is no special indication of closure in 25:16. A new paragraph in indicated simply by the topic shift to the atonement cover in 25:17 and the parallelism of 25:10 to 25:17 in respect to "Make an X; and these (are) its dimensions." The whole sequence 25:10–22 builds up to a climax in its second paragraph, where the atonement cover and its two facing cherubim are treated in an instruction replete with paraphrase and amplification (vv. 18–20) and ending with a promissory passage (v. 22) regarding God making himself known there—"above the atonement-cover between the cherubim."

This crucial piece of furniture is, in a sense, the living heart of the whole tabernacle and entails the construction of all that accompanies and surrounds it.

In somewhat parallel fashion the construction of the ephod and its breastpiece of judgment is given in two paragraphs (28:6–14 and

28:15–30). In the former, great emphasis is placed upon the engraving of the names of the twelve tribes of Israel on the two onyx stones that are to be mounted on the shoulder pieces of the ephod. In the latter—possibly the longest paragraph in our whole text—after a long and intricate section on the six rings and cords that will bind the breastpiece to the ephod (vv. 22–28), emphasis is put on the importance of the engraving of the names of the tribes of Israel on the twelve stones that are to be mounted on the breastplate (as in vv. 17–21). In v. 29 the names on the breastpiece are again mentioned, while in v. 30 the Urim and the Thummin (divination stones in the pocket of the breastpiece) figure in a joint reference to these pieces and to the stones on the breastpiece.

In both the first paragraph, referring to the names on the shoulder pieces of the ephod, and in the second paragraph, referring to the names on the twelve stones of the breastpiece, the work of Aaron as representative and mediator for the whole nation is emphasized with considerable paraphrase and amplification (28:12 and 28:29–30). Again, the ephod and its breastpiece are presented as the crucial pieces of clothing and as such are prescribed first.

In both the sections on the tabernacle construction and on the making of the garments of the high priest and his sons, an instruction regarding the crucial item immediately follows the stage (with its imperative and cleft sentence).

In various periods of Israelite history, as represented in Judges and the books of Samuel and Kings, the Ark of the Testimony is represented as the crucial item in the worship of God, while the priest is often referred to as "one wearing the ephod." In a very real sense the Ark symbolized worship and the presence of God, while the ephod symbolized the priesthood. Both, on occasion, were objects of superstitious veneration—with the Ark carried into battle on several occasions and an ephod set up as a cult object.[4]

3.5. Peak (cumulative development)

The Peak of the whole text can plausibly be considered to be 29:38–46. That this is clearly meant to be a major section—although

---

[4] If, indeed, "ephod" in such passages as Judges 17 and 18 is to be identified with part of the clothing of the priest. Possibly the reference is to divination stones associated with the ephod.

consisting of only one paragraph—is seen by the use of a cleft sentence in its introduction (29:38).

This is, in a sense, the "target" of the whole discourse: the institution of the daily worship. Furthermore, there is a certain sonority and solemnity achieved by resort to various devices which are noted below. The shift to first person singular (Yahweh speaking) in the center of v. 42 involves an unusual shift between the main clause and the relative clause and, of course, foregrounds God as the dominant agent in the peculiar agency hierarchy of this discourse.

The whole paragraph is juridical in tone and structure. The first part of the paragraph (vv. 38–42) is prescriptive of the daily ritual of the morning and evening sacrifice. The last verse, v. 42, is somewhat of a hinge between the two halves of the paragraph:

> Ø a continual offering for your generations at the door of the Tent of Meeting before YHWH—I who will be known to you (pl.) there to speak with you (pl.) there.

The first part of the verse is a solemn injunction: "It will be a continual offering for your generations. . . ." The phrase "before YHWH" is followed by a relative (*ʾăšer*) clause with a verb in first person singular. The transition from a third person noun to a modifying relative clause in first person does not make for smooth translation and is somewhat unusual, but presents no grammatical problem. The relative clause in first person anticipates the second half of the paragraph, which involves a number of coordinated structures that are somewhat paraphrastic in function. There are several ekbalic relations (ranging semantically from result to purpose to promise) involved: (1) vv. 43–46 can be regarded as the result of the institution of the regular daily worship (= "Institute the daily worship, then I will sanctify the place and dwell among them"); (2) likewise, the last verse, v. 46 (= "I will sanctify the place and dwell there so that they will know that I am their God . . ."), can be regarded as the result of vv. 43–45. However, we might better take the primary relation of vv. 38–42 to vv. 43–46 (i.e., to the whole paragraph) to be one of a conditional promise (as suggested in 4.3.1). The pronoun *ʾănî* occurs twice in v. 46—while all the verbs from 42b on (except the third person singular niphal at the end of v. 43) are first person singular. Thus, the second half of this peak paragraph achieves a certain sonority by resorting to coordination and paraphrase, and develops in one grand crescendo the germinal idea found in the stage of the whole text: "They shall make me a sanctuary and I will dwell among them" (25:8). The whole ends on the grand chord: "I Ø YHWH their God."

3.6. The postpeak construction

Why is the construction of the altar of incense delayed until after the peak of the entire discourse rather than being given as part of the first embedded discourse, where construction of the furniture of the Tent of Meeting and of the Tent itself is given? The construction of the altar of burnt offering is given in 27:1–8, while the consecration of the altar for worship is given in 29:36–37; and the projected implementation of the altar in daily sacrifice is given in the peak (29:38–40). Here, in 30:1–10, the construction of the altar of incense and its projected implementation as a daily ritual, which is parallel to that of the daily sacrifices, are summarily given together. Both the peak and the postpeak have to do with the projected institution of daily worship.

Peak is not necessarily a discrete area, but rather a zone of turbulence and excitement. The target of all the procedures is the exciting prospect of the institution of daily worship of a God who dwells among his people. The consecration of the priests in prepeak and the construction and projected implementation of the incense altar in postpeak partake of some of the culminating tension that is expressed in the peak itself.

3.7. Order of projected construction as controlled by the macrostructure

Apparent irregularities in the order of construction procedures, e.g., the priority given to the construction of the Ark of Testimony, the Table of the Presence, and the Menorah, as well as the late positioning of the section regarding the incense altar, can now be reviewed again in the light of the macrostructure that is posited at the end of section 2 above.

In order to perceive clearly the controlling force of the macrostructure in ordering the construction procedures, it is of some interest to compare the order of projected construction in the text we are currently analyzing with the order of narrated construction as given in Exod 36:8–40:38, especially 36:8–39:31. The order of projected construction and that of narrated construction are given in parallel columns in Diagram I.

DIAGRAM I

Order of Narrated Construction Exod 36:8–39:31

(1) The Tent Curtains	36:8–13
(2) The Over-Tent	36:14–19
(3) The Tent Framework	36:20–34
(4) The Veil	36:35–36
(5) Entrance Curtain	36:37–38
(6) The Ark of Testimony	37:1–5
(7) The Atonement Cover	37:6–9
(8) The Table of the Presence	37:10–16
(9) The Menorah	37:17–24
(10) The Altar of Incense	37:25–28
(11) Anointing Oil	37:29
(12) Incense	
(13) The Altar of Burnt Offering	38:1–7
(14) The Bronze Basin	38:8
(15) The Courtyard	38:9–17
(16) Entrance Curtain	38:18–20
(17) The Ephod	39:1–7
(18) The Breastpiece	39:8–21
(19) The Robe of the Ephod	39:22–26
(20) Tunics, turbans, sashes	39:27–29
(21) The "Holiness" Tiara	39:30–31
A. *Then,* Moses inspects	39:32–42
B. God commands it to be assembled, etc.	40:1–15
C. Moses assembles it, places furniture, etc.	40:16–33
D. The glory of the Lord fills the Tent of Meeting	40:34–38

Order of Projected Construction Exod 25:1–30:10

(6) The Ark of Testimony
(7) The Atonement Cover
(8) The Table of Presence
(9) The Menorah
(1) The Tent Curtains
(2) The Over-Tent
(3) The Tent Framework
(4) The Veil (placement of furniture)
(5) Entrance Curtain
(13) The Altar of Burnt Offering
(15) The Courtyard
(W) Oil for the Menorah (cf. 37:37)
(17) The Ephod
(18) The Breastpiece
(19) The Robe of the Ephod
(21) The "Holiness" Tiara
(20) Tunics, turbans, sashes
(X) Underpants for the priests
(Y) Long bloque on the ordination of priests (cf. 40:12–15)
(Z) Institution of worship (cf. 40:22, 20)
(10) Altar of incense

Appended Discourses
(14) The Basin
(11) The Anointing Oil
(12) The incense

In the narrative which recounts the actual construction, first the tent curtains are made, then the over-tent, then the tent framework of staves, and the entrance curtains (bloques 1–5). Following this a number of cultic objects are constructed: the ark of testimony with its atonement cover, the table of the presence, the menorah, the altar of incense; the anointing oil and the incense; the altar of burnt offering, and the bronze basin (bloques 6–14). The surrounding courtyard with its entrance curtains (bloques 15–16) are constructed to enclose all the preceding.

The narrative of the construction of the above items is then followed by the narrative of the making of clothes for the priests (bloques 17–21). Finally, following the account of the construction of all these items, the narrative depicts Moses as inspecting the work for presumably both quality of workmanship and pattern-conformity (39:32–42), receiving God's command to erect the Tent of Meeting and its courtyard, placing its furnishings in the correct places, and ordaining the priests (40:1–15). Verses 40:16–33 resume the narrative, with a summary statement in v. 16: "Moses did everything just as the Lord commanded him." Verses 34–38 recount that the Lord took possession of His dwelling: "and the glory of the Lord filled the Tent."

In this narrative account of the construction, the institution of the regular worship—the morning and evening sacrifice and the offering of incense—is only summarily referred to at the end (40:27, 29). Nowhere in the narrative is the note clearly sounded that the various items were built so that God could dwell among His people—although this comes about in 40:34–38. Even the ordination of the priests is not recounted as such, although God enjoins this in summary fashion in Exod 40:12–15. Indeed, the whole account in chapters 36–40 is a rather routine recital to the effect that what was projected in chapters 25–30 was in fact carried out.

Turning again to the discourse with which this study is concerned, we are initially impressed that the order of the projected construction is less logical and harder to rationalize than the order of the narrated construction. Narrative bloques (6)–(9) precede bloques (1)–(5). Furthermore, the construction of the altar of incense (10), instead of being given after (6)–(9) is split off and forms the closure of the first long embedded discourse. Again, while in the narrated account the altar of burnt offering (13) and the bronze basin (14) (the furniture of the courtyard) appear before the construction of the courtyard (15) and its entrance (16), in the projected construction the bronze basin (14) is postponed as one of the appended discourses (30:14–21). So neither the furnishings of the Tent nor of the courtyard are given in one continuous sequence, but one item in each set is dislocated and occurs elsewhere.

As far as the making of the garments for Aaron and his sons, the various pieces of apparel in bloques (17)–(21) occur in the same order in both discourses,[5] except that in the projected construction the "Holy to the Lord" tiara or plaque (21) is mentioned before the section on tunics, turbans, and sashes (20). Furthermore, bloque X of the projected constructions, which prescribes underpants for the priests in 28:42–43, is summarized in a noun phrase in 39:20 of the narrated construction.

Again, therefore, I refer to the macrostructure that is posited at the end of the section 2. The macrostructure, a distillation from the contents of chapters 25–30, does not merely mention making the Tent (and by implication, its furnishings) nor making things according to the revealed pattern; rather, integral parts of the macrostructure are: the purpose that God may dwell among his people, the ordination of the priesthood, and the institution of daily worship. These features make

---

[5] It may well be, however, that the projected order and the narrated order are both transposed in regard to the ephod and the robe of the ephod. While in both 28:6–35 and in 39:1–26 the making of the ephod and of the breastpiece is mentioned before the making of the robe of the ephod, the order of putting on these items of apparel was apparently the reverse, i.e., the robe of the ephod was first put on, then the ephod, then the breastpiece of the ephod. Several things point in this direction: (1) Why is the robe called the robe of the ephod unless the robe and the ephod were closely related? (2) It is hardly credible that the priest's insignia of office on the ephod would have been worn under and concealed by the robe. (3) At any rate, when Moses is told to clothe Aaron for the ordination rites (29:5), he is told to put on him "the tunic, and the robe of the ephod, and the ephod and the breastpiece," and this may well be the actual order of putting on the garments (cf. also Lev 8:7). See again sections 3.4 and 3.7 above.

As to the nature of the ephod, Levine in his beautiful coffee-table picture volume portrays the ephod as a kind of apron. With this substantially agree Wendland (1985:198), Pixley (1987:200), and Cassuto (1967:372–73), who describes it as "a kind of simple pinafore that covered the loins."

I believe that this mitigates somewhat Noth's complaint that "these pieces (of apparel) do not fit together into a convincing overall picture, but to some extent stand in the way of each other" (1962:220). It is his taking the ephod to be a loincloth that is a major source of his difficulties. A waist coat or a kilt could be worn over the robe of the ephod, but if the ephod were a loincloth this would not have been possible.

these instructions quite distinct from the narrated account given in Exod 36–40. As an instructional text, the text is not only full of specifications, and thus heavily prescriptive, but is juridical in certain parts. Everything is to be done—and properly done "now and to all your generations"—with a glorious end in view. A certain atmosphere of religious excitement and awe enters the text at points where the end is envisioned (25:8; 25:22; 25:30; 27:21; 28:29–30 but especially 29:42–46 and to some degree in 30:6–10).

For this reason the apparent departures from logical order in the projected construction can be considered to be departures motivated by the need to highlight these elements of excitement and awe in the macrostructure. Thus, as already suggested, the permutation of the bloques (6)–(9) to the fore of the construction of the Tent and Overtent (1)–(3) can be likened to the presentation of an inciting incident in a story: building the Ark and its atonement cover where YHWH will dwell "between the cherubim" is an important enough step to entail everything else that is to be constructed. As far as the splitting off of the passage concerning construction of the Altar of Incense (10) and making it a postpeak procedure in the projected construction, here, as we have suggested, the incense altar with its morning and evening incense offering is effectively located after the peak, where the instruction of the morning and evening sacrifice of lambs is inculcated; both have to do with the institution of daily worship.

The dislocation of the construction of the bronze basin (14) to an appended discourse in 35:17–21, as well as that the anointing oil (11), given in 30:23–33, and of the incense itself (12), given in 30:34–38, at first blush seem not to be as well motivated. Even here, however, it is possible to conjecture that the overriding demands of the macrostructure has led to a brushing aside of certain details and their postponement to a later position. The discourse 25:1–30:10 is very evidently driving toward its culmination in the prepeak (ordination of the priesthood, 29:1–37), peak (institution of daily worship and God dwelling among His people, 29:38–46), and in the postpeak (more on the daily worship, 30:1–10). The framer of the discourse is, as it were, impatient to get on to his main objectives; and in the process certain items are set aside for later treatment lest they impede the progress of the whole.

From this perspective even the passage on underpants for the priest (28:42–43), which is not only prescriptive but juridical, needs to be considered. The worship of YHWH was to be in every way distinct from contemporary Canaanite worship, which was characterized by sexual motifs and activity. By contrast, there was not even to be accidental exposure of the genitals of an officiating priest—much less sexual activity around the Lord's altars. In the period of the judges the priests Hophni and Phineas were judged for, among other things, sexual activity with women attendants at the Tent of Meeting (1 Sam 2:22), while in the time of the reformer King Josiah it was necessary to expel sacred male prostitutes from their quarters in the Temple itself (2 Kings 23:7)

The passage of 28:42–43 constitutes, then, an urgent concern relative to the institutions of worship. Since the passage concerns the clothing of the priests, it properly finds its place at the close of the section on the priests' clothing. Nevertheless, the quasi-parenthetical nature lies in the fact that this bit of apparel concerns decency rather than dignity and is to this degree unlike the rest of the clothes-making prescriptions.

It is also of further interest here that the instructional discourse of chapters 25–30 is divided from its narrative implementation in chapters 36–40 by the interlude of the golden calf and the aftermath in chapters 32–34 (while 35 is mainly concerned with gathering materials for construction). Here the author of Exodus, in separating the projected construction from the narrated construction by means of this account of lapse into unauthorized worship and idolatry, has underscored the need for a worship according to the revealed pattern and has anticipated the struggle throughout Israel's history between such divinely instituted worship and the perennial invasions of Canaanite religious patterns.

4. A Beginning at Microsegmentation

The principles of microsegmentation that will be discussed and illustrated here are (1) the distribution and function of *waw*-conjunctival; (2) further considerations of thematicity and pronominal reference; and (3) the ranking of verb forms/clause types in a scheme of relative closeness to or departure from the main instructional line of the discourse. In respect to the latter consideration, height of ranking in the salience scheme correlates roughly with dominance within the local span (the paragraph).

4.1. *Waw*-conjunctival in the sentence and the paragraph

In accordance with a theory of BH sentence structure which has been developed elsewhere (Longacre, 1989, chap. 4), the Hebrew sentence is, for the most part, a domain set off by *waw*, whether consecutive or conjunctival. Absence of *waw* is more likely to indicate the continuation of a sentence unit than its onset. Thus a BH sentence is basically of three sorts: (a) a main clause to which may be attached subordinate clauses and relative clauses; (b) complementation sentences with a *wayhî* or *wĕhāyâ* plus a temporal expression plus the main clause; and (c) paratactic sentences—without medial *waw*—and usually chiastic in structure: $V_1N_1 + N_2V_2$ where V_2 either repeats V_1 or is a synonym of V_1. The text type here under consideration uses (a) and (c) extensively with almost no use of (b)—which occurs mainly in narrative and predictive discourses.

Very frequently, then, a Hebrew sentence begins with a *waw*. A few exceptions occur, however. In some narrative discourses (possibly in some predictive as well) a temporal phrase can begin a clause without any preceding *waw* (cf. Gen 22:4 where this marks onset of an episode). In the text under analysis here, an instructional discourse, there occurs a specialized sort of comment paragraph whose thesis is accompanied by a specification structure. Thus, the thesis of such a paragraph can be "Build an X." It is typically accompanied by: "q cubits Ø its length. And r cubits Ø its width. And s cubits Ø its height." Here the whole complex of three sentences, which specify length, width, and height is a coordinate paragraph that is embedded in the specification slot. The *waw* is omitted in the first sentence of the embedded paragraph. If, however, more than one specification structure appears, then each initiating sentence is marked by the absence of the usual introductory *waw*.

Diagram II illustrates both the operation of minus *waw* in binding together clauses in paratactic (and chiastic) sentences, and the operation of minus *waw* in indicating a specification on the paragraph level. This diagram also serves to illustrate WQTL forms as mainline of this discourse type (sec. 4.3), and considerations of thematicity in setting up embedded paragraphs (sec. 4.2). I shall present the paragraph (Exod 25:10–17) in semiliteral translation from the Hebrew via an indentation diagram in which levels of indentation represent levels of embedding. The slot class assumption of dejargonized tagmemics (Longacre, 1983) is assumed throughout.

DIAGRAM II: TREE STRUCTURE OF EXOD 25:10–17, AN INSTRUCTIONAL SEQUENCE PARAGRAPH

Sequential Thesis$_1$: (I) Comment Para.
  Thesis: And they shall make [WQTL] an ark of acacia wood.
  Spec: (E) Coord. Para.
    Thesis$_1$: $2^1/_2$ cubits Ø its L.
    Thesis$_2$: And $1^1/_2$ cubits Ø its W.
    Thesis$_3$: And $1^1/_2$ cubits Ø its H.
Sequential Thesis$_2$: And you shall overlay it [WQTL] with pure gold; inside and outside you shall overlay it [N-YQTL]
Sequential Thesis$_3$: And you shall make [WQTL] upon it a gold molding all around.
Sequential Thesis$_4$: (I) Seq. Para.
  Sequential Thesis$_1$: And you shall cast [WQTL] for it 4 rings of gold.
  Sequential Thesis$_2$: (I) Comment Para.
    Thesis: And you will attach [WQTL] them at it 4 feet.
    Spec: (E) Coord. Para.
      Thesis$_1$: 2 rings Ø on its one side
      Thesis$_2$: And 2 rings Ø on its second side.
Sequential Thesis$_5$: (I) Sequence Para.
  Sequential Thesis$_1$: And you shall make [WQTL] poles of acacia wood.
  Sequential Thesis$_2$: And you shall overlay [WQTL] them with gold.
  Sequential Thesis$_3$: (I) Comment Para.
    Thesis: And you shall insert [WQTL] the poles in the rings in the sides of the Ark to carry the Ark by means of them.
    Spec: (J) Paraphrase Para.
      Thesis: In the rings of the Ark shall be [N-YQTL] the poles.
      N.A.P.: You shall not [*lōʾ*-TQTL] take them out of it.
Sequential Thesis$_n$: And you shall put [WQTL] into the Ark the testimony which I shall give you.

In Diagram II, Sequential Theses (abbreviated ST below) 1, 4, 5 are expounded by embedded paragraphs, while ST 2, 3, and n are expounded by sentence structures. ST_2 is expounded by a paratactic chiastic sentence without any internal *waw*. This sentence has an on-the-line WQTL form that initiates it and an off-the-line YQTL form of the same verb that closes it; intervening noun phrases are assigned either to the first or to the second clause.

ST_1 is expounded by an instructional comment paragraph whose thesis is a WQTL clause. The comment slot of an instructional paragraph is so semantically specialized that I call it specification slot here and everywhere in the paper. Here the specification is expounded by what is obviously a coordinate paragraph; I term it expository coordinate in that the sentence structures which occur in it characterize expository discourse. It has three component sentences in the coordinated theses; these sentences specify the dimensions of the Ark of Testimony. Theses 2 and 3 regularly begin with *waw*, the sentence marker. The *waw* does not occur in the sentence of $Thesis_1$, since this sentence initiates the specification unit and minus *waw* marks the initiation of this structure.

Similarly, in regard to specifying the location of the rings for the carrying poles (within the I Seq. paragraph embedded under main ST_4) under ST_2 of the embedded unit, there is an expository (E) comment paragraph in which the first sentence of the specification has no *waw*, while the second does.

A slight problem—between the somewhat conflicting functions of *waw* within the sentence and within the paragraph—is found in ST_3 embedded under main ST_5. I indicate here an embedded juridical paraphrase paragraph. Both the sentence in the Thesis slot and the one in the Negated Antonym Paraphrase (N.A.P.) slot lack initial *waw*. The language is typically juridical in the prescriptive use of the verb *hāyâ*, "be," and in regard to the prohibitive use of *lōʾ*-TQTL in the next sentence. That I do not join the two as one sentence is because of the typically juridical structure in both sentences. As for the absence of *waw* in the second sentence, an N.A.P. is, in a sense, a kind of specification of the previous injunction. Possibly the semantic category of specification occurs in more than one paragraph level slot. The absence of *waw* on the first sentence is, however, quite predictable as the initial sentence in a specification slot.

This paragraph illustrates nicely the mainline role of WQTL clauses in instructional discourse. It also illustrates the manner in which considerations of thematicity lead to the positing of embedded paragraphs. While all the WQTL sentences could be considered to constitute a simple linear string of nine sequential theses, it seems better to recognize as main ST_4 a stretch whose theme is the making of the rings and whose structure is that of an embedded instructional sequence paragraph with its own ST_1 and ST_2. Similarly, it seems plausible to posit in main ST_5 a stretch whose theme is the making of the carrying poles which are to go into the rings. This stretch is considered to consist of an embedded instructional sequence paragraph with its own ST_1, ST_2, and ST_3.

DIAGRAM III: TREE STRUCTURE OF EXOD 26:15–17

ST_1: (I) Comment Paragraph
Thesis: And you shall make [WQTL] for the Tent staves of upright wood.
$Spec_1$: (E) Coor. Paragraph
$Thesis_1$: 10 cubits Ø the length of one stave.
$Thesis_2$: And $1^1/_2$ cubits Ø the width of one stave.
$Spec_2$: Two projections Ø on one stave, set woman against her sister.
Summary: Thus shall you make [*kēn* TQTL] for all the staves of the Tent.

More complicated situations regarding the absence or presence of conjunctival *waw* occur where two or more specifications are attached to one thesis rather than where the specifications constitute a coordinate paragraph, which as a unit expounds specification. Such a situation is illustrated in the opening sentences of Exod 26:15–30, which as a whole is concerned with the making of the staves for the tabernacle framework (Diagram III).[6] In this embedded comment paragraph (26:15–17) there are two specifications and one summary, all of which are ancillary to the same thesis. The thesis itself has the usual WQTL verb that is characteristic of the mainline in the discourse type. $Specification_1$ is expounded by a coordinate paragraph. As seen above, no *waw* conjunctival occurs on the first sentence of such a unit, but *waw* regularly occurs on the second sentence. $Specification_2$ as the only sentence in this repeated slot also is minus *waw* conjunctival—as in the summary with *kēn*, "thus."

4.2. Thematicity and pronominal references

As we have seen, Diagram II illustrates subparagraphing determined by thematicity. Thus in a paragraph concerning making the ark there occur two embedded sequence paragraphs on the making of the

[6] While it is not within the scope of this article to discuss architectural details of the Tabernacle, the relation of the curtains (the tent proper) to the wooden staves, pillars, and what-have-you is a moot question that has evoked considerable comment. Were the wooden pieces solid pillars of wood, which would conceal the cherubim embroidered in the inside of the tent curtains and at the same time constitute very heavy pieces to carry around—or is there some other explanation? Noth eventually considers the text to present here an incongruous picture of a tent sanctuary and a portable wooden structure capable of being dismantled (1962:110–13). Kennedy, however, in his classic description of the Tabernacle (1902) supposes the wooden pieces not to be solid but to have consisted of two parallel pieces of wood with an opening between them and joined at top and bottom. While Hyatt (1971:271) and Pixley (1987:196) agree with Kennedy in this respect, Cassuto (1967) and Levine (1968) reject this view and argue for solid boards.

rings and of the carrying poles respectively. This is a typical situation. In fact, there are none of the 27 paragraphs that I have posited and diagrammed in this text that do not have at least one such embedded paragraph determined by thematicity shifts. One of the longest embedded sequence paragraphs found in the text is in 29:4–7, where, after a preliminary N-YQTL sentence, there occurs a succession of nine WQTL sentences. This is, however, an unusually long uninterrupted run of WQTL sentences. I mention here, somewhat at random, some further examples of subparagraphs determined by thematicity.

Exod 25:23–30 is an instructional sequence paragraph concerning the construction of the table on which was to be put the Bread of the Presence. ST_3 is a three-sentence paragraph (vv. 24b, 25) which has to do with the making of a molding around the table, a rim, and a further molding on the rim. ST_4 is a paragraph (vv. 26, 27) of three sentences concerning the rings which are to be attached to the table. ST_5 is likewise a three-sentence paragraph (v. 28) which provided for the making of the carrying poles. Other ST's are single sentences (ST_2 and ST_6 and ST_n) or an instructional comment paragraph of the sort already illustrated.

Exod 26:1–6 is an instructional sequence paragraph concerning the making of the Tabernacle curtains. ST_1 is an instructional comment paragraph (vv. 1–3) with one thesis and two specifications both of which are expounded by (E) coordinate paragraphs; it specifies the dimensions of the curtains as well as which are to be coupled. ST_2 is likewise an embedded instructional comment paragraph with both thesis and specification consisting of coordinated paragraphs; it treats of the making of loops in the curtains.

Exod 26:31–35, likewise an instructional sequence paragraph, is concerned with the construction of the Veil (to divide the Holy of Holies from the Holy Place), the hanging of it, and the placement of furniture relative to it. ST_1 instructs concerning the making of the veil and hanging it upon four wood pillars overlaid with gold and equipped with hooks and sockets (vv. 31–32). ST_2 instructs concerning the placement of the furniture relative to the veil (vv. 33–35), and ST_3 instructs concerning the curtain for the entrance to the Tent (vv. 36–37). Each ST unit is expounded by a paragraph of four or five sentences (and lower-level embedding).

Exod 27:9–19 is a rather unusual paragraph that hangs four specifications upon one thesis; the whole is concerned with the making of curtains for the courtyard. The thesis (v. 9) is: "And you shall make the courtyard of the Tent." The first specification unit (9b–16) specifies in a coordinate paragraph (with multiple layers of embedding) for the south side, the north side, the west side, the east side with hanging on each side of the entrance, and finally the entrance curtain itself. We have here five coordinated theses with only the first sentence of Th_1 lacking a *waw*, while further specifications within such a unit (charcteristically dimensions) show characteristic absence of *waw* in the first sentence. Further specifications 2, 3, 4 deal with in order: the staves (v. 17), the general dimensions of the courtyard (v. 18), and further utensils and tent pegs (v. 19)—all of which are to be of bronze. Initial sentences in these specifications are minus *waw.*

The instructions for making the breastpiece of judgment in Exod 28:15–30 is the longest paragraph in the text. Essentially it is an instructional result paragraph whose thesis is expounded by an instructional sequence paragraph with three ST's. ST_1 specifies the dimensions and spells out the job for the tailor (vv. 15–16). ST_2, expounded by an instructional comment paragraph, specifies the four rows of stones engraved with the names of the twelve sons of Israel (vv. 17–21). ST_3, expounded by an instructional sequence paragraph with multiple embedding, prescribes the making of wreathen gold chains, golden rings, and blue cords to bind the breastpiece of judgment securely on the ephod "so it won't swing out" (end of v. 28). Finally, a WQTL sentence with a subject switch to Aaron signals the onset of the result: (if everything is done as specified,) then Aaron shall bear continually on his heart the names of the children of Israel—as their mediatorial representative (vv. 29–30).

4.3. Verb ranking and relative salience within the paragraph

It is obvious from the above sections that WQTL sentences occupy a position of privilege in the instructional discourse and can be considered to carry the mainline of instruction. Sentences that have a noun phrase preceding a YQTL verb act in many ways like a secondary line of instruction. Sentences in which WQTL occurs with switch reference (SR) of subject commonly indicate a sort of ekbalic construction. Clauses with initial YQTL verbs occur in this text almost exclusively as (a) second member of indirect quote construction ("Speak to them and they shall bring" > "Speak to them that they bring . . ."); and (b) purpose clauses. Participial clauses—characteristically accompanied by a form of *hāyâ*, "be"—nominal clauses, and cleft sentences occur in a specificatory, descriptive function. WQTL *hāyâ* sentences, N-YQTL *hāyâ* sentences, and *lōʾ*-YQTL sentences are more often than not prescriptive injunctive sentences in juridical discourse and are, properly speaking, not relevant to this scheme. Finally, we have also to account for the functions of the imperative and have a second look at the cleft sentence.

In the above section on the imperative (3.1.1), it was emphasized that all imperatives found in this text are 2 sg. and are addressed to Moses himself as mediator of the covenant. In this role he is the one who receives instructions and passes them on to the people. So much is he the causer of all that is built and done that very early in chapter 25, "You tell them that they do X" is replaced by, "And then you will do X." As already stated, there is an agency hierarchy assumed in the text: God, Moses, they (people, special artisans, and priests), artifacts. Imperatives are directed from God to Moses as causer/dispatcher. It is therefore necessary to realize that the use of the imperative is bound up with concerns that belong to the participant structure as formulated in the agency hierarchy.

But the same concerns also govern to some degree certain uses of WQTL that do not appear to be on the mainline of instruction. Any WQTL form characterized by switch reference from the previous subject (abbreviated WQTL-SR) has an ekbalic function. Switch reference which goes down the agency hierarchy expresses result; 26:16: "And you shall fasten the curtains to each other. And it shall be one tent." 29:21: "And you sprinkle [the blood] upon Aaron and his sons . . . and he will be holy." On the other hand, switch reference which goes up the agency hierarchy expresses promise; 25:8: "And they shall make me a sanctuary. And I will dwell among them."

This is also partially true of YQTL forms in the text. YQTL forms in purpose clauses often display a SR relative to the main clause: "And you will make an X so that it may do/may not do Q."

Except for interference from the presence of embedded juridical paragraphs, participial clauses (usually with *hāyâ*), *hāyâ*-clauses, and nominal clauses function as forms of specification or closure in the instructions. Cleft sentences are very similar in function, but often seem to be amplifying instead of simply specifying.

A further function, portmanteau to the above, of both imperative and cleft sentences is that of marking the onset of a new section (3.1.1.).

These considerations have led to the formulation of the salience scheme found in Diagram IV.

DIAGRAM IV

Band 1 IMPV (2 sg.)
command to causer/dispatcher/mediator

Band 2
a. WQTL primary line of instruction
b. N-YQTL secondary line of instruction

Band 3
a. WQTL (SR) ekbalic (result/promise)
b. YQTL (±SR) purpose

Band 4
a. participial (with *hāyâ*)
b. *hāyâ* clauses
c. nominal clauses
d. cleft sentences

Band 5 (IMPV) portmanteau
(cleft sentence) with above but articulating a new section

Promotion and demotion:
(1) 2b > 2a by explicit coordination and parallelism [non-periphrastic]
(2) clauses with WQTL forms deleted by gapping resemble nominal clauses but remain 2a.
(3) deletion of *waw* can demote 2b > 4
(4) when 3a ascends the Agency Hierarchy result > promise

A few residual problems (see notes at the bottom of Diagram IV) remain that will have to be discussed (along with full presentation of the tree structures) in a sequel to this paper. Thus, apparently some N-YQTL forms can, by explicit coordination and parallelism (non-paraphrastic), be promoted to the primary line of instruction (Exod 26:15–30, especially v. 22). This is quite exceptional to the usual use of N-YQTL clauses as preparatory or ancillary in the secondary line of instruction. In the same paragraph (v. 20) an apparent nominal clause is on the main line of instruction, but here a kind of verb gapping occurs and a WQTL can be supplied from what precedes. I also note that minus *waw* in a N-YQTL form demotes it to band 4 (specification).

Suffice it to say: secondary lines have a way of extending upward toward the primary line—whether in narrative (N-QTL) or in instructional (N-YQTL). In general, however, any scheme of salience for any discourse type in any language has to permit some systematic promotions and demotions to make it work. A system without safety valves self-destructs.

5. Conclusion

In this paper we have moved from the larger concerns of the first two sections to more detailed concerns. In moving from the larger to the smaller concerns it is important to remember that the latter sort of analysis undergirds and supplements the former. Questions of macrostructure (textual meaning) in section 2 are seen to be interwoven with matters of macrosegmentation in section 3. But these concerns are themselves seen to be linked to the study of such linguistic features as the distribution of imperatives, cleft sentences, and pronominal references—although in regard to the ordering of subsegments of the text we resorted again at the end of section 3 to the concept of the macrostructure as a control. Everywhere broader concerns interlace with the narrower details of analysis. In section 4 the linguistic structure of the text, with WQTL forms as the mainline of instruction, is further rounded out with a few details that expedite local exegesis, e.g., the absence of initial *waw* in specification constructions, and the WQTL with switch reference as indicative of result/ promise.

WORKS CONSULTED

Cassuto, U.
1967 *A Commentary on the Book of Exodus.* Trans. Israel Abrahams. Jerusalem: Magnes.

Childs, Brevard S.
1974 *The Book of Exodus.* OTL. Philadelphia: Westminster.

Cole, R. Alan
1973 *Exodus.* Tyndale Old Testament Commentaries. Downers Grove, Illinois: InterVarsity.

Hyatt, J. Philip
1971 *Exodus.* New Century Bible. Grand Rapids: Eerdmans.

Kennedy, A. R. S.
1902 "Tabernacle." Pp. 653–68 in *Hastings Dictionary of the Bible.* Vol. 4.

Knight, George A. F.
1976 *Theology as Narration.* Grand Rapids: Eerdmans.

Levine, Moshe
1968 *Mĕleket hammiškān.* Tel Aviv: Mlechet Hamishkan.

Longacre, R. E.
1979 "The Discourse Structure of the Flood Narrative." *JAAR* 47 Sup. B:89–133.
1982 "Discourse Typology in Relation to Language Typology." Pp. 457–486 in *Text Processing,* ed. Sture Allén. Stockholm: Almqvist and Wiksel.
1983 *The Grammar of Discourse.* New York: Plenum.
1989 *Joseph, A Story of Divine Providence: A Text Theoretical and Textlinguistic Analysis of Gen. 37 and 39–46.* Winona Lake, IN: Eisenbrauns.

Noth, Martin
1962 *Exodus.* OTL. Trans. John Bowden. Philadelphia: Westminster.

Pixley, George V.
1987 *Exodus: A Liberation Perspective.* Maryknoll, NY: Orbis.

Wendland, Ernst H.
1985 *Exodus.* Milwaukee: Northwestern.

2

ISAIAH 40:1–11 IN THE CONTEXT OF THE MACROSTRUCTURE OF SECOND ISAIAH

David McLain Carr

ABSTRACT

This paper addresses the problem of the structure of Isa 40:1–11. Most previous treatments of the passage have either understood it to be divided into four equal parts (40:1–2, 3–5, 6–8, 9–11) or two separate pericopes (40:1–8, 9–11). Using a text linguistic approach developed by Gühlich and Raible, this paper argues for a proposal that incorporates the observations of previous studies and locates the passage as a whole within the macrostructure of Second Isaiah.

I preface this paper with two "meta-communicative" comments (the meaning of this term will become clear in the course of the following discussion). First, this is an application paper. I do not attempt a survey of the field of text linguistics. Instead, I appropriate a particular method of descending text analysis that shows particular promise in informing biblical scholars. This method was originally developed by Elizabeth Gühlich and Wolfgang Raible in their work on modern European language texts, but they argue persuasively for the cross-linguistic applicability of their observations. The method they have developed is particularly helpful in its systematic treatment of indicators above the level of syntax and its concomitant focus on a hierarchy of text structure indicators.

Second, this paper has a structure of its own. It begins with a review of the problem in understanding the structure of Isa 40:1–11. The second section is a survey of the relevant parts of the text linguistic method adopted in this paper. In the final section the text linguistic method is applied to Isa 40:1–11.

Previous Study of Isa 40:1–11

It does not take a text linguistic approach to recognize the radical break that Isaiah 40:1 represents. A perceptive pre-critical exegete like Rashi could observe that "from here to the end of the book are words of comfort." Here he built on some Jewish interpretations that saw Isaiah as the great prophet, and the word of comfort in Isa 40:1 as typifying the greatness of Isaiah's message.[1] Likewise, in the Christian tradition, Luther in his lectures on Isaiah saw the book of Isaiah as made up of two parts: chapters 1–39 were the book of law, and chapters 40–66 were the book of grace. Such pre-critical perception of the break at the beginning of chapter 40 long preceded the widespread consensus in modern biblical scholarship that 40:1 begins the message of a "second Isaiah."

Twentieth century text linguists and form critics work with the same surface structure indicators that readers throughout the history of interpretation have, and could have, seen. Therefore, such a consensus of observations by pre-critical scholars can be useful in the analysis of text structure. Once one gets past Isa 40:1, however, there is substantial disagreement, about both the extent and the structure of second Isaiah as a whole (Westermann, 1964 [1981 reprint]:90–92; Whybray: 27; Preuss: 16–18; Scullion: 20). Nevertheless, the disagreement about Isa 40:1–11 follows consistent patterns. There is almost universal agreement that this passage breaks at 40:1, 3, 6, and 9. The issue is the significance of each of these breaks. Two basic options appear. Some divide 40:1–11 into Isaiah's call report (vv. 1–8) and a

---

[1] See in particular the comparison of prophets in *Leviticus Rabbah* 10:2 and *Pesiqta Rabbati* 29/30:4–5; 33:3 (parallels to *Pesiqta Rabbati* in the *Pesiqta de Rab Kahana* 1:16). See also the lists of places where Isaiah's word of hope contradicts Jeremiah's word of doom (*Lamentations Rabbah* 1:23; *Pesiqta Rabbati* 30:4). The *Tanḥuma* tradition (including the *Tanḥuma* Buber) includes a note about Isaiah offering double words of comfort (beginning of the *Debarim* seder). Cf. also *Genesis Rabbah* 100:9. The liturgical placement of this passage is relevant to this overview of its Jewish interpretation. Isa 40:1 begins the haftarah reading on the first Sabbath after the ninth of Ab (fast day for the destruction of the temple).

Such observations are not meant to imply that these interpreters intuited the existence of a "Second Isaiah" distinct from the first, but only that they seem to have recognized a break in the book at this point. Such intuition of separate Isaiah material does not begin to appear until Ibn Ezra. On this see Simon:257–71.

victory messenger instruction (vv. 9–11). The call report is then further divided into three parts: vv. 1–2, 3–5, 6–8 (Mowinckel:88–90; Begrich:13, 58–59; Fohrer: 15–23; Elliger:34; Krinetski:57; Loretz, 1974:489–91; Vincent:250–51, 258; Preuss:41–42).[2] In most such treatments, the call report and victory messenger instruction are not related to a macro-structure of Second Isaiah, but rather are taken as the first two of many separate pericopes that make up the Second Isaiah collection of sayings. In contrast, those who take 40:1–11 as a single unit usually understand this text to be the prologue to Second Isaiah as a whole. This pericope is then understood to be composed of four relatively equal parts: vv. 1–2, 3–5, 6–8, 9–11 (Thexton:4; Leslie:169; Westerman, 1964 [1981 reprint: 82–84], 1966:30; McKenzie:16; Bonnard:85; Lack:83; Sacon:112–13; Herbert:16; Spykerboer:182–84; Melugin:82–86; Petersen:20; Kiesow:24–26; Eaton:41; Beuken:15–18, 29–30; Ettore:303–4; Loretz, 1984:284–96; Wilson:231; Watts:78; Sweeney: 92–95).[3]

---

[2] Elliger (34) sees 40:1–8 as the original unit and the rest of chapter 40 as a whole as the prologue. Loretz's position is modified in his 1984 treatment of the same passage.

[3] In his 1984 article Loretz follows Kiesow (284–96), in contrast to his earlier treatment of the passage (1974: 489–91).

Lack (83) sees vv. 1–11 as the prologue, but chap. 40 as a whole as also introductory. In addition, the following authors argue that chap. 40 as a whole is the introduction to Second Isaiah: Rignell (9–21 [particularly 15 and 20–21]), Haran (127, 132–36) and Smart (41).

There have been some divergences from the overall trend to treat Isa 40:1–11 as consisting of four relatively equal parts (1–2, 3–5, 6–8, 9–11). Gressmann treats 40:1–2 (p. 275), 3–5, 6–8 (pp. 264–66), and 9–11 (p. 269) as separate form critical units. Rignell (9) and Ettore (296–300) are exceptions in breaking 1–11 into three parts (1–5, 6–8, 9–11). Habel (314–16) argues for dividing the unit into four units: 1–2, 3–5, 6–7, and 8–11. Muilenburg (415, 431–34) sees five parts here: 1–2, 3–5, 6–8, 9–10 and 11. Stuhlmueller (179) briefly outlines Isa 40:1–11 into two parts: 1–2 and 3–11.

Applying models from Greco-Roman rhetoric to Isaiah, Gitay argues that 40:1–11 should be divided into four parts: "the topic" (v. 1), "the thesis" (v. 2), "confirmation" (vv. 3–8), and "the epilogue" (v. 9–11). Isa 40:1–11, however, does not appear to be an argument built along the lines of Greco-Roman rhetoric. V. 1 is a command, not a "topic." Whatever "thesis" is stated in v. 2 is not "confirmed" in vv. 3–8. Rather, the statement that Jerusalem's warfare is ended and its iniquity paid for (v. 2) is followed by certain further consequences: an announcement of a procession/exodus through the wilderness (3–5) and a commissioning of a prophet (6–8). Finally, labeling 9–11 as an "epilogue" focuses exclusively on the function of these verses vis-à-vis the pericope in itself (40:1–11), ignoring their transitional role in the structure of Second Isaiah as a whole. On this, see below.

Indicators point to both options. On the one hand, the themes of Jerusalem and comfort link 40:1–2 to 40:9–11 (Kieso 38–41). In addition, there is a radical break at verse 12 from the imperatives and announcement themes of 1–11 to the disputation and creation themes of 40:12–31. These indicators favor joining vv. 9–11 with vv. 1–8. On the other hand, other indicators sharply distinguish 9–11 from 1–8. As mentioned before, form critics usually characterize 40:1–8 as a call narrative and 40:9–11 as a victory messenger instruction. Moreover, the feminine singular imperatives of v. 9 contrast with the masculine imperatives of the preceding verses. This mixture of indicators has led some exegetes to mediate between these two positions, taking 1–11 together as a prologue to Second Isaiah that has two main parts: 1–8 and 9–11. Often these two parts are then taken as introducing different parts of Second Isaiah (Melugin:82–86; Beuken:15–18, 29–30; Merendino:1–122; and Sweeney:92–95).

This review hardly sums up all of the observations made by previous exegetes of Isa 40:1–11, but it does begin to indicate the issues that dominate the discussion:

1. How are vv. 9–11 of chapter 40 related to vv. 1–8? Are vv. 9–11 the fourth part of a pericope extending from 1–11, or are they somehow separate?
2. How does the division between 40:1–8 and 40:9–11 relate to the macrostructure of Second Isaiah (whatever that might be)?

Most previous discussions have been eclectic in the kinds of indicators they have used to support different analyses of 40:1–11. The following indicators have been considered: vocabulary, theme, switches in grammatical subject, and the move in verse 40:12 from imperatives to statements. The problem is knowing how to weigh these different indicators and adjudicate between the competing proposals which they support.

Overview of the Text Linguistic Method Adopted Here

On the basis of their model of textual communication Gühlich and Raible make a primary distinction between text-internal and text-external factors. Text-internal factors are those elements governed by *langue*, the grammatical-syntactical rules shared (at least partially in common) by speaker and hearer. Examples of text-internal phenomena include pronominal substitution (use of a pronoun for a previously mentioned person or thing), renominalization (later explicit mention of the person or thing after the pronoun has been used), conjunctions, conjunctive adverbs, and word order. Text-external factors are those parts of the context of the text not governed by such grammatical-syntactical rules. The following are text-external factors: the speaker, the hearer, and the world of things and facts, both those things and facts commonly perceived by speaker and hearer and those which are not commonly perceived (Raible:33–241, esp. 230–37; Gühlich and Raible, 1975:151–60, 1977a:21–59, 1977b:133–50).[4]

By definition, text-external factors cannot occur in texts. Nevertheless, texts frequently include words or phrases that refer to text-external factors. For example, sentences at the beginning of a text can describe the text as a whole, directly address the hearer regarding the use of the text, state the speaker's intent, and direct the hearer's attention to a certain real or fictive world of things and facts commonly perceived by speaker and hearer. Such words, phrases, or sentences with text-external analogies set up the context of a text that is further divided by text-internal structure indicators.

The paradigmatic examples of such text-external structure indicators are sentences such as are commonly found in the prefaces of books. For example, West writes in the preface to the first edition of his *Introduction to the Old Testament*:

> This book is offered as a basic introduction to the collection of religious writings known to Catholics as the Old Testament . . . , to Protestants as the Old Testament with Apocrypha, and to Jews as the Tanak plus other major pre-Talmudic works. It is designed for the reader, of whatever religious or theological persuasion, who seeks to understand how these books originated, the history and culture of the people who produced them, and the characteristic ideas which they contain (xi).

These sentences play a constitutive role in introducing the body of the book that follows. They describe the text as a whole, its focus, and its intended audience. Gühlich and Raible term such statements, "metacommunicative sentences." Through thematizing the speaker, hearer,

---

[4] Heger makes some similar observations (1976:227–28, 1979:2–24), but see Raible's insightful critique (1979).

I owe my initial exposure to the field of text linguistics and Gühlich and Raible in particular to David Hellholm's 1986 article: "The Problem of Apocalyptic Genre and the Apocalypse of John." He has a more lengthy methodological discussion in the first volume of his published dissertation (1980).

text, and/or text world, meta-communicative sentences play the highest role in governing the reception of the following text. When such meta-communicative sentences occur, they mark the beginning and end of a text.

Probably the best biblical example of such metacommunicative statements are first person prophetic call reports. These reports almost always stand at the beginning of the prophetic collection and use first person narration to describe the origins and purpose of each prophet's message. Examples of such reports include Isa 6:1–13 (as the beginning of the "Testimony Book," Isa 6:1–9:7), Jer 1:4–10, and Ezek 1:1–3:27. Other biblical meta-communicative statements include the description of the "preacher" in the first of the appendices to Qohelet (Qoh 12:9–10) and prophetic word-event formulae, particularly the first person formulae found frequently in Jeremiah and Ezekiel (Jer 1:4, 11; 2:1; 13:3, 8; 16:1; 18:5; 24:4; 32:6; Ezek 3:16; 6:1; 7:1; 11:14; 12:1, 8, 17, 21, 26; 13:1; 14:2, 12; 15:1; 16:1; 17:1, 11; 18:1; 20:2; 21:1, 6, 23; 22:1, 17, 23; 23:1; 24:1, 15, 20; 25:1; 26:1; 27:1; 28:1, 11, 20; 29:1, 17; 30:1, 20; 31:1; 32:1, 17; 33:1, 23; 34:1; 35:1; 36:16; 37:15; 38:1). These latter formulae mark the beginnings of discrete prophetic oracles through thematizing the prophet and presenting the message as being of divine origin.

The next highest indicators are titles ("Little Red Riding Hood," "The Structure of Isaiah 40:1–11 . . .") or other words that designate a text or part of a text. Though these can designate the text as a whole (thus possibly concurring with meta-communicative sentences), they can also occur inside texts, as chapter headings, for example. The Bible is full of such titles. The beginning of almost every one of the prophetic collections is headed with a superscription. Mic 1:1 is an example: "The Word of the Lord that came to Micah of Moresheth in the days of Jotham, Ahaz, and Hezekiah, kings of Judah, which he saw concerning Samaria and Jerusalem." Proverbs, Qohelet, Song of Songs, and Nehemiah are among the biblical books that begin with similar superscriptions. Many books of prophecy (Isaiah, Haggai, Zechariah) are further subdivided by general headings, as are some Psalms, and parts of Proverbs.[5]

[5] Note the subtle shift from meta-communicative sentences (word-event formulae) to incomplete sentences using similar formulations but now serving as titles: Hos 1:1; Zeph 1:1; Joel 1:1. See also: Prov 1:1; 10:1; 24:23; 25:1; 30:1; 31:1; Qoh 1:1; and Cant 1:1.

Slightly lower on the hierarchy of structure indicators lie words or phrases that are used to designate a particular event or period in a text that is structured by time sequence. In Hebrew this is often done through the expression אַחֲרֵי־כֵן "after this." For example, in Genesis 23, after the text has described and summarized Abraham's purchase of the field at Machpelah, verse 19 says, אַחֲרֵי־כֵן קָבַר אַבְרָהָם אֶת־שָׂרָה אִשְׁתּוֹ "After this Abraham buried Sarah, his wife." Similarly, in Gen 45:15 the expression אַחֲרֵי־כֵן is used to refer back to Joseph's revelation of his real identity to his brothers in 45:4–14. In both cases, אַחֲרֵי־כֵן marks a text unit off (Gen 23:3–18 and 45:4–14 respectively) as describing a single event.[6]

The next set of structure indicators relates exclusively to organizing the semantic world of the text. For narrative texts such structure indicators are those which mark time and space changes, i.e., episode markers. Thus the wilderness section of the Pentateuch is divided into narratives of events at each stopping point along the way. Each stopping point represents an episode in the journey from Egypt to Canaan.

Another important signal is a shift in character groupings. For example, Knierim observed (1985a:399–404) that the final form of the Sinai pericope is divided into parts by Moses' ascents to the mountain to speak with God and descents from the mountain to speak with the people. Each ascent and descent includes a shift in characters (Moses–people, Moses–God) and place (foot of mountain versus top of mountain). He notes that though older elements in Exod 32:15–34:4 are not integrated completely into this scheme, the overarching semantic shifts are clear.

This is one point where Hellholm's system supplements that of Gühlich and Raible. Using insights from semantics, Hellholm persuasively argues that indicators of shifts in sets of worlds take precedence over episode markers and shifts in agents. "Sets of worlds" include concepts of this world (real or fictive) or of "other worlds" such as

---

[6] Other examples include Exod 34:32; Num 8:22; Josh 8:34; and 2 Chron 20:35; 33:14. אַחֲרֵי־כֵן also occurs in non-narrative contexts, particularly as a delineator in the sequence of different items in a prediction (Gen 15:14; Exod 3:20; 11:8; Jer 16:16; 21:7; 46:26; 49:6) or law (Num 4:15; 8:15). Yet more specific references to events can occur with אַחֲרֵי followed by an infinitive construct. For example, אַחֲרֵי הַכּוֹת־יְהוָה אֶת־הַיְאֹר "After the Lord struck the Nile" (Exod 7:25b referring to the event described in Exod 7:20–21).

those in a fairy tale or fantasy, or a transcendent world, e.g., heaven (1980:31–42, 87–91; 1986:40–41). Hellholm uses this approach to analyze the structures of apocalypses, which often have as one of their key components a heavenly vision.

The brief overview above results in the following hierarchy of text structure indicators:

1. Meta-communicative sentences
2. Substitution on the meta-level (chapter headings)
3. Substitution on an abstraction level (events)
4. Change in worlds (this world, other world)
5. Episode markers (change in time or place)
6. Changes in the grouping of agents

Indicators 1–3 refer to the meta-level of the text, while indicators 4–6 refer exclusively to the world of things and facts explored by the text. All six indicators have some kind of text-external analogy, and are thus distinguished from text-internal indicators which lack such an analogy, such as pronominalization.

Gühlich and Raible use these indicators for a "descending analysis" of text structure. This means that they begin with the highest indicator present in a text. This indicator divides the largest sections of the text from one another. These subsections are further divided by the next highest indicator (not already concurring with the division marked by the highest indicator). Thus, a text may be divided into a preface and a body by meta-communicative sentences and by a genre title, but the body of the text will be further subdivided by chapter headings or episode markers. Ends of subsections are indicated by the occurrence of an indicator equal to or greater than the indicator that marks the beginning of the given subsection. For example, one mark of the end of chapter one is the occurrence of the heading for chapter two. Such is an all too brief overview of some of the text linguistic methodology proposed by Gühlich and Raible, as modified by Hellholm. We turn now to an analysis of Isa 40:1–11.

Application of the Text Linguistic Method to Isa 40:1–11

Isa 40:1–2 opens with:

> Comfort my people, comfort them, says your (pl.) God.
> Encourage Jerusalem, and proclaim to her,
>
> that her time of compulsory service is completed,
> that her punishment (for guilt) is sufficient,
>
> For she has received from the hand of the Lord,
> double for all her sins.

The source of the command is God, while the masculine plural audience of the command is left unspecified. Isa 40:3–5 is a new speech act whose source is simply described as "a voice calling out." This time an unspecified audience is commanded to prepare a way in the wilderness for God. Finally, 40:6–8 is a series of three closely related speech acts:

1. Another unspecified voice commands, this time directing a male individual to "proclaim."
2. In 40:6b–7 the receiver of this command says:

   > "How can I proclaim?[7]
   > All flesh is grass,
   > and all its faithfulness like the blossoms of the field.
   > The grass dries up, the blossom withers,
   > when the breath of the Lord blows upon it.
   > Indeed, the people is grass!"

3. The giver of the command replies with another form of the proverb used in the question (Westermann, 1966:37; Melugin:84):

   > The grass dries up, the blossom withers,
   > But the word of our God endures forever."

As previous scholars have recognized, the form of this text gives the informed audience clues about the text's portrayed setting, participants, and function. First, Isa 40:1–8 is a prophetic call report. Prophetic call reports often have the following pattern: command to give a message – question/objection – reassurance. This pattern is also found in Isa 40:1–8. Like other prophetic call reports, 40:1–8 is placed at the beginning of the prophetic writing and serves to validate the following message through reference to the prophet's divine com-

[7] For discussion of the text critical problem here, see the Appendix.

mission (Mowinckel:88–89; Begrich:61, 77; Habel:314–16; Fohrer:15; Elliger:1–12, 34; Krinetski:57–58; Spykerboer:183 [with reference to vv. 6–8]; Loretz, 1974:489–91; Preuss:32–36; Melugin:83–84; Sweeney:66–67).[8]

Not only is Isa 40:1–8 a prophetic call report, but it is a report of a prophetic call given in the divine council. Two texts, Isaiah 6 and 2 Kgs 22:19–23 validate a prophet's message by describing the pro-

---

[8] Not all scholars agree that 40:1–8 is a report of a prophetic call. Kiesow (38–41, 61–62) uses the similarities between 40:1–8 (particularly 1–2) and 40:9–11 as the basis for an argument that both parts are victory messenger instructions. Though his demonstration of parallels between 40:1–8 and 40:9–11 is excellent, he fails to see the critical differences in addressee and focus of these two texts and thus draws the wrong conclusions from his comparison.

Westermann (1966:30, though see p. 38 on vv. 6–8) and Merendino (59–60) both argue that 40:1–8 diverges in significant ways from the typical call report. It lacks a direct encounter with God, and rather than narrating a past event, the emphasis is on the present (this had been previously noted by Elliger [11]). Moreover, 40:1–8 focuses on the message, not a call experience. Despite these minor objections to the call report hypothesis, neither Westermann nor Merendino denies that a call report is part of the background of 40:1–8. In addition, neither Westermann nor Merendino provides an adequate generic identification that explains the cohesiveness, form, and function of these verses as well as the call report hypothesis does. Westermann considers 40:1–11 to be a combination of Second Isaiah's major forms serving as the "prologue" to the prophecy (see also his expansion of this position [1981:82–84, particularly note 42], while Merendino takes these verses as an eschatological hymn [1–2] and a description of judgment [3–5, 6–8]).

Nielsen resembles Westermann in his contention that though 40:6 and 8 are an echo of the call experience, 1–11 is a pastiche of other forms as well. According to him, the whole is best characterized as a "Prozessionsliturgie," in the context of a divine enthronement (203–4). The procession and enthronement theses are developed at length in Vincent's work (209–17, 245–48). Since Vincent also argues against the theory that 40:1–8 is set in the divine council, I do not discuss his approach until after my discussion of the divine council setting of 40:1–8. For arguments against Vincent, see note 10.

Finally, Seitz (236–37) argues that 40:1–8 cannot be a call report because it lacks a clear statement of the prophet's acceptance of the commission, particularly after the prophet's objection in 40:6–7. Yet, Seitz does not present compelling reasons why 40:9–11 cannot be taken as the prophet's implicit acceptance of his commission through its initial execution. Moreover, his objection seems to be based on an excessively stringent definition of the call report form and what constitute parallels to its parts. Each exemplar of a given form need not, and probably will not, parallel every aspect of the other exemplars of a given form. Despite its individual characteristics, Isa 40:1–8 still shares with other call reports the characteristic commission–objection–reassurance pattern, and an authorizing function vis-à-vis surrounding material.

ceedings of the divine council.[9] This divine council setting would explain (a) the plural imperatives to a group to comfort God's people; (b) the second plural possessive pronoun without a referent on "God"; and (c) the prefix form of "say." The imperatives and 2nd plural possessive suffix would refer to members of the divine council, while the prefix form of "say" indicates that this is a communication of a divine message during the proceedings (Robinson:155; Cross:274–77; Muilenburg:422–23; Elliger:4–10; Stuhlmueller:179; Loretz, 1974:489; Melugin:83–84; Petersen:20; Preuss:33–36; Knight:7; Loretz, 1984:284, 294–95; Gitay:77, n. 2; Watts:78; Sweeney:66; Rendtorff:80; Seitz:239–40, 231–35; cf. Bonnard:85; Vincent:209–17, 245–48; Merendino:18–20; Wilson:38–39).[10]

---

[9] 1 Kgs 22:19–23 is not a call report, since the prophet is not explicitly commissioned as such. Nevertheless, it is quite close to such reports in focus on the heavenly council and validating function. As many have observed, Isaiah 6 is a prophetic call report and is particularly close to 40:1–8 (Brownlee:248–49; Habel:314; Cross:276; Melugin:83–84; Sawyer:113–15, Vincent:245–46; Kiesow:66; Ackroyd:5–6; Loretz, 1984:220; Rendtorff:79–81; Albertz:244–48; Seitz:238–43).

[10] A minority of recent studies have diverged from the view that the divine council is the setting for Isa 40:1–8, including Bonnard:85; Vincent:209–17, 245–48; Merendino:18–20; and Wilson:38–39. Usually, this position is merely asserted without much argument, but Vincent (209–17, 245–48) argues at length against the idea that 40:1–8 is a report of a prophetic call received in the divine council. Beginning with Isa 40:1–2 he argues that formal, thematic, and stylistic indicators link 40:1–2 with "Alarm calls" (*Alarmrufe*) such as Jer 4:5–12; Hos 5:8–6:6; Joel 1 and 2. These "Alarm calls" share the following elements: a call to alarm, justification and/or description of the impending disaster, call to lament, and answering cult oracle in the temple. Moreover, these "alarm calls" share with Isaiah 40 a connection to "Day of Yahweh" traditions. Of course, the comfort themes of Isa 40:1–2 make it the antithesis of the alarm call, the divine message coming after the "Day of Yahweh" has arrived and the disaster has taken place. Whereas earlier the prophet had called the people to lament, now he calls the people to comfort. In both cases, however, the prophet, not a divine being, is the speaker. The setting is not the divine council but communal ritual.

With regard to the call report hypothesis, Vincent argues that the interplay of message-objection-reassurance does not really exist in Isaiah 40:1–8. First, those who take 40:1–8 as a call report usually understand the content of the prophetic message to be given in 1–5 and the question in 6aβ to be "How can I cry out?" Vincent, however, argues that 1–5 are separate from 6–8. The command in 6aα is to simply "cry out," as in a lament, while the question which follows is a question about what to cry out (as in the more common understanding of מָה). Finally, Vincent argues that 6b–8 lack many of the typical formulae of call report reassurances ("I am with you," for example), along with a confirming sign. Rather than seeing 6b–8 as the divine reassurance section of a prophetic call report, Vincent holds that 6b–8 is a dialogue between two cultic officials in a ceremony

What does all this mean in terms of Gühlich and Raible's hierarchy? As parts of a call report, the commands to give messages and the prophet's response in 40:1–2 and 6–8 all refer to the following message, its origin, setting, and audience. As such, they are meta-communicative statements and play a critical role in setting the stage for the text in 40:9ff.

With verse 9, semantic indicators indicate a fundamental break. Using feminine imperatives, the prophet calls "Zion/Jerusalem" to her "herald" mission. The set of worlds moves from the "other world" of the heavenly divine council to the "this world" of the prophet and his earthly audience. Moreover, the set of actors changes. The heavenly scene of Isa 40:1–8 has angels, God, and the prophet as addressee as well as narrator. The earthly setting of 40:9ff. has a new group of actors prominent: the prophet (now exclusively as addressor), God, remnant, nations, their gods, and Cyrus.

Thus concurring with shifts on the meta-level of the text, these semantic shifts help highlight the authorizing function that the call report in Isa 40:1–8 plays in relation to 40:9ff. According to Second Isaiah, the prophet is the critical link between the heavenly chain of authority in 40:1–8 and the human community on earth who is called to its own mission in 40:9ff. In 40:1–8 the heavenly chain of authority

---

resembling the Babylonian New Year Festival. These cultic officials act out the divine council's deliberation about changing the fate of Israel. Just as the New Year celebration focuses on the revival of vegetation and has a universal scope, so Isa 40:6b–8 uses vegetation imagery in its discussion of "all flesh."

Vincent's analysis is convoluted and atomistic while the divine-council-prophetic-call-report thesis is elegant and unified. Vincent's analysis fails to account for the position and function of 40:1–8 (indeed he questions the existence of a break at this point), and he must build on tenuous parallels between themes in this text and themes (used quite differently) in a far distant, extra-biblical parallel (the New Year festival). Moreover, where the prophetic call report accounts for the close formal connections between the component parts of 1–8, Vincent can only posit a redactional similarity between these parts. Even his individual treatments of the form and *Sitz im Leben* of these component parts are often improbable. For example, despite thematic and stylistic similarities, his treatment of 40:1–2 does little but establish the absolute contrast between this text and "alarm calls." Whereas the call to lament in alarm calls is unproblematic, the call to comfort others in 40:la still does not make sense in Vincent's analysis. Robinson, Cross, Elliger, and others listed in the body of the text persuasively identify the audience of this command in 40:la as the heavenly council (versus the earthly recipients of comfort), but Vincent's theory does not adequately differentiate between those who are to do the comforting and those who are to be comforted. On Vincent, see also Seitz:231, 239.

runs from God-angels (40:1–2) to angel-angels (40:3–5) to angel-prophet (40:6–8). This helps support the prophet's authority vis-à-vis the addressed human community (40:9ff.).

This approach accounts for the thematic indicators linking 40:9–11 with 40:1–8, while positing a fundamental shift between the two. As expected, there are continuities in theme between these two texts. Themes such as comfort and Jerusalem occur in both the original "authorizing" message (40:1–2) and the message that is authorized (40:9–11), but this does not diminish the very different semantic focus and pragmatic function of these two texts.

These considerations lead to the following diagram of Isa 40:1–11:

I.	Authorizing Introduction: Call to Prophet	40:1–8
II.	Authorized Message	40:9–11++

I have been deliberately vague up to this point about the extent of the message authorized by 40:1–8. First person statements regarding vocation and message occur again in 49:1–7. These seem to be meta-communicative sentences marking a fundamental break in the text, a break potentially as significant as that marked by the call report in 40:1–8. Other interpreters of Second Isaiah have noted shifts in address and theme between chaps. 40–48 and 49ff. (Westermann, 1964 [1981 reprint:91–92]; Melugin:77–86 [with references]; Haran:127–48).

Be that as it may, for the present purposes it is enough to acknowledge the continuity of theme that does obtain between 40:9–11 and 40:12–48:21. The section from 40:12 to 48:21 shares a common cast of characters: the foreign nations, Cyrus, and the exilic remnant.[11] In 40:9–48:21 this exilic remnant is called to a second exodus from Babylon and a proclamation of God's power. Beginning with 40:12 the prophet supports this call with arguments regarding God's proven power in creation and history. These arguments are permeated by such themes as the new exodus (41:17–20; 43:19–20, as in 40:3–5; 48:21), God's glory being made known through this exodus (42:8, 12, 21; 43:7, 20, 21, 23, 25; 48:11, as in 40:5, 10 and 48:20), and the reliability of God's word (trial and disputation speeches; cf. Melugin: 85–86).[12]

---

[11] This remnant is alternatively addressed as a group; the herald, Zion-Jerusamem (45:14–17); Jacob; or the "servant."

[12] In contrast to chaps. 40–48, the above mentioned themes of the new exodus, God's glory being made known through it, and the reliability of God's word occur

Such thematic observations are less easy to control than the kinds of observations discussed in connection with Gühlich and Raible's work. Nevertheless, Isa 40:9–11 seems to concisely summarize the call substantiated in various ways throughout 40:12–48:19 and repeated at the conclusion of the text in 48:20–21. Given a delimitation of the text as chaps. 40–48 of Isaiah, and given these vaguer thematic observations, 40:9–11 appears to be the initial presentation of the *Leitmotiv* of 40:12–48:21, a call to the remnant to announce God's work and join in a second exodus.

These observations are reflected in the following tentative diagram of the micro-structure of Isa 40:1–11 in the macro-structure of Isaiah 40–48:

Prophetic Call to Proclamation and a Second Exodus	Isaiah 40–48
I. Authorizing Introduction: Call to Prophet	40:1–8
II. Authorized Call: Prophet's Call to Remnant	40:9–48:21
A. Call Proper	40:9–11
B. Arguments to support II.A	40:12–48:19
C. Concluding Call to Remnant	48:20–21

The above diagram incorporates the insights of the various groups of scholars who have previously treated Isa 40:1–11. In accord with many previous treatments of the structure of Isa 40:1–11, the introductory role of all eleven of these verses is acknowledged in the diagram, but (as others have observed) 40:1–8 plays a different kind of introductory role from that played by 40:9–11. The thematic continuities between 40:1–8 (the authorizing text) and 40:9–11 (the introduction to the authorized text) are natural given their authorizing-authorized relationship. Moreover, the significance of the break from call to substantiation of call in 40:12ff. is also recognized in the diagram, although this break is seen as less fundamental than the break between 40:8 and 40:9. Overall, the analysis helps highlight the function of Isaiah 40–48 as a whole. These nine chapters are designed to elicit a certain kind of behavior from the audience through emphasis on the prophet's critical role in the chain of divine authority and through argument sandwiched between two series of direct calls to action.

---

very rarely or not at all in chaps. 49–55. Moreover, 49:1–6 describes the prophet's call very differently from 40:1–8. The following chapters have a more complex view of the servant and focus on the restoration of Judah rather than the exit from Babylon.

Looking back on this analysis, the strengths and weaknesses of this text linguistic approach are clear. First of all, a detailed study of the genre, language, and movement of Isa 40:1–11 is presupposed for the application of this text linguistic method. This essay is not the "communication situation" for going into detail regarding philological, form, and text critical study of Isa 40:1–11. Nevertheless, given the interpretation of the genre, language, and movement of Isa 40:1–11 assumed here, Gühlich and Raible's indicators decisively distinguish between the function and focus of Isa 40:1–8 and 40:9ff. The structure analysis begins to lose persuasiveness as it extends to text blocks that have undergone a complex history of formation. In the Bible, older bits of material are often incompletely integrated into an overarching concept of the larger text's macrostructure. Such a history of formation produces a non-integrated system of macro-structural indicators. Therefore, methods of text analysis developed from modern "integrated" texts must be applied with care to the products of redaction. Nevertheless, this method offers potential for extended analysis of macro-structure. Then this macro-structure is the context for more detailed micro-structural observations of grammatical-syntactical features characteristic of Hebrew language texts in particular.

Appendix: The Text-Critical Problem in Isaiah 40:6aβ

Up to this point I have not yet discussed a text critical problem that potentially affects the determination of the structure of Isa 40:1–11. The issue is whether we are to read the first person (converted imperfect) here (40:6aβ) with 1QIs[a], the Old Greek, Vulgate, and some of Kennicott's manuscripts, or go with the third person (perfect) reading of the Targum, Peshitta, and Massoretic text.

If we read the first person, Isa 40:1–8 is a first person report of a prophetic call in the divine council, and contrasts with the initial execution of that call in 40:9–11. If we read a third person form, this contrast is muted, though not eliminated. Then the entire stretch of 40:1–11 (including 40:9–11) could be taken as a succession of commissions given to various figures at the divine council. At this council a "herald" is commissioned to speak a specific message (9bγ–11).[13] Only with v. 12 would the scene shift to earth and the human recipients of the herald's message. The following is a structure diagram of the possible consequences of this reading:

I.	Minutes of Divine Council: Commissioning of Herald	Isa 40:1–11
II.	Consequences of I: Execution of Commission	40:12ff.

In order to evaluate these two readings, we consider each of the three areas of text critical argument: strength of attestation of each reading, probability for a reading being original, and probability for a reading being an error.

1. **Strength of attestation**. The 3rd person reading is attested in the Massoretic (MT) and Proto-Massoretic periods (Targum, Peshitta), while the 1st person reading is attested by two witnesses formed during the earlier period of textual fluidity (1QIs[a] and the Old Greek). Since 40:6 may have been one of the familiar passages that Jerome was reluctant to modify, the Vulgate first person reading may be dependent on the Old Greek. The Kennicott manuscripts that read the first person could well be medieval variants (Goshen-Gottstein). In general, the first person reading is attested by earlier witnesses, but

[13] Note that this reading does not take the feminine imperatives of 40:9–11 as referring to Zion/Jerusalem. If these imperatives are understood to refer to Zion/Jerusalem, then the main structural break remains between 40:8 and 40:9.

given our increasing knowledge of the accuracy of the proto-Massoretic and Massoretic traditions, this evidence is not decisive in itself. Therefore, we go on to the other two factors in text critical argument.

2. **Probability for a reading being original.**
(a) *Third Person Reading*: a third person reading would be somewhat anomalous here, since the subject of the third person form is never given. Even in the earlier anonymous speech acts (40:3–5 and 6aα), the unspecified speaker was referred to as קול (if this is not interpreted as an exclamatory particle).
(b) *First Person Reading*: though a first person reading is also somewhat out of place in the present book as a whole, such a reading would have been natural if and when this text stood at the outset of an independent collection.[14] Then, the prophet presented himself in the first person at this point because this text stood at the beginning of a prophetic collection, where an account of his own call was apropos.

3) **Probability for a reading being an error.**
(a) *Third Person Reading*: the occurrence of "priests" at the beginning of verse two in the Old Greek might seem to indicate that the reading of a 1st person in 40:6 is part of a general move in the Old Greek to see 40:1–11 as earthly, not heavenly, proceedings. The Qumran Isaiah scroll's first person reading could then be seen as part of this same movement. Nevertheless, the Old Greek and Qumran scroll readings are different in a critical respect. Whereas only the Old Greek has "priests" in v. 2, both the Qumran scroll and Old Greek have a first person reading in v. 6. The Old Greek reading of "priests" in v. 2 is a clear interpretive addition and demands an earthly setting for Isa 40:1–11, while the first person reading in v. 6 can accommodate either an earthly or heavenly setting. Therefore, for text critical purposes (as opposed to history of interpretation), the Old Greek and Qumran readings of the first person must be considered independently of the Old Greek reading of "priests" in v. 2.

---

[14] Clements and Albertz (among others) have raised significant questions about the independent existence of the Deutero-Isaianic collection (Clements:95–113; Albertz:241–56). In particular, the close parallels between Isaiah 6 and 40:1–8 suggest that 40:1–8 may have been composed in relation to the earlier call report (on this see the discussions cited above in n. 9).

(b) *First Person Reading*: it is hard to explain a first person reading as a deviation from a third person reading. Though twentieth century interpreters are conscious of the appropriateness of the first person form at this point (because of the call narrative), the ancient tradents of the text were relatively unconscious of form and source critical arguments. Therefore, it is unlikely that they modified an original third person form to conform 40:1–8 to Isaiah 6, Jeremiah 1, and other call reports.[15] Rather, the more likely scenario is that the creators of the proto-Massoretic text did not see the point of a first common singular form at this point, subsumed Second Isaiah into the book of Isaiah as a whole, and adopted the third person form accordingly. We are given the earlier reading only by the independent ancient textual traditions of the Old Greek and $1QIs_a$, along with the Vulgate.[16]

---

[15] Both Barthélemy (279) and Seitz (238) argue for the probability of such a modification.

[16]Compare these arguments with those for a third person reading in the final report of the United Bible Society's Hebrew Old Testament Text Critical Project; Barthélemy:278–79.

WORKS CONSULTED

Ackroyd, Peter R.
1982 "Isaiah 36–39: Structure and Function." Pp. 3–21 in *Von Kanaan bis Kerala: Festschrift J. P. M. van der Ploeg.* Ed. W. Delsman. *AOAT* 211. Kevelaer: Butzon & Bercker; Neukirchen-Vluyn: Neukirchener Verlag.

Albertz, Rainer
1990 "Das Deuterojesaja-Buch als Fortschreibung der Jesaja-Prophetie." Pp. 241–56 in *Die Hebräische Bible und ihre zweifache Nachgeschichte: Festschrift für Rolf Rendtorff zum 65. Geburtstag.* Eds. E. Blum, C. Macholz, E. Stegemann. Neukirchen-Vluyn: Neukirchener Verlag.

Barthélemy, Dominique
1986 *Critique textuelle de l'Ancien Testament.* OBO 50/2. Göttingen: Vandenhoeck & Ruprecht.

Begrich, Joachim
1963 *Studien zu Deuterojesaja.* München: Chr. Kaiser.

Beuken, W. A. M.
1979 *Jesaja.* Deel IIA. Nijkerk: G. F. Callenbach.

Bonnard, Pierre E.
1972 *Le Second Isaie: son disciple et leurs éditeurs, Isaïe 40–66.* Paris: J. Gabalda et Cie Éditeurs.

Brownlee, W. H.
1964 *The Meaning of the Qumrân Scrolls for the Bible.* New York: Oxford University Press.

Clements, Ronald E.
1985 "Beyond Tradition History: Deutero-Isaianic Development of First Isaiah's Themes." *JSOT* 31: 95–113

Cross, Frank Moore
1953 "The Council of Yahweh in Second Isaiah." *JNES* 12:274–77.

Dijk, Teun van, and J. Petöfi, eds.
1977 *Grammars and Description: Studies in Text Theory and Text Analysis.* Research in Text Theory/Untersuchung zur Texttheorie 1. Berlin: W. de Gruyter.

Eaton, John H.
1979 *Festal Drama in Deutero-Isaiah.* London: SPCK.

Elliger, Karl
1970 *Deutero-Jesaja. BK* 11/1. Neukirchen: Neukirchener Verlag.

Ettore, Franco
1980 "Is 40:1–11: una lettura strutturale." *RivB* 28:285–304.

Fohrer, Georg
1964 *Das Buch Jesaja.* Band 3. *Kapitel 40–66.* Zürcher Bibelkommentare. Zürich: Zwingli.

Gitay, Yehoshua
1981 *Prophecy and Persuasion: A Study of Isaiah 40-48.* Bonn: Linguistica Biblica.

Goshen-Gottstein, Moshe H.
1967 "Hebrew Bible Manuscripts: Their History and Their Place in the HUBP Edition." *Bib* 48:243–90.

Gressmann, Hugo
1914 "Die literarischer Analyse Deuterojesajas." *ZAW* 34:254–97.

Gühlich, Elizabeth and Wolfgang Raible
1975 "Textorten-Probleme." Pp. 144–97 in *Linguistische Probleme der Textanalyse.* Ed. H. Moser. Jahrbuch des Instituts für deutsche Sprache 35. Dusseldorf: Pädagogischer Verlag Schwamm.
1977a *Linguistische Textmodelle: Grundlagen und Möglichkeiten.* Unitaschenbücher 130. München: Wilhelm Fink.
1977b "Überlegungen zu einer makrostrukturellen Textanalyse: J; Thurber, The Lover and His Lass." Pp. 132–75 in *Grammars and Description: Studies in Text Theory and Text Analysis.* Ed. Teun van Dijk and J. Petöfi. Research in Text Theory/Untersuchungen zur Texttheorie 1. Berlin: W. de Gruyter.

Habel, Norman
1965 "The Form and Significance of the Call Narratives." *ZAW* 77: 297–323.

Haran, Menaḥem
1963 "The Literary Structure and Chronological Framework of the Prophecies in Is XL–XLVIII." *VTSup* 9:127–55.

Hardmeier, Christof
1978 *Texttheorie und biblische Exegese. BEvT* 79. München: Chr. Kaiser.

Heger, Klaus
1976 *Monem, Wort, Satz und Text.* 2nd enlarged ed. Konzepte der Sprache- und Literaturwissenschaft 8. Tübingen: Niemeyer.
1979 "Sigmenrange und Textanalyse." Pp. 1–72 in *Linguistische Textanalyse: Überlegungen zur Gliederung von Texten.* Eds. Elizabeth Gühlich, Klaus Heger, and Wolfgang Raible. Hamburg: Helmut Buske.

Hellholm, David
1980 *Das Visionenbuch des Hermas als Apokalypse: Formgeschichtliche und texttheoretische Studien zu einer literarischen Gattung.* Vol. 1. *Methodologsiche Vorüberlegungen und makrostrukturelle Textanalyse.* ConNT 13:1. Lund: CWK Gleerup.
1986 "The Problem of Apocalyptic Genre and the Apocalypse of John." *Semeia* 36:11–64.

Herbert, Albert Sumner
1975 *The Book of the Prophet Isaiah: Chapters 40–66.* Cambridge: Cambridge University Press.

Jackson, Jared J. and M. Kessler, eds.
1974 *Rhetorical Criticism.* PTMS 1. Pittsburg: Pickwick.

Kiesow, Klaus
1979 Exodustexte im Jesajabuch: Literarkritische und motivgeschichtliche Analysen. *OBO* 24. Göttingen: Vandenhoeck & Ruprecht.

Knierim, Rolf P.
1973 "Old Testament Form Criticism Reconsidered." *Int* 27:435–68.
1985a "The Composition of the Pentateuch." *SBLSP:* 399–404.
1985b "Criticism of Literary Features, Form, Tradition and Redaction." Pp. 123–65 in *The Hebrew Bible and Its Modern Interpreters.* Ed. Douglas A. Knight and Gene M. Tucker. Philadelphia: Fortress and Chico, CA: Scholars Press.

Knight, Douglas A. and Gene M. Tucker, eds.
1985 *The Hebrew Bible and Its Modern Interpreters.* Philadelphia: Fortress and Chico, CA: Scholars Press.

Knight, George
1984 *Servant Theology: A Commentary on the Book of Isaiah 40–55.* Grand Rapids: Eerdmans; Edinburgh: Handsel.

Krinetski, Leo
1972 "Zur Stilistik von Jes 40:1–8." *BZ* 16:54–69.

Lack, Rémi
1973 *La symbolique du livre d'Isaïe.* AnBib 59. Rome: Pontifical Biblical Institute.

Leslie, Elmer Archibald
1963 *Isaiah: Chronologically Arranged, Translated, and Interpreted.* Nashville: Abingdon.

Loretz, Oswald
1974 "Die Sprecher der Götterversammlung in Is 40:1–8." *UF* 6:489–91.
1984 "Mesopotamische und ugaritisch-kanaanaische Elemente im Prologue des Buches Deuterojesaja (Jes 40:1–11)." *Or* 53:284–96.

McKenzie, John L.
1968 *Second Isaiah.* AB 20. Garden City: Doubleday

Melugin, Roy
1976 *The Formation of Isaiah 40–55. BZAW* 141. Berlin: W. de Gruyter.

Merendino, Rosario Pius
1981 *Der Erste und der Letzte: Eine Untersuchung von Jes 40–48.* VTSup 31. Leiden: E. J. Brill.

Moser, H., ed.
1975 *Linguistische Probleme der Textanalyse.* Jahrbuch des Instituts für deutsche Sprache 35. Düsseldorf: Pädagogischer Verlag Schwamm.

Mowinckel, Sigmund
1931 "Die Komposition des deuterojesajanischen Buches." *ZAW* 49:87–112.

Muilenburg, James
1956 "Isaiah 40–66." *IB* 5:381–773.

Nielsen, Eduard
1970 "Deuterojesaja: Erwägungen zur Formkritik, Traditions- und Redaktionsgeschichte." *VT* 20:190–205.

Petersen, David L.
1976 *Late Israelite Prophecy: Studies in Deutero-Prophetic Literature and in Chronicles.* SBLMS 23. Missoula, MT: Scholars Press.

Preuss, Horst Dietrich
1976 *Deuterojesaja: Eine Einführung in seine Botschaft.* Neukirchen: Neukirchener Verlag.

Qimron, Elisha
1986 *The Hebrew of the Dead Sea Scrolls.* HSS 29. Atlanta: Scholars Press.

Raible, Wolfgang
1972 *Satz und Text: Untersuchungen zu vier romanischen Sprachen.* Beihefte zur Zeitschrift für die romansiche Philologie 132. Tübingen: Niemeyer.
1979 "Vergleich mit der von Klaus Heger durchgeführten Textanalyse." Pp. 127–47 in *Linguistische Textanalyse: Überlegungen zur Gliederung von Texten.* Ed. Elizabeth Gühlich, Klaus Heger, and Wolfgang Raible. Hamburg: Helmut Buske.

Rendtorff, Rolf
1989 "Jesaja 6 im Rahmen der Komposition de Jesajabuches." Pp. 73–82 in *Le Livre d' Isaïe: Les Oracles et leurs relectures unité et complexité de l'ouvrage.* Ed. J. Vermeylan. BETL 81. Leuven: Leuven University Press.

Rignell, Lars Gösta
1956 *A Study of Isaiah 40–55.* Lund: Gleerup.

Robinson, Henry Wheeler
1945 "The Council of Yahweh," *JTS* 45:151–57.

Sacon, Kiyoshi Kinoshita
1974 "Isaiah 40:1–11—A Rhetorical-Critical Study." Pp. 99–116 in *Rhetorical Criticism.* Ed. J. Jackson and M. Kessler. PTMS 1. Pittsburg: Pickwick.

Sawyer, J. F. A.
1977 *From Moses to Patmos: New Perspectives in Old Testament Study.* London: SPCK.

Scullion, John
1980 *Isaiah 40–66.* Wilmington: Glazier.

Seitz, Christopher R.
1990 "The Divine Council: Temporal Transition and New Prophecy in the Book of Isaiah." *JBL* 109:229–47.

Simon, Uriel
1985 "Ibn Ezra between Medievalism and Modernism: The Case of Isaiah XL–LXVI." VTSup 36. Leiden: E. J. Brill.

Smart, James D.
1965 *History and Theology in Second Isaiah: A Commentary on Isaiah 35, 40–66.* Philadelphia: Westminster.

Spykerboer, H. C.
1976 *The Structure and Composition of Deutero-Isaiah with Special Reference to the Polemics Against Idolatry.* Groningen: Rijksuniversiteit.

Stuhlmueller, Carroll
1970 *Creative Redemption in Deutero-Isaiah.* AnBib 43. Rome: Pontifical Biblical Institute.

Sweeney, Marvin Alan
1988 *Isaiah 1–4 and the Post-Exilic Understanding of the Isaianic Tradition.* BZAW 171. Berlin: W. de Gruyter.

Thexton, S. Clive
1959 *Isaiah 40–66.* Epworth Preacher's Commentaries. London: Epworth.

Vincent, Jean Marcel
1977 *Studien zur literarischen Eigenart und zur geistigen Heimat von Jesaja, Kap. 40–55.* Frankfurt am Main: Peter Lang.

Watts, John D. W.
1987 *Isaiah 34–66.* WBC 25. Waco, TX: Word.

West, James King
1981 *Introduction to the Old Testament.* 2nd ed. New York: Macmillan.

Westermann, Claus
1966 *Das Buch Jesaja: Kapitel 40–66.* ATD 19. Göttingen: Vandenhoeck & Ruprecht.

1981 *Sprache und Struktur der Prophetie Deuterojesajas.* Calwer Theologische Monographien 11. Stuttgart: Calwer. (Reprint of a 1964 article: "Sprache und Struktur der Prophetie Deuterojesajas." *Theologische Bücherei* 24:92–170.)

Wilson, Andrew
1986 *The Nations in Deutero-Isaiah: A Study on Composition and Structure.* Ancient Near Eastern Texts and Studies 1. Lewiston, NY: Mellen.

Witlander, Bertil
1984 *Prophecy as Literature: A Text-Linguistic and Rhetorical Approach to Isaiah 2–4.* Malmö, Sweden: Gleerup.

Whybray, Robert North
1975 *Isaiah 40–66*. New Century Bible. London: Oliphants.

B. Theory

3

FUNCTIONAL GRAMMAR, HEBREW AND ARAMAIC: AN INTEGRATED, TEXTLINGUISTIC APPROACH TO SYNTAX

Randall Buth

ABSTRACT

Functional grammar coupled with textlinguistics is a necessary perspective for an adequate understanding of the grammar of any language, especially Hebrew and Aramaic. Functional grammars and Dik's Functional Grammar are briefly described. The interaction of several textlinguistic parameters with structures of Hebrew and Aramaic are discussed. Crucial concepts and structures include the difference between Topic [as Contextualizing Constituent, including Dramatic Pause] and Focus. A Contextualizing Constituent is related to a pragmatically defined Background distinction, and this, in turn, is part of a Continuity-Discontinuity marking system. The recognition of these structures aids in understanding how and why an author has structured one's text as it is. The larger linguistic framework also provides a rationale for "exotic" systems like the Hebrew tense-aspect systems and some diachronic adjustments within Aramaic syntax.

0.0 Introduction

Functional grammar presents a developing paradigm in linguistics, and the premise of this paper is that it is useful for biblical studies. It affects the way we look at Hebrew and Aramaic grammar and can stimulate us to explore grammatical relationships that have sometimes been ignored. By including a pragmatic perspective (see below, sections 1.0 and 2.0.) in grammar we can incorporate some insights from textlinguistics. We find a linguistic motivation for the existence of the *waw hahippuk* verbs in Hebrew. We can explain some of the motivations for the different changes throughout Aramaic. We are also able to see the detail of what is happening in texts from those languages. Not only is it possible to distinguish narrative units linguistically, but even notions from plot structure like setting and peak can interact with the grammar.

1.0 Functional Grammar

There are functional grammars with a generic, small "f," and there are specific grammar systems developed by theorists with a capital "F." A functional grammar is one that includes pragmatic information in the core of the grammar.

Since the rise of the Prague structural linguistic school it has been commonplace to think in terms of three different domains of activity in a language. The relationships of constituents like nouns and adjectives to a noun phrase, or of subject, object, and verb to a clause, are viewed as part of syntax. Thus, the subject of an English passive clause has a syntactic relationship to the verb and clause as "Subject."

Logical relationships between constituents form the semantic domain of a grammar. A label like "patient" or "goal" for a subject of a passive clause is a semantic term. Grammarians have felt a responsibility to integrate semantic information with the core of the grammar system. How to do that is, of course, what provides jobs for linguists and has led to the debates of twenty years ago between "Generative Semantics" and "Transformational Grammar." (Within transformational and government-binding theory these semantic relationships are called "thematic roles" and "theta criterion.")

The pragmatic domain raises questions because it is defined and used so differently by various schools and because it can be used to describe phenomena that lie outside the scope of a grammar of a language. Pragmatics refers to the communication situation. In a functional grammar the pragmatic part of a grammar needs to be limited to the way in which definable linguistic constructions function within the communication situation. Traditionally, that means referring to the information marking system of a language and integrating ideas like topic and focus (or old information, new information, salient information and Prague School theme-rheme). Pragmatics, as a discipline, goes far beyond this, and much of it cannot be considered part of a grammar, although it is still within the sphere of linguistic investigation. For example, a statement like "It's cold in here" may function as an imperative "Turn on the heater." Functional grammars do not yet have a way of encoding that kind of information in the core grammar of a language so that generalizations can be captured as rules. Relevance Theory discusses such communication situations, but they are not written into the grammar rules that generate the sentences of a language.

The traditional transformational grammars and "Extended Standard Theory" were designed to generate possible structures in a language by algorithms. If the rules could generate the attested surface structure, then the grammar was descriptively adequate. Simplicity and smallness were the yardsticks used to evaluate and compare grammatical descriptions. The question of when certain structures were to be used was considered to be outside the grammar itself. Functional grammars, on the other hand, assert that some pragmatic information is incorporated by a language user as part of the encoding process itself. If it affects the structural and morphological system of the language, then it is a necessary part of the grammar. It should not be discussed as an afterthought in an ad hoc manner.

A functional grammar provides a matrix and raises questions that biblical scholars need to answer in order to better understand both Hebrew and Aramaic.

2.0 Dik's Functional Grammar

Simon Dik has formalized a functional grammar that makes use of syntactic, semantic and pragmatic information in the core, clause-generating part of the grammar. The syntactic functions recognized are subject and object. The semantic functions include agent, recipient, benefactor, goal, et al. His pragmatic functions are basically topic and focus. A simplified analysis of two sentences follows which will illustrate the simultaneous functioning of the three domains:

(1) With the bat (instrument-topic) the boy (subj-agent) hit the football (object-patient) into the neighbor's yard.

(2) The football (subject-patient) was hit into the neighbor's yard.

In example (1) the fronted phrase "with the bat" is semantically instrumental to its clause (marked with "with") and would normally relate the sentence to a larger context. The primary perspective within the clause is the syntactic subject, but it is important to recognize that English, as well as other natural languages, have structure(s) for relating to perspectives that are beyond the clause. These larger perspectives are topicalizations (or contextualizations).[1] Sentence (2) has a syntactic subject and a semantic patient function, but it does not necessarily have a *marked* topic. (See further comments below, 4.0 Topic [contextualization] and focus.) A speaker may intend to set up "the football" as a topic in the larger context, but English does not usually distinguish a topicalized subject and a non-topicalized subject. (However, both Hebrew and Aramaic easily distinguish topical and contextualized subjects from pragmatically unmarked subjects.)

Dik's functional grammar (hereafter—Functional Grammar or FG) postulates that every language has a pragmatic position (P-position) at the beginning of a clause that can be used for marking a constituent. Most English clauses are formed on a subject-verb-object pattern, which would be produced by the following nuclear pattern:

(3) P-position subject verb object

A verb-initial language would form basic clauses from a pattern:

(4) P-position verb subject object

3.0 Defining Word Order

Functional Grammar helps in recognizing and defining the verb-initial nature of Hebrew. There have been two methodologies, to be explained below in 3.1 and 3.2, which have asserted that Hebrew was SVO. But, if Hebrew were SVO or if it became SVO, then when pragmatically marked constituents were placed in the initial P position, the resulting sentences would be XSV(O) and not the regularly attested XVS(O). The failure of a predicted XSVO to regularly occur in any strata of Biblical Hebrew singlehandedly nullifies SVO

---

[1]So much confusion among linguists surrounds the term "topic" that I now prefer the terms contextualization and contextualizing constituent. "Topic" in English implies subject matter and what the unit is about. However, many times the "topicalized" constituent is not the larger subject of a unit but only provides some frame of reference or connection to a larger context. This is particularly clear when the topicalized element is something other than the subject/nominative of its clause. As a result of this I prefer a name that more transparently reflects the actual function: contextualizing constituent. In this paper contextualizing constituent is used as a replacement synonym of topic. Cf. Buth, forthcoming.

theories.[2] Consequently, one must be careful in evaluating simple SV occurrences. These are not a simple "unmarked" order in Hebrew, but are pragmatically marked subjects.

3.1 Givón's Late Biblical Hebrew SVO

Talmy Givón (1976) counted an "increasing" number of SV constructions in some prophetic, didactic, and poetic materials and claimed that Late Biblical Hebrew had shifted to an SVO syntax. Such an approach actually hides what is happening in the grammar. Functional grammar recognizes that fronted constituents have pragmatic marking. If clause initial subjects had become syntactically normal and pragmatically unmarked, then we would find cases of pragmatic marking on other constituents in which they go to the beginning of the clause, where they are regularly followed by any explicit subject, producing XSV(+) clauses. This is what we find in English, but not Biblical Hebrew. Late Biblical Hebrew is still a VSO language, and all the cases of subject verb order or XV order need to be recognized as involving pragmatic marking on the fronted constituent.[3]

Givón can be praised for looking for a system and for linguistic explanation, but four faults invalidate his analysis.

A. He ignored *vayyiqtol* versus *veyiqtol*. These are pragmatically different, and only *veyiqtol* has the same tense/aspect as *noun* + *yiqtol*. All the *yiqtol*'s cannot be lumped together.

B. He ignored genre distinctions. Statistics could have pushed Isaiah into an SVO column but that would not have fit his expected time dimension.[4]

---

[2]Of course, one can postulate a basic SVO pattern for Hebrew, list XVSO sentences, VSO, and SVO sentences, and then describe various occurrences of each. But such a methodology has no explanatory power. It does not explain w h y XSVO is so rare as to be almost non-existent outside of participial clauses. Furthermore, an SVO theory is worse than a clumsy theory because it hides the fact that SVO sentences have a specially pragmatically marked element. See 3.1.

[3]Participial clauses are excepted, since participles have nominal morphology and follow verbless clause patterns.

[4]Compare what can be done with one of the most ancient poems in the Bible, Judges 5. Statistically this poem could be labelled SVO. There are, twelve [+2] clauses that begin with a subject immediately followed by the verb (Judg 3b, 4c, d, e, 5a, 6c, 13b, [+ 17a—SXV], [+ 17b—SXV], 17c, 18a, 21a, 29a, b). Five clauses begin with a verb immediately followed by a subject (Judg 5:7, 8, 19a, 24a[VXS], 28b [*waw ha-hippuk*]) In addition, there are another eleven clauses that begin with

C. Mishnaic Hebrew was set aside and ignored. Mishnaic Hebrew is statistically VSO, and it represents the continuation of spoken Hebrew down to the 2nd century CE. It would have been embarrassing to the theory to explain how a language could have shifted from VSO to SVO but then back to VSO at a time when the contact languages (Aramaic and Greek) were supposedly moving towards SVO themselves.

D. Loose analysis. E.g., Gen 3:12 "she" was called topic shifting according to Givón, while I would call it focus.

Even so, Givón assumed VSO for pre-exilic Hebrew. (For further comments, see Buth, 1987:21-25.)

In this example FG provides a framework for better defining and analyzing a proposed analysis. After exposing unresolved inconsistencies like the lack of XSVO, FG further requires an analyst to propose pragmatic explanations for the identified fronted phenomena in the texts and genres covered. These are exactly the things that researchers desire in a useful theory and are developed in sections 4.0 to 8.0 below.

3.2 SVO as a Basic, Statistical Remainder

A second incomplete approach to Hebrew word order would be to remove from consideration the *waw ha-hippuk* clauses, imperatives, and any clause that has a predictable, obligatory order. Then the remaining clauses could be counted and classified.[5] In the case of Hebrew, SVO would win. But the same theoretical shortcoming mentioned above in 3.0 and 3.1 hampers this approach and leaves it as a dead end. Such an approach does not explain why XSVO is relatively non-existent. A clause with special fronted elements should produce XSV(O) clauses according to this approach, something that does

---

something other than a verb and that have V relatively before S (Judg 5:6b, 11d [*ʾaz*], 13a [*ʾaz*], 14c, 19b [*ʾaz*], 20a, 22a [*ʾaz*], 23a, 28c, d, 31a [*ken*]).

I am not arguing that the oldest layer of Hebrew was SVO. I am pointing out that in the disjunctive genre of poetry some element frequently precedes the verb and that that element is often the subject. By judicious restrictions one can produce a statistical SV superiority over VS, 12 to 5, even though the absolute numbers for relative SV to VS are 14 to 16. If another poet contemporary to the poet of Judges 5 had written about a subject matter calling for more participles, the numbers would have been skewed much more toward SV. That is the true explanation of the figures in Song of Songs.

[5]Edward Greenstein called my attention to this approach. Cf. Greenstein: 9, n. 7.

happen with participles.[6] But the general lack of XSV(O) clauses in relation to the abundance of XVS(O) and SV(O) clauses demands a more explanatory linguistic framework for Hebrew than declaring SVO basic and listing others with ad hoc descriptions.

The FG analysis can explain the relative occurrences with the theoretical streamlining of needing only one P-V-S-O "template" for finite verbs. This covers and predicts the SV occurrences, excludes XSV[7] and leaves the VS occurrences of *waw ha-hippuk* verbs as syntactically regular and pragmatically unmarked.[8] Again, a Functional Grammar framework provides for a way to evaluate one analysis and leads to another more insightful analysis.

3.3 Value of Recognizing PVSO

Showing that there are pragmatically marked constituents in a grammar is only the first step of an analysis. The real benefit for interpretation begins when one tries to account for the pragmatic forces at work in the marking.

Much of the rest of this paper will define and show how contextualization, foreground and background, continuity and discontinuity, and plot structure affect Hebrew and Aramaic and how they can fit into FG. But before discussing these theoretical expansions within FG we will briefly look at the difference between topic/contextualization and focus.

---

[6]For example, in Jer 1:11 both SVO participle clauses have focus constituents before the subject:

WHAT (obligatory Focus) do you see? מה אתה ראה ?

I see (participle) an ALMOND STICK (Focus) מקל שקד אני ראה

[7]An XSV could occur where X was a marked contextualizing constituent and S was a marked focus. E.g., Ps 51:5 כי־פשעי אני ארע "for my-crimes *I* know" = "as for my sins, I am the one conscious of them."

Likewise, SXV would occur where a contextualized subject is followed by a marked focal element. E.g., Judg 21:25: איש הישר בעיניו יעשה "a man, the correct thing in his own eyes, he would do" = "a person did what was *right in his own eyes.*"

[8]Participles can be handled with a secondary order P-S-V-O, something that is reasonable in the light of the recognized morphological affinity of participles with nouns and nominal clauses as opposed to verbs. Participles use regular "nominal" declensions and generally fit the parameters associated with verbless clauses.

4.0 Topic/Contextualization and Focus

In FG a topic is a constituent of a clause that has received special marking (either by word order, a special particle, or intonation, depending on the language) in order to signal the intended perspective for relating the clause to the larger context. A topic (contextualizing constituent-C.C.) does not need to be the subject of a sentence, and a topic(C.C.) is functionally as distinct from focus as day from night. A marked topic is not the salient, important information of a clause. Its purpose is to help the listener understand how and on what basis some sentences are grouped together. (Within Prague School Functional Sentence Perspective, Beneś and Firbas used the term "basis" to refer to this pragmatic topic function.) Focus, on the other hand, is a way of specially marking the salient, important information of a sentence. Consider the following:

(5) He hit it with a bat (unmarked). ["bat" is unmarked salient information]

(6) He hit it with a BAT (focus). [high-falling intonation used to mark salient information as a focus]

(7) It was a BAT (focus) he hit it with. [cleft sentence to precisely mark salient information]

(8) Then with a BAT (focus) he hit it. [intonation and fronting to mark focal salient information]

(9) Then with the bat (topic/C.C.) he hit it. [normal intonation on fronted topic with "hitting" the salient information]

(10) In the morning (topic/C.C.) he played football. [fronted topic where "morning" is not part of the salient information and does not receive special intonation]

(11) He played football in the morning. ["morning" is part of the salient information and is not a topic/C.C.]

(12) In the morning (topic/C.C.) she kissed him,
in the EVENING (topic/C.C. + focus) she hit him. [fronting plus focus intonation for a contrastive topic. This last example merges the "contrast" inherent in focus with the relational function of a contextualizing constituent. To use the analogy of night and day, languages have "eclipse" structures as well.]

The above examples should be sufficient to illustrate the difference between topic (contextualizing constituent) and focus, though each example would be better if listed as part of an appropriate text. The discerning reader will see that within this major distinction there are different kinds of focus and different kinds of topic. However, one would be mistaken to conclude that there is an undifferentiated continuum along a topic-focus line. Languages have discrete structures, and an author or speaker must choose whether or not to use a particular topic or focus construction. In any case, marked topic/C.C. and marked focus are vital distinctions for understanding the pragmatic packaging of communication, and it is a major advancement over the general catch-all "emphasis."

5.0 Foreground

The study of texts has opened a new field within linguistics and pragmatics. Whether it is called textlinguistics, discourse analysis or חקר השיח, the larger framework of a text requires some new concepts for grammars. A pair of concepts from gestalt theory is foreground and background.[9] These terms have been widely used in understanding linguistic narrative structure. When properly defined they can distinguish facets of language structure that were either misunderstood or ignored in previous studies. It turns out that some psychological enigmas in the morphological systems of languages are readily explained. Hebrew can never be taught the same way after these foundational concepts are understood.

How many students of Hebrew have asked about the purpose of having a *waw-hahippuk* verb system? The traditional answer, that it is a "nice way to continue marking the tense-aspect of the verb," is intuitively found to be suspect. Why bother having two ways to mark the same tense-aspect? An answer based on historical development is

---

[9]Foreground and background do not appear to be identical to the theses of Schneider (1974), adapting Weinreich (1971) to Hebrew. (I have not been able to obtain copies of their work.) Secondary descriptions suggest that Schneider has attempted to interpret the verb and tense system of the language with primary categories of narrative (*erzählt*) versus discoursive (*besprochen*). Such a system is too confined and would fail by ignoring the basic tense-aspect-mode opposition. In effect, the system tries to replace semantic distinctions with pragmatic ones instead of defining how both interact. Walter Gross (1980) represents a positive development in this regard, though one that is somewhat confusing or inconsistent. He asserts that background (*Hintergrund*) and foreground (*Vordergrund*) are necessary categories for Hebrew grammar, but he does not define the terms, leaving them somewhat in the realm of literary criticism. For example, he contrasts background with a circumstantial clause (139), and most inexplicably he attributes Gen 1:2 to foreground at the end of his article (145), though the verse unquestionably exhibits the structures of backgrounding.

only partially satisfying. Such an answer explains where the forms came from, but it does not explain why the language continued to use both forms and why it continued to do that for over a thousand years.

The foreground of a narrative is usually defined to be the sequential chain of completed events. This is a strictly semantic definition of foreground. However, a problem arises when one tries to match that definition with a particular structure, form, or lexeme of a language.

In Hebrew the obvious candidate for foreground is the *waw-hahippuk* verb. Certainly, most of the sequential, completed events in a narrative are encoded in the *waw-hahippuk* verb forms. But what do we do about the *waw-hahippuk*'s that are not sequential or complete?[10] Studies that relate the *waw-hahippuk* verbs with sequentiality can only give a percentage of clauses that fit the definition (cf . Lowery, 306–8). If foreground is limited to an objective definition in the semantic field of grammar, then one must say that the *waw-hahippuk* is sometimes foreground and sometimes not. It is sometimes sequential and sometimes not.

(13) Jon 1:16-2:1

ויזבחו־זבח ליהוה וידרו נדרים
וימן יהוה דג גדול לבלע את יונה

[Foregrounded, verb initial clauses with *waw ha-hippuk* verbs are in italics]
and they *sacrificed* a sacrifice to the LORD
and they *vowed* vows
and the LORD *appointed* a great fish to swallow Jonah.

The sacrifice of the sailors took a bit of time and appears to have followed the calming of the sea. The appointing of the big fish could have taken place before or during the time of sacrifice, perhaps during the storm itself. In English we might mark the ambiguous temporal relationship between the sailors' actions and the Lord's appointment with "meanwhile" if we were concerned with temporal precision, i.e., "Meanwhile, the LORD (had) appointed a big fish." The Hebrew storyteller recounts the appointing of the big fish as though it were the next event in the story, but we must not assume that absolute sequentiality was intended. From his pragmatic viewpoint the storyteller proceeds from the sacrifices and vows directly to the fish. Appointing the fish is the next "mainline" event in the story. Assuming that real-time sequentiality is ignored, we can attribute this to the pragmatic

[10]See below under "continuity and discontinuity" for more neutral and helpful terms than foreground and background.

constraints of organizational sequentiality and the author's desire to recount these specific events as structurally equal without any narrative pause or distraction.

A more absolute mismatch of semantic sequentiality and pragmatic foregrounding is the following example 14.

(14) Judg 11:1

ויפתח הגלעדי היה גבור חיל
והוא בן זונה
ויולד גלעד את יפתח
ותולד אשת גלעד לו בנים
ויגדלו בני האשה
ויגרשו את יפתח

a and Yiftaḥ the Gilʿadi was a great warrior
b and he was the son of a prostitute
c and Gilʿad (had) fathered Yiftaḥ
d and the wife of Gilʿad birthed for him sons
e and the sons of the wife grew up
f and they drove away Yiftaḥ.

Sentence 14c above is certainly a temporal back-reference since a warrior's birth happens before he becomes a warrior. This was reported as a mainline event of the story by using the *waw ha-hippuk* structure, even though this breaks the normal sequentiality of the *waw ha-hippuk* (see Buth, 1991 for further details). Sentences 14d-14f follow in apparent sequentiality once the reader reorients to the time of Yiftaḥ's birth.

If we define foreground as a pragmatic function, instead of semantically, we get around the impasse of non-sequential events being encoded with a "sequential-foregrounding" structure. The advantages of this redefinition are that it corresponds with real language data and allows more objective mapping between surface structures and their functions. The disadvantage is that the definition of foreground becomes "subjective" and is not able to be measured by comparison to a referential world. We would not be able to point to an event in a narrative and say categorically, based only on the referential nature of the event itself, that it is or is not a foregrounded event. We must look and see how the author structured and encoded the event and then, after looking at the surface structures of the language, we can say that it is or is not foreground. The advantages of including foreground as a pragmatic function greatly outweigh the disadvantage. In fact, the disadvantage is only an artificial constraint. If languages develop structures that are subjectively used, then we must make room for that in our grammar. Nothing else would be scientific.

In this definition foreground is a structuring, packaging device of the grammar; it does not communicate referential meaning by itself. This partly explains why it has not been defined or properly discussed in traditional grammars. It may help to rename foreground as "mainline event" to emphasize its pragmatic structural character. And since foreground only contrasts with background, a two-valued name like "on-line" and "off-line" would also work for 'foreground-background. However, for Hebrew and Aramaic, continuity and discontinuity may prove to be the most general, neutral and useful terms. See section 11.0 below.

As an aside for those biblical scholars who may think that the above discussion only applies to an "exotic" system like the Hebrew verb, I would mention that that pedigree of Indo-European languages, Classical Greek, distinguishes between narrative events encoded as aorist participles and as finite aorist verbs. The difference between them is a similarly subjective and pragmatic function of thematic demotion. There is not any semantic difference between "having got in the boat he sailed away," and "he got in the boat and sailed away." But they are different in their pragmatic structure. The first has one demoted verb and only one foregrounded verb, "sail," while the second has two foregrounded verbs, "got in" and "sailed."

6.0 Background

Foreground is a binary notion bundled with background. Background is the material in a narrative that is not foreground. Usually, this means material that is not temporally sequential. Simultaneous material, pluperfect past reference, negation, stative descriptions, habitual actions, reason and purpose clauses are usually part of the background of a narrative.

In the Bible, Hebrew uses verb-second word order and a separate tense-aspect system to mark a clause as "background" ("not foreground"). This includes what grammarians often discussed as the "circumstantial clause" when subject verb order was used. It also includes those examples that led some to say that Hebrew had a pluperfect verb tense marked by word order.

(15) Jon 1:5b

ויונה ירד אל־ירכתי הספינה
וישכב וירדם

[Foregrounded, verb initial clauses with *waw ha-hippuk* verbs are in italics]
AND Yonah (had) gone down to the bottom of the boat [subject verb order]
and he *lay down and fell soundly asleep.*

This is a nice example of a backgrounded structure being used for a pluperfect event. The verb is pushed to second place by the subject. The subject can be said to be tagged as a contextualizing constituent (here a pseudo-topic) and has been placed in the P1 pragmatic slot.

7.0 Contextualizing Constituent, Setting and Paragraph Unit Borders

The existence of background clauses with nouns apparently marked like "topics," but without an apparently motivated topicality related to the noun itself, led me to recognize a pragmatic form-function fusion within FG: contextualization by a contextualizing constituent, used for topic, setting, paragraph unit borders and dramatic pause.

Within expository non-narrative discourse where information is logically structured hierarchically, it is common to find noun phrases marked as C.C. and placed in the P1 position, which provide topic spans for the text. However, quite often in Hebrew narrative one encounters nouns in the P1 position which do not provide specifically topical organization for the following clauses, but simply serve to set the clause off from the sequence of on-line foregrounded-continuity clauses. They are used as a discontinuity structure to break up and mark off time, paragraph, or episode divisions. An example will help illustrate this.

(16) Gen 4:1

והאדם ידע את־חוה אשתו
ותהר ותלד את־קין
ותאמר—קניתי איש את יהוה

[Foregrounded, verb initial clauses with *waw ha-hippuk* verbs are in italics]
AND the Man knew Havah his-wife [SV order]
and she *conceived*
and gave birth to Qayin
and said—I have gotten a man from the Lord

This passage does not deal primarily with the man, Adam, but with Eve and her children. Any topic marking on the Subject, Adam, is best explained as a structure affecting the clause as a whole in relation to other clauses, not just the noun "Adam." The clause opens a whole new episode with a new setting and new characters. The purpose of a backgrounded clause here is closely tied to the idea of a unit boundary marking. This marks a new paragraph and episode as beginning. At times this structure may coincide with a unit that we call paragraph: at other times it is best seen as something larger. A comparison with Gen 4:17 suggests that here 4:1 is beginning a large unit. This reinforces the new setting and new characters.

It appears that Gen 4:1 is a sequential event that follows chapter 3. The impression of chapter 3 is that transgression and punishment were swift enough to preclude 4:1. This leads the reader to interpret this background construction as a unit marker rather than a pluperfect event.

For linguists who do not want redundant labeling of both contextualization and background in the same clause in the grammar, the contextualizing constituent is the general structure and can be said to mark a clause for a wide range of relationships which includes a backgrounding-discontinuity where the discontinuity does not refer to a switch of a "topic," but to a higher level of discontinuity. The name contextualizing constituent is intended to be flexible enough to include such non-topical, packaging situations as Gen 4:1. To say it another way in reference to Gen 4:1, the author chose a structure that said "Let's talk about Adam/let's relate to Adam" because he was beginning something new, not because he was going to talk about Adam. He proceeded to talk about (Eve), Cain and Abel.

8.0 Peak and Dramatic Pause

A more radical expansion to FG is the idea that a literary notion like peak or climax can be part of the grammar. Most phenomena that have been attributed to marking a literary peak cannot be called grammatical (cf. Longacre, 1983). However, an investigation into both Hebrew and Aramaic reveals some structures that clearly show the interaction of such a literary notion as peak with the core grammar of the language. (The term "literary notion" would be a part of the domain of pragmatics, the packaging of a message in a particular communication situation.)

It turns out that there is a relationship between marking peak and background-discontinuity structures in both Hebrew and Aramaic. Such a relationship is quite special because the C.C. normally puts clauses off the main line of events, while at a peak the structure can be clearly marking main line events of the story. Two examples from Hebrew will illustrate this use of contextualizing constituents as "background-discontinuity structures" for marking a "foregrounded" peak in a story

(17) Esth 7:6–10

ותאמר אסתר—איש צר ואויב המן הרע הזה
והמן נבעת מלפני המלך והמלכה
והמלך קם בחמתו ממשתה היין אל גנת הביתן
והמן עמד לבקש על־נפשו מאסתר המלכה
כי ראה כי־כלתה אליו הרעה מאת המלך
והמלך שב מגנת הביהן אל־בית משתה היין
והמן נפל על־המטה אשר אסתר עליה
ויאמר המלך—הגם לכבוש את־המלכה עמי בבית
הדבר יצא מפי המלך
ופני המן חפו
ויאמר חרבונה אחד . . .
ויאמר המלך—תלהו עליו
ויתלו את־המן על־העץ אשר־הכין למרדכי
וחמת המלך שככה

[Foregrounded, verb initial clauses with *waw ha-hippuk* verbs are in italics]
and Esther *said*—such a cruel enemy is this wicked Haman
AND Haman trembled before the king and queen [SV]
AND the king rose in rage from the banquet to the garden [SV]
AND Haman stood to plead for his life from Esther the queen [SV]
for he saw that the king wanted to condemn him for his evil
AND the king returned from the garden to the banquet [SV]
AND Haman was prostrate on the couch where Esther was [SV]
and the king *said*—You'd violate the queen right here!
The word went forth from the king [SV]
AND the face of Haman contorted [SV]
and one of the bodyguards *said* . . .
and the king *said*—Hang him!
and they *hanged* Haman on the gallows he prepared for Mordechai
AND the rage of the king subsided [SV]

This is a remarkable string of contextualizing constituents used with sequential narrative events. The most credible explanation of this is that the author has pragmatically suspended the marking of foregrounding-continuity in the story in order to hold the audience's attention at a dramatic peak.[11]

---

[11]The SV order is not a reflection of Late Biblical Hebrew (LBH) syntax. The rest of the book of Esther faithfully uses normal, classical *waw ha-hippuk* VS constructions. Accordingly, an analyst should not hypothesize that at verse 7:6 the author was hit on the head, started spewing forth a non-existent SV syntax, and then at 8:1 reverted to normal Classical Hebrew. Linguistics and Relevance Theory would demand that we first assume a coherent author. When we do, we find a perfectly rational and pragmatically perceptive composition that reveals an ability

A good name for such a function might be dramatic pause: "pause," because the C.C. structure normally stops the flow of sequential events, "dramatic," because of the association of this grammatical inversion at major turning points and climaxes. It is the grammatical equivalent of a slow motion technique or of a freezing of a frame at an emotional point of a motion picture film. The X-V structure can be distinguished from a simple contextualizing constituent by being used with a sequential event, and it can be differentiated from unit-boundary settings by its logical connections to the surrounding context as non-initial. In a string like this Esther example or in the following example from Genesis the repetition of the structure helps us isolate the phenomenon and recognize what is happening.[12] Consequently, it would seem justified and useful to at least include dramatic pause as a sub-set of the background-discontinuity function of the contextualization structure.

In the Esther example there are other items of special interest. When one of the clauses was used circumstantially, "and" was not used so as not to mimic the chain of dramatic pause "backgrounds." Also, several of the verbs are ambiguous morphologically as to whether they are participles or suffix verbs. It would be interesting to see whether or not the ratio of ambiguous forms to unambiguous forms turns up significantly more often in background clauses than in foreground clauses. Morphologies and word-formation in languages sometimes mirror such functional compatibility. It is clear, though, that the typical subject-plus-suffix-verb construction has been intended most of the time in the above example because חפו, "contorted" and שככה, "subsided" are unambiguously suffix verbs. In addition, most of the events are sequential: "trembled," "got up," "stood," "returned."

---

to use Classical Hebrew structures and incidentally produces the longest syntactical narrative SV chain in the Bible. Besides, LBH is normatively VSO, as Esther, Chronicles, Ezra, Daniel and any temporally structured Hebrew text will show. On the other hand, there were major syntactic developments in LBH: e.g., the *waw ha-hippuk* system dropped out of normal speech. That partially accounts for Qohelet's simple *wĕqātal* forms according to the later Mishnaic system.

[12] It can also be used individually, though that requires recognizing that it does not come at the beginning of a paragraph-like unit but as a climax. See further Buth, forthcoming.

(18) Gen 44:3

הבקר אור
ואנשים שלחו, המה וחמריהם
הם יצאו את־העיר
לא הרחיקו
ויוסף אמר לאשר על־ביתו—קום רדף . . .

The morning dawned
and the men were sent, they and their donkeys
they departed the city
they did not go far
and Joseph said to the man over his house—Go, chase down

The chain of "backgrounded" clauses prolongs the setting for an unusual length. More importantly, there are three sequential events, including the speech frame: "Joseph said." Again, we need to invoke a dramatic pause intended by the author. This passage is different from Esther, though, because the events do not describe the climax or, peak events themselves. They open the scene and set the stage for the dramatic confrontation at the height of the Joseph story, where Joseph reveals himself to his brothers. This is another example where the grammar is directly affected, inverted as it were, by very high level considerations of literary structure. Properly configured, FG will handle this. In order to mark a special point of tension in the story, the author of Genesis marks the clauses as "background-discontinuity" by using subjects as contextualizing constituents. The FG assignment rules place the contextualizing constituent in the initial P1 pragmatic slot as the clause is generated in the core of the grammar.

9.0 Aramaic

It appears that most of the above discussion on background-discontinuity and related functions applies to Old Aramaic. By Old Aramaic we mean the scanty, but very valuable, inscriptional remains before the seventh century BCE. They reveal an Aramaic language that was basically ordered as verb-subject-object and which used the P1 position to mark topic/C.C. (including background-discontinuity clauses) or focus by putting some constituent before the verb.

Imperial Aramaic, the international diplomatic and commercial language from the seventh to third centuries BCE, is noted for very diverse word orders. It is obvious that a major syntactic change took place in the language. This paper is not the place to discuss the complex details, but we can outline some of the most significant conclusions from a study of this dialect along functional lines.

9.1 Aramaic Change and FG

The use of a single P1 position before the verb expanded to include more than one function. For example, both a subject topic/C.C. and a setting topic/C.C. could precede a verb (cf. Dan 2:19). Old Aramaic was a more restrictive VSO language because it only allowed one pragmatic function to be marked before the verb. (Multiple initial pragmatic positions are a necessary expansion to Dik's model.)

Imperial Aramaic developed a new way of marking background-discontinuity. The grammar could reserve the verb for the end of a backgrounded clause. Narrative topic marking in the P1 position of foregrounded clauses was also developed. Thus, many foreground clauses in Daniel have SV(+) word order. The result of these far reaching changes was a language whose power to order constituents had hidden its VSO structure from casual reading. Nevertheless, Imperial Aramaic remained a VSO language, and the Aramaic dialects that emerged after the Alexandrian Greek conquests returned to more restrictive VSO grammars (see Buth, 1987 for further details).

FG can recognize a major structural and grammatical distinction where one grammar allows a single pragmatic function before a VSO core, while another grammar allows multiple functions before a VSO core. The multiple P1-Pn grammar of Imperial Aramaic is attested in Aramaic from before the Persian period, so we must conclude that the structure-changing foreign influence on Aramaic word order came from Akkadian and not Persian. The beginning of that influence can already be seen in the bilingual Tell Fakhariyeh inscription (cf. Buth, 1987:164–7).

The fact that foreground-continuity was not as simply marked in Imperial Aramaic as in Old Aramaic led to the development of adverbial sentence conjunctions expressing sequentiality—"then": אדין, באדין, אחר, קרבתא. So FG lets us watch, measure and understand some of the changes taking place in the language. For Aramaic examples and a full discussion of the developments in Aramaic word order the reader is referred to Buth, 1987 and 1990.

10.0 Examples

Four examples of various complexity in Hebrew and Aramaic follow.

(19) Num 17:13–15

ויעמד בין־המתים ובין החיים
ותעצר המגפה
ויהיו המתים במגפה 14,000 . . .
וישב אהרן אל־משה אל־פתח אהל מועד
והמגפה נעצרה

and he *stood* between the dead and the living
and the plague *stopped*
and there were 14,000 dead in the plague
and Aharon *returned* to Moshe . . .
AND the plague stopped

The second mention of the plague stopping has nothing to do with verb-tense parallelism of poetry. It is closing out the episode by mentioning the result. The plague had already stopped, so the second mention of the "stopping" would not be expected in the narrative foreground form. The author clearly signals this distinction by putting the first "stopping" in the *waw ha-hippuk* form while using the contextualizing, background SV construction for the second mention.[13]

(20) Num 16:35

ויהי ככלתו לדבר את כל־הדברים האלה
ותבקע האדמה אשר תחתיהם:
ותפתח הארץ את־פיה
ותבלע אתם ואת־בתיהם ואת כל־האדם אשר לקרח ואת כל־הרכוש:
וירדו הם וכל־אשר להם חיים שאלה
ותכס עליהם הארץ
ויאבדו מתוך הקהל:
וכל־ישראל אשר סביבתיהם נסו לקלם
כי אמרו
פן־תבלענו הארץ:
ואש יצאה מאת יהוה
ותאכל את החמשים ומאתים איש מקריבי הקטרת:

[Foregrounded, verb initial clauses with *waw ha-hippuk* verbs are in italics]
And it happened when he finished speaking these words
and the land which was under them *split-up*
and the earth *opened* its mouth
and swallowed them and their houses and . . .
and they and all they had *went down* alive to Sheol

[13]From a viewpoint of tense marking the same result is reached. Here the SV order is used for a pluperfect event, a correlation that has long been noted by Hebraists as significant but not exclusive for SV structures. Pluperfect tense markings are by definition off-line and background.

and the earth *covered* them
and they *perished* from the midst of the assembly
AND all Israel around them fled at their cries
for they said lest the earth swallow them
AND fire went forth from the Lord
and devoured the 250 men, presenters of incense.

In Hebrew the events of "fleeing" and "fire going forth" are marked as "off-line" background-discontinuity events from the earlier narrative. Semantically, the "fleeing" and the "going forth" may be simultaneous to the main story. This could explain the C.C. structures. However, if the clauses are understood to be semantically sequential, then the "fleeing" and "fire going forth" would be examples of dramatic pause, a formal, grammatical pause to mark peak events.

The final clause "devour" continues the narration about the fire, as both sequential and foreground in relation to the previous clause ("went forth") but not necessarily in relation to the earlier clauses. Naturally, a binary distinction cannot differentially mark several levels of structure but has to be used within each one. Literary and theological readings of the passage can be tested to see that they conform to the structures the author has chosen. The grammar cannot complete an analysis, but when properly understood it serves as a useful tool.

(21 Aramaic) Dan 5:3, 23

5:3 [Foreground-Continuity—Verb Subject Object]
באדין היתיו מאני דהבא די הנפקו מן . . .
ואשתיו בהון מלכא ורברבנוהי שגלתה ולחנתה

Then they brought the golden utensils which had been . . .
[or passive: "then were-brought the golden utensils"]
and they drank with them, the king and his nobles. . . .

5:23 [Background-Discontinuity—P1 Pn Subject Object Verb x]
ועל מרא־שמיא התרוממת
ולמאניא די־ביתה היתיו קדמיך
ואנתה ורברבניך שגלתך ולחנתך חמרא שתין בהון
ולאלהי כספא־ודהבא . . . שבחת
ולאלהא . . . לא הדרת

and [because] over the Lord of heaven you exalted yourself
and the vessels of his house they brought to you
and you and your nobles . . . wine were-drinking in them
and the gods of silver and gold . . . you praised
and God . . . you did not honor

Dan 5:3 is foreground-continuity in the main narrative and uses a verb initial structure. Dan 5:23 recounts the same incidents in a non-narrative, expository framework where the first clause "exalt" presents a conclusion followed by a listing of four clauses as evidence but which are not structured as narrative. These all have verb-final structures.

(22 Aramaic) Dan 6:19, 20

6:19 [Foreground-Continuity] אדין אזל מלכא להיכלה
Then went the king to his palace

6:20 [Background-Discontinuity, Dramatic Pause, Peak]
באדין מלכא בשפרפרא יקום בנגהא
ובהתבהלה לגבא די־אריותא אזל

Then the king at dawn got up at sunrise
and with haste to the pit of lions he went

Dan 6:19 and 20 use the same verb but use different word orders to distinguish pragmatic structures. (The first clause of 6:20 may have an added gloss בנגהא "at sunrise," or, it may be a parenthetic afterthought.) The unusual use of a prefix verb for a punctiliar event may also be related to peak, dramatic pause, and background.

11.0 Continuity and Discontinuity

There are some problems with the above descriptions that can be avoided by adapting a framework with the terms continuity and discontinuity.[14] The problems stem from the incongruity of comparing contextualizing constituents in narrative and non-narrative. In narrative the topic/C.C.'s break the normal temporal progress while in much non-narrative material there is no time-line to break. But why is it that a "topic" structure should be chosen to break-up narratives and mark the relation of clauses to each other? Why is the time-breaking structure the same as topic-changing structures in non-narratives? What is the similarity that is reflected in these structures?

A text is based on an assumption of literary continuity. If there were not some kind of underlying continuity, then the assumed text

---

[14]I would like to thank Stephen Levinsohn of SIL Colombia for calling my attention to the importance of these terms. The terms are explained in Givón, 1983. One of the ironies of that work is that the terms are excellent for categorizing what some language structures actually do, but the focus of the book is on a quantitative analysis that only measures indirect results of the structures. The studies do not elucidate the linguistic functions themselves.

would not be a text but only a random gathering of sentences or words. Givón (1983:5–10) has tentatively proposed a ranking of the various notions that give a text continuity. First of all, there is a general "thematic continuity." This is the subject matter of the text. It may be difficult to define and different analysts may describe the theme slightly differently, but a text would not usually be a text without some underlying abstract "theme." Then there are smaller continuities within a text that continue the same situation or the same series of actions or the same topic-character. The reason for ranking these three aspects of continuity in the above order is that this represents the order in which continuity is most resistant to being broken by discontinuities. Topic continuities can be broken up by switching to new topic continuities, yet one or more of these different topic continuities may hold together as an overarching action continuity. And the action continuities may be broken by other gapped or nonsequential action continuities. Yet they may all hold together to form a larger continuity of a situation.

Now the interesting aspect of this description of text continuity is that it provides a way of unifying the functions of various discontinuities. Both "topic" level and action level discontinuities can be grouped together as "discontinuities" despite the different aspects of their "discontinuity." This will be most easily seen in the descriptions of "topic" for Hebrew. A "pure" topic marks a nominal constituent of a clause in order to set up that constituent as a unifying aspect for a series of clauses and as distinct from other series of clauses dealing with other topics. Such a topic provides a base for continuity, but it is itself a marked discontinuity in that it had to displace some other "base of continuity." A marked topic that does not itself serve as the "base" for a topic continuity could be called a "pseudo-topic." It marks a discontinuity and breaks the text up into a smaller continuity that is based on something other than the marked "pseudo-topic" nominal. Thus, topic/C.C.'s and pseudo-topic/C.C.'s can be categorized together as discontinuity markers that divide a text into smaller units of cohesion. This also resolves some of the tension involved in marking a "clause-level feature" on a nominal argument.

In Hebrew the XV structures are structures of discontinuity. If the discontinuity concerns a change of nominal topic/C.C., then the marking system and the discontinuity are congruent. If the discontinuity marks a change of action or situation like a parallel series of actions or another grouping of events, such as a paragraph or episode, then the XV construction is still a discontinuity but not necessarily related primarily to the nominal of the marked form. It is the larger sequence of events that receives the discontinuity marking and not the "X" item itself. Furthermore, the function of XV structures as a dramatic pause at peak and peak setting is appropriately included under discontinuity.

For Hebrew and Aramaic syntactic studies it will prove easier in the long run to use terms like continuity and discontinuity as a replacement for the pragmatically defined foreground and background. The *waw ha-hippuk* is the tense-aspect system to mark continuity, while the XV structures are the system to mark pragmatic discontinuity. This is diagrammed in the following chart.

Tense-Aspect

	Past ± Perfective ± Realis	*Non-Past ± Imperfective ± Irrealis*	
Continuity	wayyiqtōl	wĕqātal	Discourse Continuity
Discontinuity	X + qātal	X + yiqtōl	

12.0 Conclusion

This brief description of functional grammar and the examples from Hebrew and Aramaic have shown how such a grammatical theory can help to clarify our understanding of the grammars of the particular languages. Furthermore, the application of discourse analysis from within functional grammar leads us to recognize new phenomena and gives us a theoretical matrix with which to understand it.

With foreground-continuity (VS) versus background-discontinuity (XV) we are dealing with a binary structure that can be manipulated in many circumstances to produce quite an array of subtle distinctions. The text is able to signal foreground-continuity and is able to break-up that continuity to report parallel actions, out-of-sequence actions, new topics, new units and even to mark dramatic pause in a grammatical inversion. Overlaid on these organizational structures (contextualizations) is a separate focus function.

If we were to use spatial metaphors, the importance of functional grammar for language in general and for Hebrew and Aramaic in particular is the difference between a two-dimensional framework and a three-dimensional one. Many things may be discussed on the two-dimensional plane, but ultimately the three dimensional plane is necessary in order to grapple with the real world. In my estimation, a shift to a functional language theory is more fundamental than the shift from data definition to general rule definition that has taken place under the name of generative linguistics.

For exegesis, a better understanding of grammar allows us to more accurately assess the structure and development of text. Our "close" readings can be tighter and can have more precise grammatical confirmations.

WORKS CONSULTED

Beneś, E.
1962 "Die Verbstellung im Deutschen von der Mitteilungsperspektive her betrachtet." *Philologia Pragensia* 5:6–19.

Buth, Randall
1987 *Word Order in Aramaic from the Perspectives of Functional Grammar and Discourse Analysis.* University of California, Los Angeles dissertation. Ann Arbor: University Microfilms International.

1990 "*ʾEdayin/Tote*—Anatomy of a Semitism in Jewish Greek." *Maarav* 5–6: 33–48.

1994 "Methodological Collision between Source Criticism and Discourse Analysis: The Problem of 'Unmarked Temporal Overlay' and the Pluperfect/Non-Sequential *Wayyiqtol*." Pp. 138-54 in *Biblical Hebrew and Discourse Linguistics.* Ed. Robert L. Bergen. Winona Lake, IN: Eisenbrauns.

Forth-coming "Contextualizing Constituent as Topic, Non-Sequential Background and Dramatic Pause: Hebrew and Aramaic Evidence." In *Selected Papers from the 4th International Colloquium on Functional Grammar, Copenhagen, 1990.*

Dik, Simon
1980 *Studies in Functional Grammar.* New York: Academic.

Firbas, J.
1974 "Some Aspects of the Czechoslovak Approach to Problems of Functional Sentence Perspective." Pp. 11–37 in *Papers on Functional Sentence Perspective.* Ed. František Daneš. Prague: Academia/The Hague: Mouton.

Givón, Talmy
1976 "The Drift from VSO to SVO in Biblical Hebrew: The Pragmatics of Tense-Aspect." Pp. 181-254 in *Mechanisms of Syntactic Change.* Ed. Charles Li. Austin: University of Texas Press.

Givón, Talmy, ed.
1983 *Topic and Continuity in Discourse.* Amsterdam: John Benjamins.

Greenstein, Edward L.
1988 "On the Prefixed Preterite in Biblical Hebrew." *HS* 29:7-17.

Gross, Walter
1981 "Syntaktische Erscheinungen am Anfang althebräischer Erzählungen: Hintergrund und Vordergrund." *VTSup* 32:131–45.

Hopper, Paul J.
1979 "Aspect and Foregrounding in Discourse." Pp. 213-41 in *Discourse and Syntax.* Ed. Talmy Givón. *Syntax and Semantics 12.* New York: Academic.

Levinsohn, Stephen H.
1987 *Textual Connection in Acts.* SBLMS 31. Atlanta: Scholars Press.

Longacre, Robert E.
1983 *The Grammar of Discourse.* New York: Plenum.

Lowery, Kirk E.
1985 *Toward a Discourse Grammar of Biblical Hebrew.* University of California, Los Angeles dissertation. Ann Arbor: University Microfilms International.

Schneider, Wolfgang
1974 *Grammatik des biblischen Hebräisch: Ein Lehrbuch.* München: Claudius.

Weinreich, Harald
1971 *Tempus, Besprochene und erzählte Welt.* Stuttgart: W. Kohlhammer.

4

THE THEORETICAL FOUNDATIONS OF HEBREW DISCOURSE GRAMMAR

Kirk E. Lowery

ABSTRACT

Which approach to discourse analysis (text linguistics) is most appropriate to apply to the Hebrew Bible? To answer this question the major approaches to discourse analysis are surveyed and classified into four groups: the psycho-social, anthropological, cognitive, and grammatical. Seven criteria are offered for determining the most useful approach for the Hebraist. The conclusion is that if these axioms are accepted, then the grammatical approach is the only real option. Finally, an outline of a prospective discourse grammar of Biblical Hebrew is presented with a discussion of its form and organizing principles.

1. Introduction

Since the late 1960s there has been a change in the development of method in the study of the Hebrew Bible. A dissatisfaction with previous methods and perspectives grew among biblical scholars. Even as early as 1938, Gerhard von Rad (1) felt he had come to a dead end with form criticism. The dissatisfaction was expressed in James Muilenberg's 1968 presidential address to the Society of Biblical Literature, which suggested that the older methodologies were incapable of answering the questions biblical scholars were asking.

> Persistent and painstaking attention to the modes of Hebrew literary composition will reveal that the pericope exhibits linguistic patterns, word formations ordered or arranged in particular ways, verbal sequences which move in fixed structures from beginning to end. It is clear that

> they have been skillfully wrought in many different ways, often with consummate skill and artistry. It is also apparent that they have been influenced by conventional rhetorical practices. This inevitably poses a question for which I have no answer. From whom did the poets and prophets of Israel acquire their styles and literary habits (Muilenburg: 18)?

The most significant characteristic of this dissatisfaction had to do with the direction of perspective. Since the beginning of this century, analysis of the Hebrew Bible had moved from large units of text toward the ever smaller. This was driven by a desire to discover sources and origins of ideas. The aim was to identify the smallest literary unit in the text and trace how these units were combined together to form the canonical text. This concept of the evolving text is epitomized in Otto Eissfeldt's *magnum opus, The Old Testament: An Introduction.* Source criticism identified the smallest units, form criticism characterized the *Sitz im Leben* and usage of the units, and tradition history tracked the evolution of those units.

The problem, of course, is that the biblical data to answer such questions are sparse. Often hypothesis was built upon speculation. Agreement was rare. Further, James Barr focused attention upon the misuse of etymology and linguistic evidence in theology (206–62). He showed just how linguistically naive biblical scholarship was at the time. To their credit, biblical scholars hastened to repair their oversight and neglect. It seemed that these older approaches to the text had taken us as far as they could.

Muilenburg's essay reflected a change in perspective. Rather than downward, the focus was now outward. Regardless of the history of the text, the text appeared in a final form. Why was the text placed in the form that it was? Here was a question which could be explored profitably without knowing the history of that text. Whether by an editor, a team of editors or the original author, there was a purpose to the text as it now stands.

Objectivity is a *sine qua non* for any scientific analysis and no less so for biblical scholars. How can we approach the text (an admittedly subjective product) with the greatest measure of objectivity, controlling for that ultimate evil, eisegesis? Biblical scholars looked outside their own discipline in an explosion of crossdisciplinary applications of anthropology, psychology, sociology, literary criticism, and linguistics to the text of the Hebrew Bible.

Many turned to linguistics for help. The descriptive linguists of the 1930s and 1940s concentrated upon how language was actually used, moving away from the idea of grammatical "right" and "wrong." Since the biblical text was a product of language, it was natural that the theory and praxis of linguistics would be applied to the Hebrew Bible. Hebrew Bible studies had long been concerned with classical philology, tracing the history of words and their meanings. With the discovery of the Ugaritic texts, along with the vast store of Akkadian, comparative philology began a revolution in Hebrew lexicography.[1] Careful application of phonological analysis to the Semitic languages in general produced new insights into how Biblical Hebrew formed words.[2]

But what began with phonology and morphology did not continue with syntax. While much refinement went on during the first half of the twentieth century, the theoretical foundations of modern syntaxes of Biblical Hebrew are essentially the same as that of Eduard Koenig in 1909. Only since 1970 has research gone forward to explore new theories of syntax and their possible value for Hebrew. For evidence of this lack of attention to syntax, note that Hosper's *Basic Bibliography* and Moscati's *Introduction* do not include anything specifically treating comparative Semitic syntax.[3]

This is odd, for general syntactic theory has made revolutionary advances since World War II. The most famous are the insights of

---

[1]For a historical summary of these developments in our knowledge of the languages of the ancient Near East, see Albright (32–49) and Hospers (365–75).

[2]It is fascinating to trace the literary history of GKC. As it moved through its various stages and as other scholars carried on the work, one can see the history of modern linguistics acted out in its pages.

[3]The earliest attempt to apply post-Chomskyan grammatical theory to Biblical Hebrew I have been able to document is Longacre (1961). Greenstein is an early application of transformational syntax. F. I. Andersen's pioneering *The Verbless Clause in the Hebrew Pentateuch* (1970) must be contrasted with the recent monumental compendium of Waltke and O'Connor (1990). Andersen takes a single syntactical construction in Biblical Hebrew and uses modern linguistic theory to describe and then evaluate the underlying semantic connotations. Waltke and O'Connor, while lingustically literate and taking all such research into account, consciously eschew modern perspectives for the "traditional" (55). They do not allow such perspectives to control the organization of their material, nor to change their goal. They effectively describe the operations of Hebrew syntax. They do not offer explanations as to why the distributions occur as they do when they do. In my view, their description of Hebrew syntax is therefore incomplete.

Noam Chomsky. It was he who showed that syntax had its own semantics and that the form of the sentence can be linked to or uncoupled from its corresponding meaning. The idea that "deep structure" can be "transformed" by consistent and discoverable rules into the "surface structure" of the actual sentence profoundly affected the direction of the study of language (Chomsky, 1965:15–18). Still, it must be noted that the unit being analyzed was the sentence. Bloomfield (20) insisted that the sentence was the proper object of inquiry for linguistics, and Chomsky did not depart from this conception of language.

Chomsky's link between syntax and semantics led others to explore this relationship in greater detail. In 1968 Charles Fillmore wrote a seminal article on the semantics of syntax. He argued that there was a relationship between the nouns and verbs in a sentence that was systematically consistent and that the idea of "case" should not be linked with the morphology of the noun, but was, in fact, a semantic notion, part of what Chomsky would call the deep structure of the sentence (Fillmore:3). There could be other ways (in the surface structure) to indicate case, such as constraints on word order or particles (Fillmore:21).

In arguing that the set of cases found in a sentence are determined by the semantic character of the verb in that sentence, Wallace L. Chafe (1970:10) significantly developed the implications of Fillmore's theory. However, contrary to Fillmore (27), who said that the selection of the verb depended upon the set of noun cases in the sentence, Chafe (1970:96) argued that the choice of the verb conditioned the available choices of noun cases for that particular sentence. Further, he showed how verbs could be classed semantically based upon the set or grouping of cases that are associated together.[4]

These basic insights have influenced many researchers' conceptions of language, but Simon Dik's *Functional Grammar* brought a theoretical rigor to these many ideas. Simply put, Dik views the kernel of any clause to be the predicate[5] and its corresponding arguments. This

---

[4]See also Walter A. Cook, who took these ideas to their logical conclusion.

[5]This is Chafe's terminology (1970:96), used also by Dik (25–54). I use the term "predicate" for the deep structure notion of state, process or action, whereas the term for the corresponding surface structure is "verb." Similarly, entities referring to objects—abstract or concrete—will be called "argument" when speaking of the

"nuclear predicate" can be extended by other arguments, often the traditional adverbial ones, called "satellites." Predicates are classed according to their case/argument "frames" and are mapped to surface structures. The term "nuclear" evokes the image of atoms combining with other atoms according to a specified and predetermined "valence." The metaphor is exact, as it illustrates the relationship between the predicate and its arguments.

The stage is now set for the next conceptual step. Language can be viewed as having levels. Phonology, studying the smallest components of linguistic utterances, is essential for a comprehensive grasp of the morphology of a language. The study of syntax completes the understanding of morphology. We would also expect phonology to clarify syntactic matters from time to time. However, there remains much of syntax, and Biblical Hebrew syntax in particular, which is not well understood. Could it be that this is because syntactic usage is conditioned by yet another level of language, that of text, which has yet to be taken into consideration?[6]

Of course, there has been a concern with text since ancient times. The uniqueness of discourse analysis is that it is motivated from a linguistic perspective, a desire to understand how language works and discover universal features of language, whereas classical rhetoric concerned itself with oratory and the effective delivery of speeches.

2. Theoretical Orientation

Attempts to understand the nature of text have not been limited to purely linguistic concerns. De Beaugrande and Dressler[7] surveyed the field in 1981 and came to this conclusion:

---

semantic level of language and "noun" when taking the perspective of the surface structure of the clause.

6There is a terminological ambiguity here. In Europe the study of this level of language is called "text linguistics." In the United States linguists have adopted the unfortunate term "discourse analysis." It is unfortunate because modern usage understands the primary meaning of "discourse" to be "a conversation," or "dialogue." Of course, the term can also mean "an extended essay," and it is in this metaphoric sense that it denotes the linguistic discipline.

7This is the best place to begin reading in discourse analysis. The bibliography and references to the literature are excellent, and the summary of the state of the art is highly useful, as we shall see below.

> The picture that emerges from these works is diffuse and diversified, because there was no established methodology that would apply to texts in any way comparable to the unified approaches for conventional linguistic objects like the sentence (14).

The reason for this lack of an "established methodology" is due, in part, to the newness of the discipline and also to the manifold goals of the investigators. Whereas the sentence might only interest the linguist, exegete, or literary critic, both oral and written texts are of interest to the psychologist, anthropologist, and sociologist as well. Why? Unlike the phoneme, morpheme, or sentence, whose context was another linguistic construct, the context of the text is the larger world of human interaction. How human beings dialogue with each other, for example, has implications for culture (e.g., how cultures maintain their distinctiveness) and for psychology (e.g., cognition and how reality is encoded by speakers).

The best way to maintain one's orientation to the often confusing variety of approaches to the study of text is to classify the goals of investigators. What motivates them to study text? And for any particular research, what are the specific questions that are used to interrogate the text? Those questions and goals will often determine the type of text examined. Sociologists, for example, often examine dialogue to discover how speech and interactions reveal and express social relationships. These goals seem to group themselves into four broad classes. I call these the *psycho-social, anthropological,* and, from linguistics, the *cognitive* and *grammatical* approaches.

The goals of the psycho-social approach revolve around the user of language rather than the text (oral or written) itself. One study focused strictly upon written materials.

> The written word provides a major means of transmitting ideas and feelings freely through the human community. As such, it has been explored widely by linguists, anthropologists, philosophers, and educationalists each from their own particular orientation. Our approach is psychological—to analyze those processes by which the written word comes to be understood by the reader (Sanford and Garrod: xiii).

Questions asked by such investigators have to do with comprehension of the text. What happens when a speaker deliberately violates rules of discourse? What sort of psychological constraints operate to make communication comprehensible? What common knowledge must the speaker and hearer share in order for meaning to be effectively transferred? How does the person process discourse information, and what sort of mental representations in human memory result? What is the significance of paragraphs and other groupings for efficient processing of discourse information?

Sociologists are interested in discourse for related, but different reasons. One study looked at how word order was constrained by social considerations and how word order conditioned following interactions

> In summary, we find that word order, in particular the initial position of utterance, is sensitive to social interaction in two ways. First, word order is shaped by social interaction, in the sense that the initial item should be socially warranted. Second, word order is a shaper of subsequent social interaction. The initial item in an utterance can determine who will speak next, who will occupy the next turn. These functions of word order can be as important and in some cases more important than the function of encoding inherently salient information (Ochs, 1979b:219).

The study of discourse has had implications for the understanding of psychoses such as the "verbal salad" of some types of schizophrenia (Bateson: 177–93). Other types of linguistic phenomena looked at from the social perspective include left-dislocation,[8] turn-taking in dialogues, pronominalization, the use of quantifiers and comparatives, verb tenses, and the connections between sentences.[9] These studies begin with social phenomena and ask the basic question, What role do language and language elements play in these social interactions and exchanges?

The distinction between an anthropological approach and a sociological one is sometimes blurred and no more so than when considering the analysis of discourse. However, there is a distinct shift in interest when questions of culture come into focus.[10] For example, an

---

[8]The shifting of a sentence constituent from its normal position in a sentence to the beginning for the purpose of emphasizing that constituent. In many languages, the function is to establish the sentence topic.

[9]The following list of articles illustrate the sociological concern I am speaking of. The references contained in these studies will direct the interested reader to related material: Gumperz and Tannen, Linde and Labov, Levinson, and Ochs (1979a).

[10]This blurring of goals between the two disciplines is reflected in discourse studies as well. It is often difficult to tell whether the research goal is anthropological or sociological, according to strict disciplinary boundaries. Of course,

examination of the cultural expectations regarding films was made among Greek-speaking people. A culture will develop expectations around certain situations which then affect language production.

> What unifies all these branches of research is the realization that people approach the world not as naive, blank-slate receptacles who take in stimuli as they exist in some independent and objective way, but rather as experienced and sophisticated veterans of perception who have stored their prior experiences as "an organized mass," and who see events and objects in the world in relation to each other and in relation to their prior experience (Tannen: 144).

This particular project was interesting in that a film about a man picking pears was prepared without dialogue and then shown to various cultures. The participants were asked to tell the story that they saw portrayed in the film, and the resulting "Pear Stories" were analyzed from various perspectives. The film was carefully constructed to create various types of difficulties for people to see how they would react linguistically (Chafe, 1980).

The classic anthropological study of discourse was very early and not consciously discourse analysis. Propp's The *Morphology of the Folktale*[11] was the attempt of a Russian formalist[12] to evaluate the function of a text and to examine the common structural elements of characterization and plot within a culture.

The confusion of methodology noted by de Beaugrande and Dressler above is due in part to the interdisciplinary nature of the origins of discourse analysis. Researchers from many disciplines turned to the analysis of text to further their own agendas. Naturally, many borrowed from linguistic methodology. However, there is a subtle difference to be noted here. Some studies set as their goal to understand human behavior. Other studies focus upon language itself, its nature and operation and only secondarily upon human beings themselves. For this reason, many linguistically oriented studies borrow hypotheses, terminology, and methodologies from other disciplines in their

---

such a strict separation is not necessarily possible or even desirable. Making finer distinctions, however, is beyond the scope of this essay.

[11]See also Hendricks for a discussion of Propp's methodology.

[12]"Formalist" was a term given to the Moscow Linguistic Circle formed in 1915 by, among others, Roman Jakobson. The group included not only linguists, but also poets and folklorists. See Holenstein (1976) for more information on the history of this group and its impact on linguistic theory.

search for understanding discourse. This is the source of the lack of a cohesive theory and method for the heterogeneous collection of studies called "discourse analysis."

Thus, I distinguish between two types of linguistic approach to text analysis. The first borrows much from the sociological and psychological disciplines and uses them to understand the processes which then explain the present condition of a text. This cognitive approach, nevertheless, has as its primary goal the understanding of the nature of text. This type of research has produced much of the terminology of discourse analysis and many useful concepts of the semantic nature of texts.

De Beaugrande and Dressler's "standards of textuality" summarize most clearly the various ways a text may be viewed, although Dressler's approach above would probably not be classified as exclusively cognitive. The seven standards are divided into two groups: *text*-centered (cohesion and coherence) and *user*-centered (intentionality, acceptability, informativity, situationality, and intertextuality). Cohesion has to do with how components of a text are connected to each other, the primary means of which in language is syntax. Coherence has to do with the "textual world," or "frame" (not to be confused with case frames), which underlie the text, provide a context for interpretation, and can be viewed as the "deep structure" for which cohesion is the "surface structure." Coherence and cohesion are established by the producer's intentionality and are then evaluated by the receiver for acceptability—the attitudes necessary for communication to occur and the definition of the border between text and non-text.[13] Informativity deals with the extent to which information in a text is expected as opposed to unexpected. When a text could be interpreted in more than one way, its situationality helps the receiver to use texts to monitor and manage situation. So does intertextuality,[14] those factors which make the proper understanding of one text dependent upon knowledge of other texts exhibiting similar or contrasting characteristics (de Beaugrande and Dressler: 3–11).

---

[13]Many of the sociological and anthropological research goals for the study of discourse could be classified here.

[14]Hebrew Bible form criticism might very well be fitted into discourse analysis here.

Teun van Dijk also belongs to the cognitive group. He, among others, attempted to describe a grammar of texts using the abstract approach of generative grammar, itself a development of Chomsky's transformational grammar. His *Some Aspects of Text Grammars* (1972)[15] introduced the important concept of "macro-structure," the statement of a text as a whole. He formulated grammatical "operations" on texts (parallel to the transformations in Chomsky's syntax) which required a process model of textual formation borrowed from cognitive psychology. His discussion of the pragmatics of discourse examines the systematic relationships between the text and its context, i.e., its macro-structure and the textual world it invokes. Macro-structures are irreducible atoms of meaning for the text as a whole and correspond to Chomsky's deep structure for texts rather than sentences (van Dijk, 1977).

Among more recent cognitive studies of discourse are two arising out of the anthropological study of story telling mentioned above (Chafe, 1980). Clancy explored the relationship between the structure of narratives and the decision to use nouns or pronouns to refer to an object or person by Japanese as compared to English speakers. She found that in both languages new sentences would begin when a new object was introduced or an old one reintroduced. At episode boundaries there was a change from implicit forms of reference (e.g., pronouns) to explicit ones (e.g., nouns). She concluded that:

> one source of unusual referential choices, such as the use of implicit forms despite potential ambiguity or use of a noun phrase when the identity of a referent is entirely obvious, is the presence of various types of discourse boundaries. Such referential marking usually occurs at larger, episode boundaries, but can also be found even at extremely brief changes in point of view, as when the narrator makes a single-clause comment about the story he is recounting (177–8).

Du Bois also uses the data from the pear film project to examine how objects are introduced into a narrative and then how they are tracked through the story.

> When an important object first appears in the story line, the speaker often shifts into the descriptive mode to introduce it and provide background information, subsequently returning to advance the story line in the narrative mode. If this critical introduction period has elapsed—or if it has

---

[15]Cf. also van Dijk and Petöfi (1977).

> not yet begun—the speaker will usually fail to indicate that the referent is being newly introduced. This, plus evidence from the distribution of adjectives and of narrative or descriptive verbs, suggests that speakers direct their attention either to the task of introducing or to the task of advancing the story line, but not to both at once (273).

Note that these studies, although using anthropological and psychological perspectives, have as their goal the understanding of language itself, rather than the understanding of a culture or type of mental process. This difference is the reason that I classify the cognitive approach to discourse with other linguistic approaches.

From the earliest attempts to analyze discourse, there have been those whose concern was primarily grammatical. Their conviction was that, just as with the other levels of language, speakers would organize text in some systematic fashion with the forms of language. In short, we ought to be able to describe a grammar of the discourse of any language. Literary criticism has always recognized the value of grammar and linguistics in service of the interpretation and understanding of literature.

> We can write the grammar of a literary work of art or any group of works beginning with phonology and accidence, going on to vocabulary (barbarisms, provincialisms, archaisms, neologisms), and rising to syntax (e.g., inversion, antithesis, and parallelisms). But linguistic study becomes literary only when it serves the study of literature, when it aims at investigating the aesthetic effects of language—in short, when it becomes stylistics (at least, in one sense of this term) (Wellek and Warren: 176–77).

Grammar tends to concern itself with the melding of form and meaning, what de Saussure (15) called the "sign." The Prague Linguistic Circle used this concept to analyze how information was ordered in a sequence of sentences. Their interest was primarily syntactic, and word order in particular. Yet their functional sentence perspective[16] was remarkably textual in its orientation and application. Each sentence has two parts, according to this theory. *Theme* is the information assumed to be already known to the hearer in a sentence, and *rheme* is the portion of the sentence which adds new information to the old. It suggests that grammatical (syntactical) means are used to organize the information in a sentence. Of course, the problem is to objectify the theme so that we could identify it in any

---

[16]The earliest formulation was by V. Mathesius (1882–1945).

particular sentence, but even the most recent attempts failed to do so adequately (see Firbas; cf. M. A. K. Halliday, 1966, 1967, 1968). But they did show that syntax has a significant role to play in the ordering of discourse information.

From the very beginning, the Tagmemic school of linguistics looked at language from the broadest perspective and tried to set language into the general context of human behavior.[17] De Beaugrande and Dressler (19) dismiss tagmemics as being of limited usefulness for discourse analysis because, while it provides for the systematic relationship between language and its setting, it does not provide a system for recognizing how such structures are selected and built up.

There are four principles offered by tagmemics which deeply affect one's view of discourse. First, the viewpoint of the observer affects the way he formulates his concepts of discourse. One may take the perspective that the data is static (words, constituents), dynamic (looking at events as a whole on a continuum, such a string of phones or words or sentences) or a network (paradigms, conjugations, declensions). Second, form cannot be divorced from meaning, because language behavior is structured rather than random. Form-meaning composites are the goal of analysis. These are the only controls for "reading into" a language linguistic (either formal or semantic) structures which are really there. Third, humans tend to process information in chunks or pieces, and these units need to be ordered in some way. Thus, language is hierarchical. This means that each form will be embedded in a higher form. Fourth, each unit or chunk has a place in the system (a "slot"), what may fill that slot (a "class" or "set") and how it relates to other slots and sets ("cohesion," Pike, 1976:91–127; cf. also Pike, 1982).

A number of studies began to appear in the mid-1970s which employed the method of discovering form-meaning composites, some under the direct influence of tagmemic theory.[18] Others took a more direct approach, generalizing from common grammatical functions, such as the relationship between a pronoun and its referent, and applied it as broadly as possible. In this case, Halliday and Hasan approached the question of "cohesion" in all of its aspects, not only

---

[17]Pike (1967) is the classic statement of tagmemic theory.

[18]See Longacre (1976) for a history of the development of discourse analysis from within the tagmemic school.

including the idea of discourse but also that of lexical cohesion. We see here the attempt to bootstrap upwards toward a discourse concept from a lower level of language through the medium of grammar.

Another concept derived from traditional grammar and transformed into a discourse notion is transitivity. Note that the ordinary definition of transitivity is a formal syntactic notion for those verbs which require an object. Hopper and Thompson showed that transitivity is a clause-level property and its presence, absence, and specific form are conditioned by discourse factors.

> Transitivity involves a number of components, only one of which is the presence of an object of the verb. These components are all concerned with the effectiveness with which an action takes place, e.g., the punctuality and telicity of the verb, the conscious activity of the agent, and the referentiality and degree of affectedness of the object. These components co-vary with one another in language after language, which suggests that Transitivity is a central property of language use. The grammatical and semantic prominence of Transitivity is shown to derive from its characteristic discourse function: high Transitivity is correlated with foregrounding, and low Transitivity with backgrounding (251).

It is significant that this study on transitivity requires the use of Fillmore's case grammar to interface the semantics of syntax with a discourse motivated concept. The case role of various sentence elements will significantly mark the presence or absence of transitivity (Hopper and Thompson: 294). Discourse form-meaning composites, then, are not easily separated from syntactic ones.

Paul J. Hopper provides us with a clear example of the exploration of form-meaning composites at the text level of language. He shows the actual marking of a discourse concept—tracing the plot line of a story—by grammatical forms of the language. He shows how this tracing of the plot, called foregrounding, is done through the tense-aspect systems of the verb (e.g., in Russian and French) and by word order (in Germanic languages). I have shown elsewhere that Biblical Hebrew follows a word order system of marking foreground (Lowery: 144–52, 302–8).[19]

The definitive synthesis of the grammatical approach by a discourse linguist to date must be Robert Longacre's *The Grammar of Dis-*

[19]This is a somewhat simplistic assertion, since there may be more than word order giving cues for foregrounding. Cf. Longacre's thesis of "verb rank" in Hebrew.

course (1983; cf., too, Grimes). It brings together the theoretical notions which must underlie any language-specific discourse grammar. He argues that only discourse grammar can solve certain problems in the study of language, and he summarizes those features of language which have been found to organize texts.

> Among these problems have been deixis and the use of articles; pronominalization, and other anaphoric ways of referring to a participant; better understanding of tense, aspect, mode, and voice in verbs; use of optional temporal and spatial expressions; the function of extraposition, left dislocation, and other such features; subject selection, object selection, and other focus phenomena; the function and thrust of conjunctions and other sequence signals; and the function of mystery particles which occur in connected context in some languages, which the native speaker knows where to use and where not to use, but which defy translation (xv).

Longacre's approach is not limited to a "bottom-up" look at discourse. Perhaps the most seminal of his ideas is the concept of discourse genres, defined in grammatical terms, or, as he calls it, "discourse typology." He uses two axes to divide types of discourses: how the text is oriented to time and the orientation of its agents. The result is four broad classes of text: narrative (agent oriented, temporal succession), procedural (non-agent oriented, temporal succession), behavioral (hortatory; agent oriented, non-temporal succession), and expository (non-agent oriented, nontemporal or logical succession) (Longacre, 1983:5).

Still another contribution to discourse theory, and perhaps his most important, is the linguistic specification of a literary concept: plot structure. In the tradition of Auerbach,[20] Longacre has applied linguistic rigor in providing objective criteria to define and analyze plot and plot development in a narrative (1983:20–42). In a more recent work (Longacre, 1989), he applies his theories to a Biblical Hebrew narrative text. A number of ideas previously advanced are now highlighted in their application to Hebrew texts. Interwoven like the DNA double-helix are the two strands of a discourse: the story line and the participant/thematic referent tracing (1989:18). He makes major strides in defining how episodes, climaxes and other elements of

[20]Eric Auerbach saw the relationship between poetics and language: an author uses the forms of the language and its grammar to achieve his literary effect and purposes. See especially pp. 6–7 and 23 for some of the clearest statements about the relationship between language form and an author's use of them.

stories are grammatically identified (marked) in Biblical Hebrew (1989:30). He insists that tense, verb, and aspect cannot be properly understood without being related to Hebrew discourse genres (1989:59). Most important, the roles of direct discourse and dialogue are dealt with in a systematic fashion, examining how dialogue moves the story forward (1989:158–205).

Longacre's discourse theory emerges out of the study of various languages, especially the Asian and Pacific. He and his colleagues were forced, by the very attempt to identify the meaning of language elements, to consider non-traditional (read: "non-Indo-European") concepts to explain their presence and use. Discourse grammars have been written, modeling the grammatical approach to discourse analysis (Ballard, Conrad, and Longacre; Jones; Longacre, 1971; Longacre and Woods; Walrod).

I have attempted to classify discourse methodologies on the basis of the type of questions they ask and the central object which is being analyzed. We have made a broad grouping of psycho-social, anthropological, and linguistic approaches. Among the linguistically oriented methods, we saw the use of other disciplines for solving linguistic questions. It finally comes to this: Are we attempting to understand a feature of language or something else, such as human behavior, culture, or interaction?

Discourse analysis is still in its infancy. Much of the fundamental nature of text we still do not understand. But discourse analysis offers a way to examine meaning in texts that significantly complements classic hermeneutics and literary criticism. The biblical scholar cannot ignore such a powerful tool, for it holds out the promise of solving some of the perennially nagging problems of language and interpretation. This becomes even more critical for the Hebraists, who work outside of the Indo-European language group and cannot fully trust their own intuitions about language structures as they can with Greek or Latin.

3. The Choice of Method

The great weakness of the present state of discourse analysis is lack of focus in the design of questions. It is often unclear what the researcher wishes to discover. For those who are not interested in discourse theory per se, but rather in what discourse theory might offer in understanding the texts of a particular language, I offer this solution to the problem of what it is that you wish to know. If we wish to understand our psychological nature as we process information, our theory and the hypotheses we derive from them must reflect that concern. If we wish to understand the nature of a certain language, then, of necessity, our theory and goals are going to be substantially different.

What follows are propositions about the nature of Biblical Hebrew texts. Those who share these basic assumptions, will, I argue, be driven to the same methodological choices I have made.

The Nature of the Data

It must be axiomatic that *the nature of the data determines the choice of method and goal.* Semiticists in general and Hebraists in particular have long faced the fact that most of their languages are no longer spoken. Attestation of the language of the Hebrew Bible remains almost exclusively within the biblical text. For lack of native speakers, entire classes of questions simply cannot be answered, including many of anthropological and psycho-social concern. We cannot compare the text of the Bible with that of either the common spoken or written language.

The data is outside the Indo-European language group. This means that traditional syntactic categories for Biblical Hebrew are suspect, coming out of grammatical categories which historically were developed to explain Latin grammar. Western notions of literature must be kept distinct in analysis. It is wrong to assume that literary features of ancient Near Eastern texts will exactly parallel those of the West. In fact, it is best to assume that no literary feature is parallel with Western notions unless it can be explicitly confirmed.

Verification of the Reality of Discourse Notions

How do we know that the ancient Hebrews "felt" the reality of any specified discourse concept? How can we confirm as fact that a discourse notion actually existed for Biblical Hebrew? We have a very limited sample of the language, and that sample is a very stylized form of literature. In addition, the text has had a long history. We have to allow for the fact that discourse features of a language will change over time, just as other features of a language change. The intuition of the scholar, while valuable for hypothesizing, must always be corroborated by some concrete and, if possible, quantifiable means.

One useful way to confirm any linguistic reality in Biblical Hebrew is the use of statistical procedures.[21] That is, the high and low correlation of language elements is taken to confirm the existence of any sign at any level of language, from phonetic to text. And we have a clear and objective way to do this. Using the definition of the sign we can use the statistical concept of dependent and independent variables. The grammatical forms of Biblical Hebrew are the dependent variables. Dependent variables remain constant.

Discourse notions are, as a matter of hypothesis, given operational definitions in terms of the language forms. If the text actually groups or organizes itself in a consistent way, then the discourse notion is confirmed as a reality for the language. If not, the investigator has two choices. One must either discard the discourse notion as invalid or change the operational definition (the hypothesis). Discourse notions or concepts are therefore the independent variables. Why this formulation? Because grammatical forms must function in a consistent way to the predictions of a hypothetical discourse construct.[22]

Discourse analysis has sometimes been accused of circularity in reasoning. The problem is that the identification of semantic values (of which discourse concepts are an example) involves an intuitive element. Semantic values are slippery concepts. There is also a question of whether form-meaning constructs on the syntactic and lower levels are allowable dependent variables for the operational defining of discourse concepts. These are legitimate and open questions.

---

[21]Statistics have their own pitfalls for the researcher. How they are used and then interpreted is a matter of great concern. For example, the construction of a linguistic measure can create patterns which are a function of the nature of the measure rather than reflecting the nature of the data. I have addressed this issue in my attempt to create a statistical measure of cohesion (Lowery: 98–143, 299–302). A concise introduction to statistics may be found in Hays. A comprehensive treatment of the subject, especially in creating statistical measures and the inherent dangers, is Loether and McTavish (1974a, 1974b). More advanced texts are Ferguson, and Kleinbaum and Kupper. To courageous souls I recommend Hoel's more theoretical *Introduction.*

[22]An early application of statistical theory to literary works is Yule; see also Beatie, Kemp, Moskovich and Caplan, Thomson (1973, 1974a, 1974b, 1974c, 1975a, 1975b), and Ule.

The Goal Is Grammar

While useful concepts and ideas may be occasionally borrowed, the goals and objectives of the psycho-social, anthropological, and cognitive approaches to discourse analysis are difficult to achieve using the Hebrew Bible. Hebrew grammar has always served the needs of the interpreter. We discourse analysts wish to know how this language organizes its texts and how it informs us of that organization. What parts of the Hebrew language have we misunderstood because we are unaware of their function in discourse?

Discourse grammar is the choice of greatest potential for Hebraists. Its focus upon the language forms and the application of discourse genres hold out the greatest promise for fruitful research. It provides a systematic way to deal with the diverse phenomena of a language and easily incorporates the insights from other disciplines and approaches where they are pertinent.

4. A Structural Outline

The Organizing Principle

Perhaps the earliest attempts to treat the biblical text in a unified way began in the early 1970s with the application of structuralism and the appearance of such journals as *Semeia*.[23] In the last decade a number of applications of discourse analysis have been made. The appearance of new work is accelerating.[24] It would seem that we are ready to chart the future progress of research. What would a discourse grammar of Biblical Hebrew look like?

The first problem that faces us is the question of the structure of the grammar. What should be our organizing principle? Should we begin with discourse genres and work our way down to syntax? Should we focus upon language forms, describing the discourse function of each? Traditional grammar would lead us in the direction of moving

[23]For a general introduction to structuralism and its literature see Robey (1972) and Hawkes (1977). For an example of a structuralist treatment of the biblical text see Patte and Patte (1978).

[24]Much of the work before 1980 is in unpublished papers read before scholarly societies. One unpublished bibliography lists nearly one hundred entries just for biblical discourse studies during the period of 1983 to 1987. The most significant feature of this bibliography is the number of doctoral dissertations present. These works are laying the foundations of a new discipline within biblical scholarship.

from the bottom upwards, that is, moving from the smaller units (phonemes, morphemes, syntactical elements) to the higher units. But the very uniqueness of the discourse perspective is that it is a linguistic view of literary concerns. De Beaugrande and Dressler, for example, organized discourse based upon discourse features of text, that is, upon what makes up "textuality."

The question is important, for the way we organize our thinking about discourse will impact the way that we interrogate the text and pursue the nature of discourse. One is tempted to amalgamate all viewpoints together. Must one separate forms of the language from discourse notions?

In the outline below I have opted for an emphasis upon grammar. Form rules. The search is for discourse signs, a combination of form and meaning. We should expect that discourse signs will be a set of options available to the speaker to accomplish certain tasks in the text.

The traditional movement from smaller to larger units of language is reversed. I begin with asking, What strategies are used by Hebrew authors to organize their texts? I end with the lower levels of the language, asking, What elements of Biblical Hebrew have discourse functions? Obviously, the semantics of syntax and case grammar have a large part to play. Here is where de Beaugrande and Dressler's canons of textuality help to guide our search. In an ideal world, we would go on to ask, what constellations of grammatical features of Biblical Hebrew mark discourse units? What units higher than the sentence are marked in Biblical Hebrew texts?

The State of the Art

The grammar is conceived as a descriptive rather than a pedagogic grammar. Thus the "General" section is fuller than would otherwise be the case. Much basic research remains to be done to find useful and validated statistical measures. The "Index of Cohesion" barely scratches the surface. Narrative is the best understood of all the discourse genres. Basic questions remain to be answered, such as, are there analogues to plot structures, foreground/background, and participants in the other genres? Are paragraphs constructed in the same way? Do direct speech and dialogue function differently in the other genres? Are these four genres indeed the only ones?

The analysis of poetic texts from a discourse grammar perspective has barely begun. I have noted that Hebrew syntax is not well understood and suggested that the reason is that many of the phenomena are motivated, marked, and ordered by discourse concerns. In particular, inter-clausal relations have not been conclusively delineated. In general, there ought to be a review of all perennial linguistic problems in Hebrew (e.g., tenses, verbal patterns, infinite absolute, etc.) from a text linguistic perspective to see if solutions might present themselves.

I propose here an outline of a Hebrew discourse grammar. It is as yet tentative. Better ways of organizing the material will be found as we come to a better understanding of the subject. But as the basic elements of discourse grammar are now clear, we can attempt to systematically fill in the holes. The reader will note that some areas are quite well-developed, while others are not. This outline is meant to reflect the present state of the art.

Outline of a Hebrew Discourse Grammar

0. General
0.1 Linguistic Presuppositions
0.1.1 The Sign
0.1.2 Form and Meaning
0.1.3 Deep and Surface Structures
0.2 Syntactic Theory
0.2.1 The Centrality of the Verb
0.2.2 The Nuclear Predication
0.2.3 The Extended Predication
0.3 Discourse Theory
0.3.1 Fomal Constituents
0.3.2 Semantic Notions
0.3.3 Discourse Hierarchy
0.3.4 Discourse Genres
0.3.5 Deep and Surface Structure Mapping
0.3.6 Relation to Phonology, Morphology and Syntax
0.3.7 Macrostructures
0.3.8 Discourse Pragmatics
0.4 Statistical Verification
0.4.1 Applied Mathematical Linguistics
0.4.2 Computer-Aided Processing
0.4.3 Application of Descriptive Statistics
0.4.4 Application of Inferential Statistics
0.4.5 Creating Statistical Measures
0.4.6 Dependent and Independent Variables
0.5 The Northwest Semitic Interface
0.5.1 Ugaritic Discourse Features
0.5.2 Aramaic Discourse Features
0.5.3 Syriac Discourse Features
0 5.4 Phoenician Discourse Features
0.6 Bibliography
0.6.1 General Linguistics
0.6.2 Syntax
0.6.3 Discourse Analysis and Text Linguistics
0.6.4 Hebrew Discourse Analysis
1. Discourse Strategies
1.1 Mainline Development
1.1.1 Foreground
1.1.2 Topic Focus
1.1.3 Plot
1.2 Off-mainline Development
1.2.1 Background
1.3 Participant Tracking
1.3.1 Case Roles
1.3.2 Pronominalization
1.3.3 Theme/Subject development
1.4 Pragmatics
1.4.1 Text-centered Notions
1.4.1.1 Cohesion
1.4.1.2 Coherence
1.4.2 User-centered Notions
1.4.2.1 Intentionality
1.4.2.2 Acceptability
1.4.2.3 Informativity
1.4.2.4 Situationality
1.4.2.5 Intertextuality
1.5 Macrostructures
2. Discourse Genres in Biblical Hebrew
2.1 Narrative
2.1.1 The Metaphor of Drama
2.1.1.1 Actors
2.1.1.2 Sets
2.1.1.3 Props
2.1.1.4 Plot
2.2 Expository
2.3 Predictive/Procedural
2.4 Hortatory
2.5 Direct and Indirect Speech
2.6 Poetic Discourse
2.6.1 Prophetic
2.6.2 Wisdom
2.6.3 Hymnic
3. Discourse Constituents
3. 1 Plot Structures
3.1.1 Deep Structures
3.1.1.1 Exposition
3.1.1.2 Inciting Moment
3.1.1.3 Developing Conflict
3.1.1.4 Climax (Peak)
3.1.1.5 Denouement
3.1.1.6 Final Suspense
3.1.1.7 Conclusion
3.1.2 Surface Structures
3.1.2.1 Introduction

Works Consulted

Albright, William F.
1957 *From the Stone Age to Christianity.* 2nd ed. Garden City, NY: Doubleday.

Andersen, Francis I.
1970 *The Hebrew Verbless Clause in the Pentateuch.* SBLMS 14. Nashville: Abingdon.

Auerbach, Eric
1953 *Mimesis: The Representation of Reality in Western Literature.* Trans. Willard R. Trask from German (1946). Princeton: Princeton University Press.

Ballard, D. Lee, Robert J. Conrad, and Robert E. Longacre
1971 "The Deep and Surface Grammar of Interclausal Relations." *Foundations of Language* 7:70–118.

Barr, James
1961 *The Semantics of Biblical Language.* Oxford: Oxford University Press.

Bateson, G.
1972 *Steps to an Ecology of Mind.* New York: Ballantine.

Beatie, Bruce A.
1979 "Measurement and the Study of Literature." *Computers and the Humanities* 13:185–94.

Beaugrande, Robert-Alain de, and Wolfgang U. Dressler
1981 *Introduction to Text Linguistics.* Longman Linguistics Library 26. London: Longman.

Bloomfield, Leonard
1933 *Language.* New York: Holt, Rinehart & Winston.

Chafe, Wallace L.
1970 *Meaning and the Structure of Language.* Chicago: University of Chicago Press.

Chafe, Wallace L., ed.
1980 *The Pear Stories: Cognitive, Cultural, and Linguistic Aspects of Narrative Production.* Norwood, NJ: Ablex.

Chomsky, Noam
1965 *Aspects of the Theory of Syntax.* Cambridge, MA: MIT Press.

Clancy, Patricia M.
1980 "Referential Choice in English and Japanese Narrative Discourse." Pp. 127–202 in Chafe (1980).

Cook, Walter A.
1979 *Case Grammar: Development of the Matrix Model (1970–1978).* Washington, DC: Georgetown University Press.

Dijk, Teun A. van
1972 *Some Aspects of Text Grammars.* The Hague: Mouton.
1977 *Text and Context. Explorations in the Semantics and Pragmatics of Discourse.* Longman Linguistics Library 21. London: Longman.
1979 *Macro-Structures.* Hillsdale, NJ: Erlbaum.

Dijk, Teun A. van, and János S. Petöfi, eds.
1977 *Grammars and Descriptions.* Berlin: W. de Gruyter.

Dik, Simon C.
1981 *Functional Grammar.* 3rd rev. ed. Publications in Language Sciences 7. Dordrecht: Foris.

Du Bois, John W.
1980 "Beyond Definiteness: The Trace of Identity in Discourse." Pp. 203–74 in *The Pear Stories: Cognitive, Cultural, and Linguistic Aspects of Narrative Production.* Ed. Wallace L. Chafe. Norwood, NJ: Ablex.

Eissfeldt, Otto
1965 *The Old Testament: An Introduction.* New York: Harper and Row.

Ferguson, George A.
1976 *Statistical Analysis in Psychology and Education.* 4th ed. New York: McGraw-Hill.

Fillmore, Charles J.
1968 "The Case for Case." Pp. 1–88 in *Universals in Linguistic Theory.* Eds. Emmon Bach and Robert T. Harms. New York: Holt, Rinehart & Winston.

Firbas, Jan
1966 "On Defining the Theme in Functional Sentence Perspective." Pp. 267–80 in *Travaux du Cercle linguistiques de Prague,* 1. Prague: Academia.

Givón, Talmy, ed.
1979 *Discourse and Syntax.* Syntax and Semantics, 12. New York: Academic.

Greenstein, Edward L.
1974 "Two Variations of Grammatical Parallelism in Canaanite Poetry and Their Psycholinguistic Background." *JANES* 6:87–105.

Grimes, Joseph E.
1976 *The Thread of Discourse.* The Hague: Mouton.

Gumperz, John J., and Deborah Tannen
1979 "Individual and Social Differences in Language Use." Pp. 305–25 in *Individual Differences in Language Ability and Language Behavior.* Eds. Charles Fillmore, D. Kempler, and W. Wang. New York: Academic.

Halliday, M. A. K.
1966 "Notes on Transitivity and Theme in English. Part 1." *JL* 3:37–81.
1967 "Notes on Transitivity and Theme in English. Part 2. *JL* 3:199–244.

1968 "Notes on Transitivity and Theme in English. Part 3." *JL* 4:179–308.

Halliday, M. A. K., and Ruqaiya Hasan
1976 *Cohesion in English.* English Language Series 9. London: Longman.

Hawkes, Terence
1977 *Structuralism and Semiotics.* Berkeley: University of California Press.

Hays, William L.
1967 *Basic Statistics.* Basic Concepts in Psychology. Belmont, CA: Brooks/Cole.

Hendricks, William O.
1970 "Folklore and the Structural Analysis of Literary Texts." *Language and Style* 3:83–121.

Hoel, Paul G.
1971 *Introduction to Mathematical Statistics.* 4th ed. New York: John Wiley.

Holenstein, Elmar
1976 *Roman Jakobson's Approach to Language: Phenomenological Structuralism.* Trans. Catherine Schelbert and Tarcisius Schelbert from French (1974). Bloomington: Indiana University Press.

Hopper, Paul J.
1979 "Aspect and Foregrounding in Discourse." Pp. 213–42 in Givón (1979).

Hopper, Paul J., and Sandra A. Thompson
1980 "Transitivity in Grammar and Discourse." *Language* 56:251–99.

Hospers, J. H.
1973 *A Basic Bibliography for the Study of the Semitic Languages.* Leiden: E. J. Brill.

Jones, Linda K., ed.
1979 *Discourse Studies in Mesoamerican Languages.* 2 vols. SILPL 58. Dallas: University of Texas Press.

Kautzsch, E., ed.
1910 *Gesenius' Hebrew Grammar.* Trans. A. E. Cowley. Oxford: Clarendon.

Kemp, Kenneth W.
1976 "Personal Observations on the Use of Statistical Methods in Quantitative Linguistics." Pp. 59–77 in *The Computer in Literary and Linguistic Studies.* Proceedings of the Third International Symposium. Cardiff: University of Wales Press.

Kleinbaum, David G., and Lawrence L. Kupper
1978 *Applied Regression Analysis and Other Multivariable Methods.* North Scituate, ME: Duxbury.

Koenig, Eduard
1897 *Historisch-comparative Syntax der hebräischen Sprache. Schlusstheil des historisch-kritischen Lehrgebaudes des hebräischen Sprache.* Leipzig: J. C. Hinrichs.

Levinson, Stephen C.
1981 "Some Pre-Observations on the Modelling of Dialogue." *Discourse Processes* 4:93–116.

Linde, Charlotte, and William Labov
1975 "Spatial Networks as a Site for the Study of Language and Thought." *Language* 51:924–39.

Loether, Herman J., and Donald G. McTavish
1974a *Descriptive Statistics for Sociologists: An Introduction.* Boston: Allyn and Bacon.
1974b *Inferential Statistics for Sociologists: An Introduction.* Boston: Allyn and Bacon.

Longacre, Robert E.
1961 "From Tagma to Tagmeme in Biblical Hebrew." Pp. 563–92 in *A William Cameron Townsend en el vigésimoquinto aniversario del Instituto Lingüístíco de Verano.* Mexico: Instituto Lingüístíco de Verano.
1976 "Discourse." Pp. 1–44 in *Tagmemics, Volume 1: Aspects of the Field.* Ed. Ruth M. Brend and Kenneth L. Pike. Trends in Linguistics, Studies and Monographs. The Hague: Mouton.
1983 *The Grammar of Discourse.* Topics in Language and Linguistics. New York: Plenum.
1989 *Joseph: A Story of Divine Providence. A Text Theoretical and Textlinguistic Analysis of Genesis 37 and 39–48.* Winona Lake, IN: Eisenbrauns.

Longacre, Robert E., ed.
1971 *Philippine Discourse and Paragraph Studies in Memory of Betty McLachlin.* Pacific Linguistic Series C, 22. Canberra: Australian National University Press.

Longacre, Robert E., and Fran Woods, eds.
1976–77 *Discourse Grammar: Studies in Indigenous Languages of Columbia, Panama, and Ecuador, Parts 1–3.* SILPL 52. Dallas: University of Texas Press.

Lowery, Kirk E.
1985 *Toward a Discourse Grammar of Biblical Hebrew.* Ph.D. dissertation. University of California, Los Angeles.

Moscati, Sabatino, ed.
1969 *An Introduction to the Comparative Grammar of the Semitic Languages: Phonology and Morphology.* Wiesbaden: Otto Harrassowitz.

Moskovich, Wolf, and Ruth Caplan
1979 "Distributive-Statistical Techniques in Linguistic and Literary Research." Pp. 245–63 in *Advances in Computer-Aided Literary and Linguistic Research.* Proceedings of the Fifth International Symposium on Computers in Literary and Linguistic Research. Ed. D. E. Ager, F. E. Knowles, and J. Smith. Birmingham: AMLC.

Muilenburg, James
1969 "Form Criticism and Beyond." *JBL* 88:1–18.

Ochs, Elinor
1979a "Planned and Unplanned Discourse." Pp. 51–80 in *Discourse and Syntax.* Syntax and Semantics, 12. Ed. Talmy Givón. New York: Academic.
1979b "Social Foundations of Language." Pp. 207–21 in *New Directions in Discourse Processing.* Ed. Roy O. Freedle. Advances in Discourse Processing 2. Norwood, NJ: Ablex.

Patte, Daniel, and Aline Patte
1978 *Structural Exegesis: From Theory to Practice.* Philadelphia: Fortress.

Pike, Kenneth L.
1967 *Language in Relation to a Unified Theory of the Structure of Human Behavior.* 2nd ed. The Hague: Mouton.
1976 "Toward the Development of Tagmemic Postulates." Pp. 91–127 in *Tagmemics, Volume 2: Theoretical Discussion.* Ed. Ruth M. Brend and Kenneth L. Pike. The Hague: Mouton.
1982 *Linguistic Concepts: An Introduction to Tagmemics.* Lincoln: University of Nebraska Press.

Propp, Vladimir
1968 *The Morphology of the Folktale.* 2nd ed. Ed. Louis A. Wagner. Trans. Laurence Scott from Russian (1928). Austin: University of Texas Press.

Rad, Gerhard von
1938 *The Problem of the Hexateuch and Other Essays.* London: SCM.

Robey, David, ed.
1972 *Structuralism: An Introduction.* Wolfson College Lectures 1972. Oxford: Clarendon.

Sanford, Anthony J., and Simon C. Garrod
1981 *Understanding Written Lanauage: Explorations of Comprehension beyond the Sentence.* Chichester: John Wiley & Sons.

Saussure, Ferdinand de
1959 *Course in General Linguistics.* Ed. Charles Bally and Albert Sechehaye. Trans. Wade Baskin from the 3rd French ed. (1909–11). New York: McGraw-Hill.

Tannen, Deborah
1979 "What's in a Frame? Surface Evidence for Underlying Expectations." Pp 137–81 in *New Directions in Discourse Processing.* Ed. Roy O. Freedle. Advances in Discourse Processing 2. Norwood, NJ: Ablex.

Thomson, N. D.
1973 "Literary Statistics I: On the Small Print of Statistics." *BALLC* 1:10–14.
1974a "Literary Statistics II: On Probability Distributions." *BALLC* 2:10–15.
1974b "Literary Statistics III: On Estimations." *BALLC* 2:42–47.
1974c "Literary Statistics IV: On Hypothesis Testing." *BALLC* 2:55–61.

1975a "Literary Statistics V: On Correlation and Regression." *BALLC* 3:29–35.

1975b "Literary Statistics VI: On the Future of Literary Statistics." *BALLC* 3:166–71.

Ule, L. A.

1974 "Cluster Analysis." *BALLC* 2:16–21.

Walrod, Michael R.

1979 *Discourse Grammar in Ga'dang.* SILPL 63. Dallas: University of Texas Press.

Waltke, Bruce K., and Michael P. O'Connor

1990 *An Introduction to Biblical Hebrew Syntax.* Winona Lake, IN: Eisenbrauns.

Wellek, René, and Austin Warren

1963 *Theory of Literature.* 3rd ed. New York: Harcourt Brace Jovanovich.

Yule, G. Undy

1944 *The Statistical Study of Literary Vocabulary.* Cambridge: Cambridge University Press.

5

STYLISTICS FOR THE STUDY OF ANCIENT TEXTS: WANDERINGS IN THE BORDERLANDS

Tova Meltzer

ABSTRACT

Selected approaches to textual style in the Western tradition are surveyed, showing how changes in our conception of style are directly dependent upon changes in how we perceive language and text. The debt to classical and neo-classical theories is acknowledged, prefatory to a focus on twentieth century developments in modern stylistics. The two parallel developments of linguistic stylistics and literary studies are traced from early, often antagonistic, positions to the current increasing rapprochement, brought about in large part by a growing concern in both linguistics and literary criticism with discourse and semiotic dimensions.

While the term "style" has practically evaporated in much recent linguistic and literary-critical analysis, the actual language elements traditionally labeled "stylistic criteria" are being researched, analyzed, deconstructed, and reconstructed with more fervor and rigor than ever before. This change in our conception of "style" is directly dependent upon changes in how we perceive language and text. For linguists and literary critics whose chief informants are ancient texts, "style" is an especially slippery and elusive concept. This essay is intended as a limited survey of approaches to textual style as they have developed in the Western intellectual tradition, focusing on themes of relevance to those who study ancient texts. The latter sections of the bibliography which closes this volume will provide samples of such work. For surveys of textual stylistics in other non-

Western cultures, one may consult A. Aklujkar for the Sanskrit tradition, and W. K. Archer and Forough Al-Zaman Minou-Archer for the Persian tradition. Such a historical perspective can form the basis for a deeper understanding both of the questions we are asking of our text-informants and of why we are now asking these particular questions.

The beginnings of stylistics in the West have predictably been seen in classical Greek and Roman rhetoric (Hough, Hartmann, Segre). Modern stylistics is indebted to the classical, as well as later medieval, writers on rhetoric for certain basic terms and concepts. Ancient rhetoricians set down guidelines along which future formal analysis of texts could develop. Ancient rhetoric, of course, was prescriptive criticism, concerned with the production of texts rather than their analysis. The concept of style in ancient rhetoric depended on a distinction between an originally unadorned context and the addition of ornaments or colorings. As we shall see, this idea of style as deviation from a norm has been fundamental to most modern approaches as well. In addition, the stages in composing an oration point to what we now recognize as the sociolinguistic variables of discourse, while the different types of oratory foreshadow the genre/style connection. There are, of course, recognizable limitations to ancient rhetoric as a model for discourse (Hartmann: 11–12): it is static; it is dependent on a single, literary, written standard; it gives little attention to principles of textual organization or to correlations with situational factors; and, finally, it is unsuitable for cross-cultural application.

Beginning in late antiquity and lasting well beyond medieval times, neo-classical theories of literary kinds connected style with genre, with the understanding that each genre has its own appropriate style. These theories developed within more broadly encompassing frameworks, linking not just style and genre, but human types, onomastics, and environment. According to the European literary scholar, Cesare Segre (262), the style/content relation was no longer obvious after the coming of Christianity. Rather, choice of genre became more closely related to choice of language; style choice was no longer just a choice of Latin registers—it became a choice of Latin or the vernacular. Other illuminating perspectives on the socio-historical significance of style in the West are to be found in the works of Auerbach (1946, 1958) and Foucault (1970).

The dominance of classical and neo-classical theories of rhetoric began to decline from approximately the eighteenth century, with style being understood more in the Romantic mode, as an individual manner of expression, the most intimate evidence of the thought of the author. The greatest impetus to modern stylistics, however, was the work of de Saussure. The diachronic/synchronic and *langue/parole* distinctions in language study allowed for a more sophisticated expression of the idea that there is some impersonal norm of which style is the specialized variation. This specialized variation, the *parole*, was not a dimension with which de Saussure was especially concerned. This was left to his student Bally, who was probably the first to use the term "stylistics," though not in the modern sense.

Modern stylistics is a twentieth century development. Historical surveys all give founding father status to Bally and to Spitzer (Segre: 266). Hough (12) also sees a dual impetus to the modern study of style: one from literary criticism, largely Anglo-American, and the other from the historical linguistics of continental Europe. For Hough, writing in 1969, these two impulses led to fundamentally separate endeavors:

> It is not likely that the stylistic study of literature will ever become a science, but there is no need for it to be a riot of subjective fancy. Professional linguists are apt to say that their science has literary bearings to which students of literature pay insufficient attention. I think it is obvious that *most* of what the science of linguistics now does cannot be usefully related to literature at all; but there are bridges to be built, and it is in the area of stylistics that the opportunities for doing this are the greatest (Hough: 19).

Literary stylistics, which developed in response to the need for a close comparative description of different language varieties, has taken many forms. Hartmann draws our attention to the division of Pierre Guiraud (1974), who classifies literary stylistics as descriptive, functional, genetic, or quantitative. This division has some chronological dimensions, descriptive stylistics being the first on the scene and quantitative the last to arrive. From the perspective of linguists, the literary approach to stylistics has been highly questionable because of the required "leap of faith," best illustrated by the frequently quoted words of Leo Spitzer:

> Why do I insist that it is impossible to offer the reader a step-by-step rationale to be applied to a work of art? For one reason, that the first step, on

> which all may hinge, can never be planned: it must already have taken place. This first step is the awareness of having been struck by a detail, followed by a conviction that this detail is connected basically with the work of art; it means that one has made an "observation"—which is the starting point of a theory—that one has been prompted to raise a question—which must find an answer (Spitzer: 226).

Various individuals, coming originally from linguistics as well as literary criticism, have sought to control the intuitive leaps, usually by ostensibly more "scientific" linguistic approaches (e.g., Fowler, 1981). This early history of the quest for a rapprochement between linguistics and literary criticism, which in important respects is not over yet, was filled with impassioned and often vitriolic pleading from all sides. Increased understanding of the role of intuition in the natural sciences has blunted the edge of most of these arguments, if not destroyed their foundations. The disdain for the position of "the other side" has been rightly castigated as contrary to the spirit of humane inquiry (Freeman: 4). In spite of developing complexities and sophistication in both theory and method, early twentieth century stylistics was still based presuppositionally in the ancient rhetorical concept of ornamentation. This can be illustrated by Riffaterre's understanding of style as textual marking: remove style and we have a neutral, unmarked context. A useful summary of the positions of some of the chief practitioners of early literary stylistics may be found in Hough (59–102), while Widdowson may be consulted for a similar summary of the positions of some of the chief stylistic linguists.

Freeman, writing in 1970, found three basic approaches in twentieth-century linguistic stylistics and in literary criticism. The first approach saw style as deviation from the norm and featured anthropologically, biographically, or philologically oriented studies (4–10). The second, viewing style as recurrence or convergence of textual pattern, was realized in text-centered, data-restricted, empirical and taxonomic studies (4–5, 10–13). The third, involving reconstruction of conscious/unconscious or surface/deep structure elements, saw style as a particular exploitation of a grammar of possibilities (4–5, 13–15).

In part as an overreaction against the "impressionism" of literary criticism, much of the early work in linguistic stylistics was so rigorously empirical that it approached being behavioristic (Freeman: 5). This dominance of method over subject has been noted in the stylistics of Riffaterre, among others (Segre: 268; Freeman: 5). Statistical analyses of style features, in part seeking quantitative techniques to assess the affective manipulation of language, have enjoyed considerable popularity (see, e.g., Dolezel, 1969; Dolezel and Bailey).

A major role in the "style as deviation" approach is that of Prague stylistics (although, properly speaking, this is more a collection of varying perspectives than a unified "school"; Mukarovsky, Dolezel and Kraus). The common denominator in early Prague stylistics was the characterization of literary (or poetic) language as a purposeful distortion of standard language. Involved was a deliberate breaking of rules in order to foreground certain features of the language. Starting in the 1930s and generally designated as functional stylistics, the rich and varied Czech developments have led to the current approach in which style is understood in the general framework of communication theory. The theoretical assumptions of "style as deviation" are also illustrated by what has been called "structural metrics" (Fowler, 1966, 1971). Freeman rightly notes the basic contribution of this work as "its raising of the possibility that surface phenomena (in this case, the rhythms of speech stress) and the deep form underlying them (the abstract metrical pattern) can differ and that a proper object of scholarly investigation is the system of rules which relates the two levels" (9). Fowler's approach, subject to the same basic influences as Prague stylistics, has likewise shown an increasingly semiotic orientation (1981, 1986).

A further refinement of the concept of "style as deviation" arose in what has been called the London or neo-Firthian school of linguistics. Here, style is not described in terms of the entire language, but rather in terms of the typical characteristics of the register (roughly equivalent to genre) and the dialect of the writer. This approach has had far-reaching implications, for it directly gave rise to the idea that each individual text exemplifies a unified language with its own specific grammar and with connections beyond the text itself. A basic theoretical impasse in the "style as deviation" approach—the fact that no way could be found to establish a normative model—prompted continuing developments. Style as a choice of alternatives became a very suspect notion as the nature of synonymy was more closely investigated. With a consensus arising that absolute synonymy cannot exist, any premise for defining style that depends on there being alternative ways of saying exactly the same thing is undercut. One should note, however, the contrary position of Hirsch, who writes with the express purpose of "defending the existence and importance of synonymity, that is, the expression of an absolutely identical meaning by means of different linguistic forms" (59).

The concept of style as "recurrence or convergence of textual pattern" was sparked by the seminal "Closing Statement" of Roman Jakobson to the otherwise indifferently regarded 1958 symposium on style at Indiana University (Sebeok [ed.]). The shift here is to an understanding of style according to which it is produced by a combination of syntagmatic and paradigmatic elements. This view strongly underlies the work of Halliday and his students (e.g., Halliday, 1978; Benson and Greaves, 1985a, 1985b; Berry, 1975, 1976; Leech, 1966, 1970), and the transformational-generative approach to stylistics (Levin, 1962, 1963). The assumptions in this view allowed for considerable openness to developments which had already taken place in semiotics. We note fairly early evidence of the view of "style as a particular exploitation of a grammar of possibilities, that is, a grammar that goes beyond the literary text." This tendency is particularly noticeable in "generative metrics" (Ohmann, 1970; Thorne, 1970a, 1970b).

Also showing influence from this direction are certain developments brought under the rubrics of systemic linguistics, functional grammar, or even systemic functional grammar. While a systemic grammar is still heavily ruled-based and should ideally function as an explicit generative model, features at the discourse level are included in it. Much of the current work in this area is on the development of the model and the formulation of generalizing theory (e.g., Benson and Greaves, 1985a, 1985b; Berry, 1975, 1976, 1981; Butler; Dik; Halliday, 1985; Kress; Morley).

Fawcett's approach in cognitive linguistics (systemic functional grammar) moves away from the position that syntactic structures are the basis for explanation of language (the early Halliday model) towards the position that these structures are merely the realizations of choice between meanings (1984a, 1984b). He thus includes semantics in a more defined and rigorous way, using a model of the "communicating mind" in which the language system is only one of the meaning-creating parameters involved. Close scrutiny of these works shows little or no use of the word "style," but they pay detailed and rigorous attention to features labeled "stylistic" in other approaches. Even where the word is retained, attempts tend more to free it from definitional constraints. Goodman reflects this when he says, "My purpose has not been to impose an elaborate and rigid system of classification upon features of style, but rather to free the theory of style from warping constraints of prevalent dogma—from the misleading opposition of style and subject, of form and content, of what and how, of intrinsic and extrinsic" (1975:259).

Important developments in the understanding of language and discourse can be seen in the changed treatment—or nontreatment—of style. Linguistic observations are no longer conceptualized as "deviations," but rather in more neutral terms, in which particularities are illustrated in terms of their grouping, cross-referencing, and contrasts. Evident is an increasing realization that while particular approaches to language understanding may be sentence-based, the notion of style depends upon consideration of text, that is, language as discourse. The trend is toward more unified analyses, intended to account in a more satisfactory manner for all the data. Critiques of these newer approaches have sometimes pointed to an abandonment of rigor and to too great a reliance upon intuition; in some instances this criticism is totally justified. Many other studies, however, show an acute awareness of the necessity for constant questioning of the grounds for one's analysis. García contrasts this newer approach with more traditional understandings:

> The (statistical) norm, which traditional grammar interprets as the results of an absolute-type categorization rooted in the logical or propositional structure imputed to the sentence, is, from our perspective, only the natural result of speakers' using the linguistic means at their disposal in the most appropriate manner. . . . The type of analysis (and of validation) presented here is certainly not subject to either formalization or strict falsification, as it relies on an in principle open-ended set of (possibly relevant) ill-defined criteria. This, however, does not make the criteria circular, irrelevant, or uncheckable. Nor does it necessarily constitute an indictment of the analysis: The coherence of the discourse itself is, by its very nature, open-ended, context sensitive, and ill-defined. And it is this coherence, after all, that constitutes the ultimate touchstone: for the use of language, just as much as for linguistic analysis (1983:205).

Moving outside of sentence-based approaches has resulted in an increasing number of studies in which anomalous usages, traditionally attributed to style, can be described in predictive and generalizing terms. Some of the most interesting of this work concerns adjective placement in Spanish (Klein-Andreu) and in French (Waugh 1976, 1977). Klein-Andreu not only draws attention to the failures of sentence grammars in predicting these so-called stylistic anomalies, she points out the unnecessary and misleading use of lexical subcategorization (147). Studies such as those of Klein-Andreu and Waugh actually introduce a new level of rigor and control, for by rejecting rule-based theories of grammar they also reject the old commonplace understanding that "all grammars leak." "Style" can no longer be the comfortable category into which all data which do not fit the rules can be thrown. The importance of contextually-based explanations is pointed up by Klein-Andreu:

> Consideration of data without context, then, necessarily leads full circle: to a benighted satisfaction with "rules" capable of producing only an impoverished caricature of the language, bearing no explanatory relation to its actual use. . . . It is only when one approaches language with the assumption that it is essentially a CODE, consisting of overt signals for constant meanings, that one is tempted—indeed forced—to examine how the units postulated are deployed in actual usage. For one is then forced to assume that there must be a demonstrable coherency between the particular meanings postulated and what the context shows the speaker is trying to express (177).

At this point, developments in linguistic stylistics are so closely connected with developments in other areas that it will be profitable to bring into purview some related areas of textual analysis as they touch upon concerns of style. Hartmann (13) notes another tradition of textual analysis with significant involvement in questions of style: exegesis or "close reading." In the West the study of both sacred scripture and legal codes has a long, well-established tradition. The existence of canonical texts in both of these areas has meant a strong tendency to permit new readings only after prolonged scrutiny according to an accepted set of exegetical methods, which themselves can be seen as another type of canon. Since the canonical methods have not framed questions in terms of the relevant discourse factors, discussions of style within this tradition have likewise been dependent upon a "leap of faith." New directions in exegetical method are now opening up more controlled ways of defining style in ancient texts. Two of the greatest stimuli in this direction are to be found in the work of James Barr (1961, 1968), who has pioneered the introduction of certain linguistic considerations to the Christian exegetical tradition; and the work of Jacob Neusner, who, while not as linguistically based as Barr, has introduced radically new perspectives to the Jewish tradition.

New ways of looking at the communication process beginning in the 1930s led to a network of approaches we now generally refer to as semiotic approaches (Bartsch and Vennemann; Beale; Fawcett *et al.*, 1984a, 1984b; Fowler, 1981; Halliday, 1978). The common denominator in semiotic approaches to text is the viewing of language as discourse, understanding discourse as a communicative event with behavioral status. Interestingly, the word "style" is infrequently used, and then vaguely, in these studies. What one finds, rather, is that all of the text features which have been pointed to in literary or linguistic stylistics or in traditional exegesis as "stylistic devices" are now accounted for in a more-or-less well-controlled fashion as mean-creating factors in the communication event (Hartmann: 13–15).

Having a general relation to the focus of semiotic inquiry is speech act theory. Although the idea of speech as act can be found already in the work of Bronislaw Malinowski, this particular theoretical perspective was especially popular in the 1950s and 1960s and has been brought to bear very recently upon ancient texts in *Semeia* 41. Hartmann (16)describes the genesis of this approach as "the result of a combination of the philosopher's concern for refining the devices of ordinary language into tools of (socio-)logical analysis and the ethnographer's interest in verbal taxonomies and practices as reflections of (psycho-)cultural interaction." Once again, we have a more unified field theory intricately involving the traditional parameters of "style," with little attempt to define "style" as a discrete category. Related to speech act theory, but with an applied focus is the "New Rhetoric." This approach developed to meet needs in teaching composition in American secondary and higher education. Like speech act theory, the New Rhetoric focuses on text as communicative strategy, with profound implications for how we define style.

The renewed interest in the discourse dimensions of language may be seen in two other approaches which began to take shape in the late 1960s. Wolfgang Dressler (1972) distinguished these as the "whole-text" approach (discourse analysis) and the "sentence-sequence" approach (text grammar or text linguistics). The roots of discourse analysis are usually understood to lie primarily within American anthropology and British sociology, while the impetus for text grammar was primarily European deductive linguistics. Hartmann amplifies this by describing discourse analysis as an approach which "starts with the outer frame of the situational context and works inward to find out which verbal features correlate with specific communicative settings" and text grammar as one which "starts from within the linguistic patterns of the message and asks how they might be used in certain contexts" (17). There now exists a vast array of models and methods in both areas: to keep the work prior to 1977 ordered, the survey by Gülich and Raible is especially helpful. With the focus on "text-ness" as a more appropriate way to understand communicative events, rather than a focus on individual components such as phonemicity, grammaticality, or semanticality, we again find the traditionally conceived "stylistic features" evaporating into the details of the text pattern as it creates meaning.

Semiotic approaches have been attractive to both linguists and literary scholars. Linguists see in these approaches a possible way to understand language in terms of the most inclusive package of parameters producing variations. Literary scholars see in these studies important features which were usually absent in earlier linguistic work: an appreciation of the aesthetic qualities and of the way literary texts make their total impact. It is thus precisely in the area traditionally designated "stylistics" that linguistics and literary criticism now share the most common ground. When we add the dimensions of culture and experience required in semiotic analysis, we find that anthropology is now also involved in dimensions of textual analysis formerly considered outside the domain of that discipline. One new approach, in which anthropology intersects with linguistics, literature, and folklore, has been designated "ethnopoetics" (Bauman, Bauman and Sherzer, Casson, Fox, Sherzer, Sherzer and Woodbury). For those of us who work with ancient texts, that is, who by definition work crossculturally, the approach of ethnopoetics offers a powerful tool for approaching questions of variation in our ancient materials. This is of special value for understanding such dimensions as oral versus written discourse and genre or text types. Ethnopoetic studies point out the special dangers of analyzing texts in terms of referential function only; equal attention must be paid to the expressive, poetic, and pragmatic functions of the language in its socio-cultural context. Since anthropological approaches have been so typically dependent upon the existence of living informants, we should note that some anthropologists are now also directing their ethnopoetic approaches to the analysis of written texts with no contemporary language or culture source (e.g., Sherzer, Sherzer and Woodbury).

As Hough commented in 1969: "The study of language and the study of literature obviously have a common frontier, and stylistics is the border area" (ix). We may now observe that what was once the borderland has become a large and populous territory with well-mapped and frequently traveled roadways. Gray's description of the concept of style as analogous to the concept of ether in 18th-19th century physics (108–10) was correct in certain basic essentials. The word "style" has evaporated as a meaningful term in language description; the "data of style," however, have stimulated exciting new dimensions in language research. Analysis of ancient Near Eastern texts reflects aspects of all approaches to descriptions of style discussed here (including ancient rhetoric, if one takes this view of the intent of Weingreen's work on Hebrew composition!). Regardless of whether we retain the term "style" or not, we are looking for particular patterns to account for variabilities in our texts; and the way we structure our searches determines to a large extent which types of patterns we will be able to perceive. The cross-cultural investigation of how texts mean (which is what we are about when we read ancient texts) requires that particularly sensitive care be taken in controlling the structure of our searches.

This brief survey of dominant approaches to style in the Western tradition has studiously avoided parading a spectrum of specific definitions of style. Nonetheless, it has been the quest for a definition of style which has stimulated our new understandings of textual complexities. In the words of Cesare Segre, "The history of stylistics is the history of a never-ending hunt after evidence on the part of literary critics" (274).

WORKS CONSULTED

Aklujkar, Ashok

1972 "Stylistics in the Sanskrit Tradition." Pp. 1–14 in *Current Trends in Stylistics.* Ed. Braj B. Kachru and Herbert F. W. Stahlke. Edmonton: Linguistic Research.

Allen, John P. B., and S. Pit Corder, eds.

1974 *The Edinburgh Course in Applied Linguistics, Volume 3: Techniques in Applied Linguistics.* London: Oxford University Press.

Anttila, Raimo

1975 "Linguistics and Philology." Pp. 145–56 in *Linguistics and Neighboring Disciplines.* Ed. Renate Bartsch and Theo Vennemann. Amsterdam: North-Holland.

Archer, William K., and Forough Al-Zaman Minou-Archer

1972 "Some Observations Concerning Stylistics Amongst the Persians." Pp. 15–36 in *Current Trends in Stylistics.* Ed. Braj B. Kachru and Herbert F. W. Stahlke. Edmonton: Linguistic Research.

Auerbach, Erich

1946 *Mimesis: Dargestellte Wirklichkeit in der abendländischen Literatur.* Bern: Francke.

1958 *Literatursprache und Publikum in der lateinischen Spätantike und im Mittelalter.* Bern: Francke.

Babb, Howard S., ed.

1972 *Essays in Stylistic Analysis.* New York: Harcourt Brace Jovanovich.

Bakhtin, Mikhail M.

1981 *The Dialogic Imagination.* Austin: University of Texas Press.

Bally, Charles

1905 *Précis du stylistique.* Geneva: Eggiman.

Barr, James

1961 *The Semantics of Biblical Language.* London: Oxford University Press.

1968 *Comparative Philology and the Text of the Old Testament.* Oxford: Clarendon.

Barthes, Roland

1971 "Style and Its Image." Pp. 3–15 in *Literary Style: A Symposium.* Ed. Seymour Chatman. London: Oxford University Press.

Bartsch, Renate, and Theo Vennemann, eds.

1975 *Linguistics and Neighboring Disciplines.* Amsterdam: North-Holland.

Bauman, Richard

1986 *Story, Performance, and Event: Contextual Studies of Oral Narrative.* Cambridge: Cambridge University Press.

Bauman, Richard, and Joel Sherzer, eds.
1974 *Explorations in the Ethnography of Speaking.* Cambridge: Cambridge University Press.

Beale, Walter H.
1987 *A Pragmatic Theory of Rhetoric.* Carbondale: Southern Illinois University Press.

Benson, James D., and William S. Greaves, eds.
1985a *Systemic Perspective on Discourse, Volume 1: Selected Theoretical Papers from the Ninth International Systemic Workshop.* Norwood, NJ: Ablex.
1985b *Systemic Perspectives on Discourse, Volume 2: Selected Applied Papers from the Ninth International Systemic Workshop.* Norwood, NJ: Ablex.

Berry, Margaret
1975 *An Introduction to Systemic Linguistics, Volume 1: Structures and Systems.* London: B. T. Batsford.
1976 *An Introduction to Systemic Linguistics, Volume 2: Levels and Links.* New York: St. Martins.
1981 "Systemic Linguistics and Discourse Analysis: A Multi-Layered Approach to Exchange Structure." Pp. 120–45 in *Studies in Discourse Analysis.* Ed. M. Coulthard and M. Montgomery. London: Routledge and Kegan Paul.

Brisau, A.
1969 "Sentence Structure as a Characteristic of Prose Style." *Revue des Langues Vivantes* 35:159–74.

Burton, D.
1981 "Analyzing Spoken Discourse." Pp. 61–81 in *Studies in Discourse Analysis.* Ed. M. Coulthard and M. Montgomery. London: Routledge and Kegan Paul.

Butler, Christopher S.
1985 "Discourse Systems and Structures and Their Place Within an Overall Systemic Model." Pp. 213–28 in *Systemic Perspectives on Discourse, Volume 1.* Ed. James D. Benson and William S. Greaves. Norwood, NJ: Ablex.

Callary, R. E.
1974 "Status Perception Through Syntax." *Language and Speech* 17:187–92.

Carpenter, Ronald H.
1969 "The Essential Schemes of Syntax: An Analysis of Rhetorical Theory's Recommendations for Uncommon Word Orders." *Quarterly Journal of Speech* 55:161–68.

Casson, Ronald W., ed.
1981 *Language, Culture, and Cognition: Anthropological Perspectives.* New York: Macmillan.

Chatman, Seymour
1967 "Stylistics: Quantitative and Qualitative." *Style* 1:29-43.

Chatman, Seymour, ed.
1971 *Literary Style: A Symposium* (Bellaggio, Italy, 1969). London: Oxford University Press.

Ching, Marvin K. L., Michael C. Haley, and Ronald F. Lunsford, eds.
1980 *Linguistic Perspectives on Literature.* London: Routledge and Kegan Paul.

Cluysenaar, Anne
1975 *Aspects of Literary Stylistics: A Discussion of Dominant Structures in Verse and Prose.* New York: St. Martins.

Connor, Ulla, and Robert B. Kaplan, eds.
1987 *Writing Across Languages: Analysis of L2Text.* Reading, MA: Addison-Wesley.

Corbett, Edward P. J.
1965 *Classical Rhetoric for the Modern Student.* New York: Oxford University Press.

Coulthard, M., and M. Montgomery, eds.
1981 *Studies in Discourse Analysis.* London: Routledge and Kegan Paul.

De Vito, J. A.
1967 "Levels of Abstraction in Spoken and Written Language." *Journal of Communication* 17:354–61.

Dik, Simon C.
1978 *Functional Grammar.* Amsterdam: North-Holland.

Dillon, George L.
1978 *Language Processing and the Reading of Literature: Toward a Model of Comprehension.* Bloomington: Indiana University Press.

Dolezel, Lubomir
1969 "A Framework of the Statistical Analysis of Style." Pp. 10–25 in *Statistics and Style.* Ed. Lubomir Dolezel and Richard W. Bailey. New York: American Elsevier.

1971 "Toward a Structural Theory of Content in Prose Fiction." Pp. 95–110 in *Literary Styles: A Symposium.* Ed. Seymour Chatman. London: Oxford University Press.

Dolezel, Lubomir and Richard W. Bailey, eds.
1969 *Statistics and Style.* New York: American Elsevier.

Dolezel, Lubomir and Jirí Kraus
1972 "Prague School Stylistics." Pp. 37–48 in *Current Trends in Stylistics.* Ed. Braj B. Kachru and Herbert F. W. Stahlke. Edmonton: Linguistic Research.

Dressler, Wolfgang U.
1972 *Einführung in die Textlinguistik.* Tübingen: Niemeyer.

Dressler, Wolfgang U., ed.
1978 *Current Trends in Textlinguistics.* Berlin: W. de Gruyter.

Ellis, J. M.
1970 "Linguistics, Literature and the Concept of Style." *Word* 26:65–78.

Enkvist, Nils E.
1964 "On Defining Style." Pp. 95–110 in *Linguistics and Style.* Ed. Michael J. Gregory. London: Oxford University Press.
1971 "On the Place of Style in Some Linguistic Theories." Pp. 47–64 in *Literary Style: A Symposium.* Ed. Seymour Chatman. London: Oxford University Press.
1973 *Linguistic Stylistics.* The Hague: Mouton.

Fawcett, Robin P. , et al, eds.
1984a *The Semiotics of Culture and Language, Volume 1: Language as Social Semiotic.* London: Frances Pinter.
1984b *The Semiotics of Culture and Language, Volume 2: Language and Other Semiotic Systems of Culture.* London: Frances Pinter.

Fillenbaum, Samuel
1973 *Syntactic Factors in Memory.* The Hague: Mouton.

Fish, Stanley E.
1973 "What Is Stylistics and Why Are They Saying Such Terrible Things About It?" Pp. 109–52 in *Approaches to Poetics.* Ed. Seymour Chatman. New York: Columbia University Press.

Foucault, Michel
1970 *The Order of Things: An Archaeology of the Human Sciences.* New York: Vintage Books (French original 1966).

Fowler, Roger
1966 "Linguistic Theory and the Study of Literature." Pp. 1–28 in *Essays on Style and Language.* Ed. Roger Fowler. London: Routledge and Kegan Paul.
1971 *The Languages of Literature.* London: Routledge and Kegan Paul.
1981 *Literature as Social Discourse: The Practice of Linguistic Criticism.* Bloomington: Indiana University Press.
1986 *Linguistic Criticism.* New York: Oxford University Press.

Fowler, Roger, ed.
1966 *Essays on Style and Language: Linguistic and Critical Approaches to Literary Style.* London: Routledge and Kegan Paul.

Fox, James J.
1988 *To Speak in Pairs: Essays on the Ritual Languages of Eastern Indonesia.* Cambridge: Cambridge University Press.

Freeman, Donald C.
1970 "Linguistic Approaches to Literature." Pp. 3–17 in *Linguistics and Literary Style.* Ed. Donald C. Freeman. New York: Holt, Rinehart and Winston.

Freeman Donald C., ed.
1970 *Linguistics and Literary Style.* New York: Holt, Rinehart and Winston.

Friedrich, Paul
1986 *The Language Parallax: Linguistic Relativism and Poetic Indeterminacy.* Austin: University of Texas Press.

Fucks, Wilhelm
1971 "Possibilities of Exact Style Analysis." Pp. 51–76 in *Patterns of Literary Style.* Ed. Joseph Strelka. University Park: Pennsylvania State University Press.

García, Erica C.
1975 *The Role of Theory in Linguistic Analysis.* Amsterdam: North-Holland.
1983 "Context Dependence of Language and of Linguistic Analysis." Pp. 181-207 in *Discourse Perspectives in Syntax.* Ed. Flora Klein-Andreu. New York: Academic.

Goodman, Nelson
1975/87 "The Status of Style." Pp. 254–66 in *Twentieth-Century Literary Theory: An Introductory Anthology.* Ed. Vassilis Lambropoulos and David N. Miller. Albany: State University of New York Press.

Goodman, Paul
1971 *Speaking and Language: Defense of Poetry.* New York: Random House.

Gray, Bennison
1969 *Style: The Problem and Its Solutions.* New York: Humanities.

Guiraud, Pierre
1971 "Modern Linguistics Looks at Rhetoric: Free Indirect Style." Pp. 77–89 in *Patterns of Literary Styles.* Ed. Joseph Strelka. University Park: Pennsylvania State University Press.
1974 "Rhetoric and Stylistics." Pp. 943–55 in *Current Trends in Linguistics,* Vol. 12. Ed. Thomas A. Sebeok et al. The Hague: Mouton.

Gülich, Elisabeth, and Wolfgang Raible
1977 *Linguistische Textmodelle. Grundlagen und Möglichkeiten.* München: Fink.

Gumperz, John J.
1982 *Discourse Strategies.* Cambridge: Cambridge University Press.

Halliday, Michael A. K.
1978 *Language as Social Semiotic: The Social Interpretation of Language and Meaning.* London: University Park.
1985 *An Introduction to Functional Grammar.* London: Edward Arnold.

Hartmann, Reinhard R . K.
1980 *Contrastive Textology: Comparative Discourse Analysis in Applied Linguistics.* Studies in Descriptive Linguistics 5. Heidelberg: Julius Groos.

Hayes, Bruce
1981 *Metrical Theory of Stress Rules.* Bloomington: Indiana University Linguistics Club.

Hendricks, William O.
1976 *Grammars of Style and Styles of Grammar.* Amsterdam: North-Holland.

Hirsch, E. D.
1975 "Stylistics and Synonymity." *Critical Inquiry* 1:559–79.

Hough, Graham G.
1969 *Style and Stylistics.* London: Routledge and Kegan Paul.

Ihwe, Jens
1975 "Linguistics and the Theory of Literature." Pp. 131–44 in *Linguistics and Neighboring Disciplines.* Ed. Renate Bartsch and Theo Vennemann. Amsterdam North-Holland.

Jakobson, Roman
1958/60 "Closing Statement: Linguistics and Poetics." Pp. 350–77 in *Style in Language.* Ed. Thomas A. Sebeok. Cambridge, MA: MIT Press.
1968 "Poetry of Grammar and Grammar of Poetry." *Lingua* 21:597–609.

Kachru, Braj B., and Herbert F. W. Stahlke, eds.
1972 *Current Trends in Stylistics.* Edmonton: Linguistic Research.

Klein-Andreu, Flora
1983 "Grammar in Style: Spanish Adjective Placement." Pp. 143–79 in *Discourse Perspectives on Syntax.* Ed. Flora Klein-Andreu. New York: Academic.

Klein-Andreu, Flora, ed.
1983 *Discourse Perspectives on Syntax.* New York: Academic.

Kress, Gunther R., ed
1976 *Halliday: System and Function in Language: Selected Papers.* London: Oxford University Press.

Lakoff, George
1972 "Hedges: A Study in Meaning Criteria and the Logic of Fuzzy Concepts." Pp. 183–228 in *Papers from the Eighth Regional Meeting, Chicago Linguistic Society.* Ed. Paul M. Peranteau, Judith N. Levi, and Gloria C. Phares. Chicago: Chicago Linguistic Society.

Leech, Geoffrey N.
1966 "Linguistics and the Figures of Rhetoric." Pp. 135–56 in *Essays on Style and Language: Linguistic and Critical Approaches to Literary Style.* Ed. Roger Fowler. London: Routledge and Kegan Paul.
1970 "'This Bread I Break'—Language and Interpretation." Pp. 119–28 in *Linguistics and Literary Style.* Ed. Donald C. Freeman. New York: Holt, Rinehart and Winston.

Levin, Samuel R.
1962 *Linguistic Structures in Poetry.* The Hague: Mouton.
1963 "Deviation—Statistical and Determinate—in Poetic Language." *Lingua* 12:276–90.

Levinson, Stephen C.
1983 *Pragmatics.* Cambridge: Cambridge University Press.

Lybbert, E. K., and D. W. Cummings
1969 "Rhetorical Syntax, Economy, and the Theme-Rheme Distinction." *Language and Style* 2:244–56.

McLendon, Sally
1982 "Meaning, Rhetorical Structure, and Discourse Organization in Myth." Pp. 284–305 in *Analyzing Discourse: Text and Talk.* Ed. Deborah Tannen. Georgetown University Round Table on Language and Linguistics 1981. Washington, DC: Georgetown University Press.

Malinowski, Bronislaw
1929/87 *The Sexual Life of Savages.* Boston: Beacon.

Martini, Fritz
1971 "Personal Style and Period Style: Perspectives on a Theme of Literary Research." Pp. 90–115 in *Patterns of Literary Style.* Ed. Joseph Strelka. University Park: Pennsylvania State University Press.

McSpadden, George E.
1971 "Phonetics, Intonation, Metrics, and Stylistics." Pp. 116–29 in *Patterns of Literary Style.* Ed. Joseph Strelka. University Park: Pennsylvania State University Press.

Messing, Gordon M.
1971 "The Impact of Transformational Grammar Upon Stylistics and Literary Analysis." *Linguistics* 66:56–73.

Milic, Louis T.
1971 "Rhetorical Choice and Stylistic Option: The Conscious and Unconscious Poles." Pp. 77–94 in *Literary Style: A Symposium.* Ed. Seymour Chatman. London: Oxford University Press.

Moerk, Ernst
1973 "An Objective, Statistical Description of Style." *Linguistics* 108:50–58.

Morley, G. D.
1985 *An Introduction to Systemic Grammar.* London: Macmillan.

Mukarovsky, Jan
1970 "Standard Language and Poetic Language." Pp. 40–56 in *Linguistics and Literary Style.* Ed. Donald C. Freeman. New York: Holt, Rinehart and Winston.

Nichols, Marie H.
1971 "Rhetoric and Style." Pp. 130–43 in *Patterns of Literary Style.* Ed. Joseph Strelka. New York: Holt, Rinehart and Winston.

Ohmann, Richard
1959 "Prolegomena to the Analysis of Prose Style." Pp. 1–24 in *Style in Prose Fiction.* Ed. Henry C. Martin. New York: Columbia University Press.

1964 "Generative Grammars and the Concept of Style." *Word* 20:423–39.

1969 "Speech, Action and Style." Pp. 241–78 in *Literary Style: A Symposium.* Ed. Seymour Chatman. London: Oxford University Press.

1970 "Generative Grammars and the Concept of Literary Style." Pp. 258–78 in *Linguistics and Literary Style.* Ed. Donald C. Freeman. New York: Holt, Rinehart and Winston.

1972a "Literature as Sentences." Pp. 353–61 in *Essays in Stylistic Analysis.* Ed. Howard S. Babb. New York: Harcourt Brace Jovanovich.

1972b "Instrumental Style: Notes on the Theory of Speech as Action." Pp. 115–42 in *Current Trends in Stylistics.* Ed. Braj B. Kachru and Herbert F. W. Stahlke. Edmonton: Linguistic Research.

Pavel, Thomas G.
1980 "Some Remarks on Narrative Grammars." Pp. 187–212 in *Linguistic Perspectives on Literature.* Ed. Michael K. L. Ching. London: Routledge and Kegan Paul.

Pike, Kenneth L.
1981 *Tagmemics, Discourse, and Verbal Arts.* Ann Arbor: Michigan Studies in the Humanities.

Poole, M. E., and T. W. Field
1972 "Social Class and Code Elaboration in Written Communication." *Language and Speech* 15:1–7.

Riffaterre, Michael
1959 "Criteria for Style Analysis." *Word* 15:154–74.

Ross, Donald
1985 "What Surface-Structure Parsing Can Tell Us about Style." Pp. 225–40 in *Systemic Perspectives on Discourse, Volume 2.* Ed. James D. Benson and William S. Greaves. Norwood, NJ: Ablex.

Sandall, Rolf G.
1977 *Linguistic Style and Persuasion.* European Monographs in Social Psychology 11. London/New York: Academic.

Saussure, Ferdinand de
1915 *Cours de linguistique générale.* Lausanne: Payot.

Sebeok, Thomas A., ed.
1960 *Style in Language.* New York: Mitchell.

Segre, Cesare
1988 *Introduction to the Analysis of the Literary Text.* With T. Kemeny. Trans. J. Meddemmen. Bloomington: Indiana University Press.

Sherzer, Joel
1983 *Kuna Ways of Speaking: An Ethnographic Perspective.* Austin: University of Texas Press.

Sherzer, Joel, and Anthony C. Woodbury, eds.
1987 *Native American Discourse: Poetics and Rhetoric.* Cambridge Cambridge University Press.

Shopen, Tim
1972 "Logical Equivalence Is Not Semantic Equivalence." Pp. 340–50 in *Papers from the Eighth Regional Meeting, Chicago Linguistic Society.* Ed.

Paul M. Peranteau, Judith N. Levi, and Gloria C. Phares. Chicago: Chicago Linguistic Society.

Silverstein, M
1976 "Shifters, Linguistic Categories and Cultural Description." Pp. 103–37 in *Meaning in Anthropology*. Ed. Keith H. Basso and Henry A. Selby. Albuquerque: University of New Mexico Press.

Spitzer, Leo
1948/87 "Linguistics and Literary History." Pp. 207–38 in *Twentieth-Century Literary Theory: An Introductory Anthology*. Ed. Vassilis Lambropoulos and David N. Miller. Albany: State University of New York Press.

Spencer, John, and Michael J Gregory
1964 "Approaches to the Study of Style." Pp. 57–105 in *Linguistics and Style*. Ed. Michael J. Gregory. London: Oxford University Press.

1970 "An Approach to the Study of Style." Pp. 73–95 in *Linguistics and Literary Style*. Ed. Donald C. Freeman. New York: Holt, Rinehart and Winston.

Steinmann, M., ed.
1967 *New Rhetorics*. New York: Scribner's.

Strelka, Joseph, ed.
1971 *Patterns of Literary Style*. University Park: Pennsylvania State University Press.

Tannen, Deborah
1982 "Oral and Literate Strategies in Spoken and Written Narratives." *Language* 58:1–21.

Tannen, Deborah, ed.
1984 *Coherence in Spoken and Written Discourse*. Norwood, NJ; Ablex.

Thorne, James P.
1970a "Stylistics and Generative Grammars." Pp. 182–96 in *Linguistics and Literary Style*. Ed. Donald C. Freeman. New York: Holt, Rinehart and Winston.

1970b "Generative Grammar and Stylistic Analysis." Pp. 185–97 in *New Horizons in Linguistics*. Ed. John Lyons. Harmondsworth: Penguin.

Todorov, Tzvetan
1971 "The Place of Style in the Structure of the Text." Pp. 29–45 in *Literary Style: A Symposium*. Ed. Seymour Chatman. London: Oxford University Press.

Traugott, Elizabeth C., and Mary L. Pratt
1980 *Linguistics for Students of Literature*. San Diego: Harcourt Brace Jovanovich.

Turner, G. W.
1973 *Stylistics*. Harmondsworth: Penguin.

Uitti, Karl D.

1971 "Literary Discourse: Some Definitions and Approaches." Pp. 198–215 in *Patterns of Literary Style.* Ed. Joseph Strelka. University Park: Pennsylvania State University Press.

Ullmann, Stephen

1966 *Language and Style: Collected Papers.* Oxford: Basil Blackwell.

1971 "Two Approaches to Style." Pp. 217–25 in *Patterns of Literary Style.* Ed. Joseph Strelka. University Park: Pennsylvania State University Press.

1973 *Meaning and Style: Collected Papers.* Oxford: Basil Blackwell.

van Dijk, Teun A.

1972 *Some Aspects of Text Grammars: A Study of Theoretical Linguistics and Poetics.* The Hague: Mouton.

1977 *Text and Context: Explorations in the Semantics and Pragmatics of Discourse.* Longman Linguistics Library 21. London: Longman.

Waugh, Linda

1976 "The Semantics and Paradigmatics of Word Order." *Language* 52:82–107.

1977 *A Semantic Analysis of Word Order: Position of the Adjective in French.* Leiden: E. J. Brill.

Wells, Rulon

1960 "Nominal and Verbal Style." Pp. 213–20 in *Style in Language.* Ed. Thomas A. Sebeok. New York: Wiley.

1970 "Nominal and Verbal Style." Pp. 297–306 in *Linguistics and Literary Style.* Ed. Donald C. Freeman. New York: Holt, Rinehart and Winston.

Widdowson, H. G.

1974 "Stylistics." Pp. 202–31 in *The Edinburgh Course in Applied Linguistics, Volume 3: Techniques in Applied Linguistics.* Ed. J. P. B. Allen and S. Pit Corder. London: Oxford University Press.

Winter, W.

1962/64 "Style as Dialects." Pp. 324–30 in *Proceedings of the Ninth International Congress of Linguists, Cambridge, MA, August 27-31, 1962.* Ed. H. G. Lunt. The Hague: Mouton.

Wolfson, Nessa

1979 "The Conversational Historical Present Alternation." *Language* 55:168–82.

C. Grammar

6

Discourse Functions of Quotative Frames in Biblical Hebrew Narrative[1]

Cynthia L. Miller

ABSTRACT

This paper presents a preliminary account of direct and indirect speech in Biblical Hebrew narrative with examples drawn primarily from 2 Samuel[2]. On the basis of both the syntactic form of the quotative frame and the syntactic relation of the frame to the quotation, three categories of direct speech and four categories of indirect speech are isolated. Particular attention is given to quotations introduced with לאמר. It is suggested that traditional expositions, which view this form as the usual marker for direct speech or, conversely, as a marker of rhetorical verbosity, are misleading. A linguistic analysis is presented which accounts for the usage of quotative frames with לאמר within the discourse context.

[1]This paper was written in 1988 with subsequent minor revisions for publication. I regret that Meier's work (1992) appeared too late for interaction here. I am indebted to a number of readers for their comments and criticisms on this paper and its various antecedents: Adele Berlin, W. Randall Garr, Gene B. Gragg, James D. McCawley, M. O'Connor, Dennis G. Pardee, Jerrold M. Sadock, Philip C. Schmitz, David Testen, Sandra Thompson.

[2]This study uses the instances of reported speech in 2 Samuel as a sample of Biblical Hebrew dialogue. For a comprehensive analysis of all instances of reported speech in Genesis through 2 Kings, see my doctoral dissertation, "Reported Speech in Biblical and Epigraphic Hebrew: A Linguistic Analysis" (Ph.D. diss., University of Chicago, 1992).

1.0 Introduction

In reports of speech acts, language turns back upon itself to reveal its expressive and communicative functions (Banfield, 1983:23). This reflexive (or metapragmatic) use of language, in which one speech act reports another, is remarkable in that it brings together two discourse events: that in which something was originally expressed and that in which it is cited by another (Sternberg, 1982a:107; Silverstein: 132–40). However, the relation between these two discourse events may be grammatically represented in a variety of ways.

This study presents an account of reported speech in Biblical Hebrew narrative in terms of the syntactic form of the quotative frame.[3] Particular attention is given to quotations introduced with the infinitive construct לאמר and the discourse pragmatic function of such quotations within the larger narrative. A limited corpus as found in 2 Samuel was chosen for the study with additional examples drawn from the remainder of the Deuteronomistic History.

2.0 Direct and Indirect Speech

Traditionally, reported speech has been divided into two categories, direct speech (*oratio recta*) and indirect speech (*oratio obliqua*). In Hebrew the distinction between the two may be formally described in terms of (1) the relation of the quotative frame to the quotation and (2) the form of the frame itself.

2.1 The Relation of the Quotative Frame to the Quotation

2.1.1 Direct Speech

The syntactic relation of the quotative frame to the quotation differs in direct and indirect speech. A direct quotation is syntactically independent of the frame. It follows that only within direct speech may a quotation contain sentence fragments, such as exclamations, or

[3]The term "quotative frame" refers to the speech of the reporting speaker and "quotation" refers to the speech of the reported speaker. Sternberg (1982a) uses the terms "frame" and "inset." Banfield (1983) uses the terms "parenthetical" and "quotation." Rebera uses "transitional formulae" or "quotative formulae" to refer to the frame. Longacre (160–62) expands the notion of "quotative formula" to include clauses which precede the speech verb and which express movement of the speech participants (e.g., "they drew near and they said") or psychological orientation (e.g., "and they feared greatly and they said").

a language different from that of the quotative frame.[4] Because direct speech recreates, in a sense, the original discourse context of speaker and addressee, a direct quotation may also contain vocatives, imperatives, and addressee-oriented adverbials (Banfield, 1983:30–34).

The independence of quotation and frame in direct speech is also reflected in pronominal usage. Pronominal reference within direct quotation is not identical to that of the frame, but usually exhibits indexical concord with the frame in accordance with two general principles.[5] A first principle is that first and second person pronouns within the quotation are co-referential with the reported speaker and the reported addressee in the preceding frame, as illustrated in (1):[6]

(1) ויאמר לו דוד אל־תירא כי עשה אעשה עמך חסד בעבור יהונתן אביך

And David$_i$ said to him$_j$, "Do not be afraid because I$_i$ will certainly show loyalty to you$_j$ on account of Jonathan your$_j$ father. . . ." (2 Sam 9:7).

A second principle is that third person pronouns in the quotation must not be co-referential with either the reported speaker or the reported addressee in the preceding frame, as illustrated in (2):

(2) ויבא יואב אל־המלך ויאמר מה עשיתה הנה־בא אבנר אליך למה־זה
שלחתו וילך הלוך׃

So Joab$_i$ went to the king$_j$ and he$_i$ said, "What have you$_j$ done? Look, Abner$_k$ came to you$_j$. Why did you$_j$ let him$_k$ go? And now he$_k$ is gone!" (2 Sam 3:24).

Thus, pronominal elements in direct speech must be determined with reference to the clause that frames the quotation; that is, pronominal reference is opaque.[7]

Although pronominal reference is a primary means for distinguishing direct and indirect speech, pronominal reference may differ from the principles given above in some speech situations and in the direct reports of those situations. Three of these pragmatic contexts are as

[4]These issues are discussed in Coulmas, 1985:42–43. Gumperz (57–99) discusses the complexities of code-switching (the juxtaposition of two distinct language systems) within reported speech.

[5]These principles are set forth by Li (30–32). See also the general formulation for Biblical Hebrew given by Givón (10–11), though without the exceptions given below.

[6]The subscripted indices "$_i$", "$_j$", and "$_k$" are used to indicate co-referential noun phrases and/or pronouns in accordance with standard linguistic practice.

[7]For the phrases "opaque pronominal reference" and "transparent pronominal reference," see Munro (302–3).

follows. First, in deferential language, noun phrases with pronominal suffixes may regularly be substituted for pronouns (for example, "your servant" for "I" and "my lord" for "you"):

(3) ויאמר ציבא אל־המלך ככל אשר יצוה אדני המלך את־עבדו כן יעשׂה עבדך

And Zibah$_i$ said to the king$_j$, "Whatever *my lord the king*$_j$ commands *his servant*$_i$ thus will *your servant*$_i$ do" (2 Sam 9:11).

Second, in oath formulas the speaker may refer to him/herself in the third person:

(4) ויאמר הראשׁ כלב אנכי... כה־יעשׂה אלהים לאבנר וכה יסיף לו....

And he [Abner]$_i$ said, "Am *I*$_i$ a dog's head? . . . Thus may God do to *Abner*$_i$ and thus may he add to *him*$_i$. . . ." (2 Sam 3:8-9).

In the first part of the quotation Abner refers to himself as "I," but within the oath formula he refers to himself by his proper name and by the third person "to him." However, the use of third person to refer to the speaker within oath formulas is optional; more commonly the first person is used (see, for example, 1 Kgs 2:23).

Third, the addressee occasionally is not addressed as second person within direct speech, if the speaker wishes to express sarcasm or reproach:

(5) ותצא מיכל בת־שׁאול לקראת דוד ותאמר מה־נכבד היום מלך ישׂראל אשר
נגלה היום לעיני אמהות עבדיו

And Michal the daughter of Saul went out to meet David and she said, "How *the king of Israel* has been honored today who disrobed today before the eyes of the maidservants of *his* servants. . . ." (2 Sam 6:20).

By referring to the addressee with third person pronouns and noun phrases, the speaker distances herself from the addressee and mocks him.

Thus, the relation between direct quotation and its frame is one of independence. This independence is manifested in two ways. First, the quotation is syntactically independent of the frame. Second, pronominal reference within the quotation is not identical to that of the frame, but is determined with reference to the frame and in accord with the pragmatic context.

We may go on to consider two sub-categories of direct speech: semidirect speech and internal speech. The first distinction relates to the form of the quotation; the second relates to the pragmatic context of the quotation.

2.1.1.1 Semidirect speech

The discourse feature referred to as "semidirect speech" has been described by Robert Alter (71) and Adele Berlin (99–101), although the term was coined later by M. O'Connor (forthcoming). It refers to a quotation in which specific details of the original discourse are replaced by more general terms such as כה "thus," זאת "this," or פלני אלמני "so-and-so." Such a quotation does not purport to be a verbatim account of the speech act, or even a paraphrase of it. It is a literary construct used to condense information in the narrative. An example is given in (6):

(6) ויאמר חושי אל־צדוק ואל־אביתר הכהנים כזאת וכזאת יעץ אחיתפל
את־אבשלם ואת זקני ישראל וכזאת וכזאת יעצתי אני:

And Hushai said to Zadok and Abiathar, the priests, "Ahithophel has advised Absalom and the elders of Israel to do *such and such*, but I have advised to do *such and such*" (2 Sam 17:15).

A verbatim account of the dialogue would have related the particular advice of Ahithophel and Hushai as recorded in the preceding narrative.

Semidirect speech may be used when a customary exchange between persons is reported. For example, 2 Sam 15:2–4 reports a representative exchange of numerous conversations between Absalom and citizens seeking justice. The part of the exchange which varied with each individual (their city of origin) is reported in semidirect speech:

(7) והשכים אבשלום ועמד על־יד דרך השער ויהי כל־האיש אשר־יהיה־לו־ריב
לבוא אל־המלך למשפט ויקרא אבשלום אליו ויאמר אי־מזה עיר אתה ויאמר
מאחד שבטי־ישראל עבדך:

Absalom would get up early and stand by the side of the road leading to the city gate. Whenever anyone came with a complaint to be placed before the king for a decision, Absalom would call out to him, "What town are you from?" He would answer, "Your servant is from *one of the tribes of Israel*" (2 Sam 15:2).

The other examples of semidirect speech in 2 Samuel occur in 17:6; 17:21.

The phenomenon of semidirect speech is significant in light of accounts of quotation which differentiate direct and indirect speech on the basis of the recoverability of the original speech. Direct speech is said always to have a *de dicto* reading, whereas indirect speech has a *de dicto* or a *de re* reading depending upon how the reporter chooses to process the quotation.[8] Semidirect speech does not match either category perfectly. On the one hand, semidirect speech resembles direct quotation in linguistic form, but it does not allow a *de dicto* reading. On the other hand, semidirect speech resembles many indirect quotations in having a *de re* reading, but the source of that reading may be different. A *de re* reading of indirect speech reflects the perspective of the reporting speaker. A *de re* reading of semidirect speech may reflect the perspective of the reporting speaker or the perspective of the narrator.[9]

2.1.1.2 Internal speech

Although Hebrew has a number of verbs for the representation of mental processes (e.g., חשב "to think, esteem, reckon"; זכר "to remember, recall"; הגה "to utter, muse"), these verbs are infrequently found in quotative frames to introduce the content of thought. Most often internal speech is not distinguished from external speech; both may be introduced by the verb אמר "to say." If internal speech is marked at all, it is marked by a prepositional phrase with the verb, thus אמר בלבו "he said in his heart," or אמר אל לבו "he said to his heart."[10]

In 2 Samuel only the unmarked variety of internal speech occurs; thus there is some dispute concerning whether a particular speech act should be classified as internal speech. The following examples, however, seem to be clear from the context. In (8) Absalom's reason for setting up a pillar is presented as internal speech:

(8) ואבשלם לקח ויצב־לו בחיו את־מצבת אשר בעמק־המלך כי אמר אין־לי בן
בעבור הזכיר שמי

Now Absalom had taken and set up in his lifetime a pillar which was in the valley of the king because he *thought* (lit. said), "I have no son to carry on the memory of my name" (2 Sam 18:18).

---

[8]The classic example is: *Oedipus said that his mother was beautiful.* According to the *de dicto* reading, the original utterance would have been something like: *My mother is beautiful.* According to the *de re* reading, Oedipus could have made any of the following utterances: *Jocasta is beautiful,* or *my wife is beautiful,* etc. If his original utterance were any of the latter sentences, then the descriptive phrase "his mother" would be made from the perspective of the reporting speaker, not the reported speaker. See Coulmas, 1986:3–4.

[9]For contrastive examples, see 1 Sam 21:3 for the perspective of the reporting speaker (as noted by Berlin, 1983:100) and Ruth 4:1 for the perspective of the narrator.

[10]Conroy (130–131) calls this "inner direct speech" or "interior quotation."

In (9) the reason that the men brought provisions to David and his people when they were fleeing from Absalom is given as internal speech:

(9) ...הגישו לדוד ולעם אשר־אתו לאכול כי אמרו העם רעב ועיף וצמא במדבר:

. . . They brought [provisions] to David and to the people who were with him to eat because they *thought* (lit. said), "The people have become hungry and tired and thirsty in the desert" (2 Sam 17:29).

Were this an example of direct speech, the pronouns and deictics would reflect it (i.e., "*You* are hungry and tired and thirsty *here*").

Internal speech may also be embedded within direct speech as in (10):

(10) ויאמר אדני המלך עבדי רמני כי־אמר עבדך אחבשה־לי החמור וארכב עליה

And he [Mephibosheth] said, "My lord the king, my servant deceived me for your servant *thought* (lit. said), 'I will have my donkey saddled and I will ride upon it . . .'" (2 Sam 19:27).

Other examples of internal speech within 2 Samuel are 6:9; 9:1; 10:2; 14:15; 16:3.

2.1.2 Indirect Speech

In indirect speech, the quotation is syntactically dependent upon the frame. Most importantly, indexical concord of persons is transparent. Pronouns within the quotation reflect the same perspective as that outside of the quotation in accordance with the conventions of the language with respect to anaphora and deixis. Similarly, there must be concordance of deictic and demonstrative elements referring to the time or place of the speech act (Banfield, 1983:25).

The types of syntactic dependence present in indirect speech are a reflection of the types of dependency present in sentences of the language in general. Thus indirect speech may be introduced by: (1) כי "that" plus an independent clause; (2) the preposition ל "to" plus an infinitival clause or a noun phrase; and (3) the object marker את plus a noun phrase or את אשר plus a dependent clause. In a fourth type of indirect speech, the quotation is an independent clause with no explicit subordination to the frame, but the sentence exhibits transparent pronominal reference, which is diagnostic of indirect speech.[11]

[11]Another non-direct way of reporting speech presents the framing speech verb in one clause with the perlocutionary effect of that verb represented in a conjoined clause. (For the term "perlocution" with reference to speech acts, see the classic work by Austin, especially 101–8.) An example is: וישלח מלאכים אחרי אבנר וישבו

The first category, כי + independent clause,[12] occurs both in narration (11) and embedded within direct speech (12):

(11) ויראו עבדי דוד להגיד לו כי־מת הילד

And the servants of David were afraid to tell him *that* the child was dead . . . (2 Sam 12:18).

(12) . . . הגדת היום כי אין לך שׂרים ועבדים . . .

". . . you have declared today *that* you have no princes or servants (i.e., they mean nothing to you)" (2 Sam 19:7).

In each case, the personal pronouns and deictics are reported from the perspective of the quoting speaker rather than the quoted speaker.

In the second category ל "to" is followed by an infinitival clause as in (13) or a noun phrase as in (14).

(13) ויהוה צוה להפר את־עצת אחיתפל הטובה לבעבור הביא יהוה אל־אבשלום את־הרעה׃

Now the LORD had commanded to overthrow the good advice of Ahithophel in order for the LORD to bring evil to Absalom (2 Sam 17:14).

(14) וישאל דוד לשלום יואב ולשלום העם ולשלום המלחמה׃

And David asked concerning the welfare of Joab and concerning the welfare of the army and concerning the welfare of the battle (2 Sam 11:7).

Example (15) may be an example of internal indirect speech:

(15) ויאמר להכות את־דוד׃

And he said to strike David (2 Sam 21:16).

At first glance, it is not certain if Ishbi-Benob actually stated that he was going to kill David, or if he gave orders to someone else to kill David, or if this sentence only expresses his intention to do so. However, a comparative example in Hebrew (Exod 2:14) points to the last case.[13]

אתו מבור הסירה, "and he sent messengers after Abner and they brought him back from the well of Sirah" (2 Sam 3:26). In this instance, the principal is the subject of the first clause, and the animators are the subject of the second clause. However, in the following example, the principal is the subject of both clauses, even though he did not physically perform the action of the second: וישלח דוד מלאכים ויקחה, "And David sent messengers and he took her" (2 Sam 11:4).

[12]For an exhaustive analysis of *kî* in Hebrew and Ugaritic, see Bandstra.

[13]Exod 2:14 reads: ויאמר מי שׂמך לאיש שׂר ושפט עלינו הלהרגני אתה אמר כאשר הרגת את־המצרי, "And he said, 'Who made you a prince and judge over us? Are you *intending* (lit. saying) *to kill me* as you killed the Egyptian?'" In the Phoenician inscription from Karatepe, we find two nearly identical imprecations: *wʾm mlk . . . ʾš ymḥ šm ʾztwd*, "and if [there is] a king . . . who effaces the name of Azitawada" (*KAI*

Other examples in narrative of indirect speech introduced with ל occur in 2 Sam 10:3; and 8:10. The only example of this construction embedded within direct speech is shown in (16):

(16) ...ועד־מתי לא־תאמר לעם לשוב מאחרי אחיהם

"... and for how long will you not tell the people to return from after their brothers?" (2 Sam 2:26).

The third type of indirect speech, introduced with את or את אשר, occurs only in narrative. In (17) the dependent clause is introduced by את. In (18) the dependent clause is introduced by את אשר and the verb of the frame is an impersonal passive:[14]

(17) וישלח יואב ויגד לדוד את־כל־דברי המלחמה׃

And Joab sent and he reported to David all the matters (lit. words) of the battle (2 Sam 11:18).

(18) ויגד לדוד את אשר־עשתה רצפה בת־איה פלגש שאול׃

And there was reported to David *everything which* Rizpah the daughter of Ayyah the concubine of Saul had done (2 Sam 21:11).

Other examples are 2 Sam 11:22 and 3:19.[15] In all of the examples, the reported information is highly condensed.

The fourth type of indirect speech has an independent clause in the quotation but no formal mark of subordination.[16] Both examples in 2 Samuel occur embedded in direct speech, but they cannot be examples of direct speech because the information within the quotation is reported from the perspective of the quoting speaker. In (19) David would presumably not have referred to his own sons as "sons of the king." Therefore the quotation must be indirect:

---

26 A III 12–14) and *wʾm mlk ʾš . . . yʾmr lmḥt šm ʾztwd* "and if [there is] a king . . . who says to efface the name of Azitawada," (*KAI* 26 C III 13–15). Whether the Phoenician example represents a king's intention to efface the inscription (as opposed to his order to efface) is debatable. (I am indebted to Adele Berlin and Philip C. Schmitz for pointing out these examples.)

[14]This construction has traditionally been analyzed as an instance in which the logical subject of the passive verb is treated as the object (by analogy to the active construction), see GKC: §121a. However, Khan (496–97) disputes this analysis, since the subjects of passives preceded by את agree in number and gender with the subject (e.g., 2 Sam 21:22; 2 Kgs 18:30).

[15]A sub-type of this category is introduced by אשר alone. The only example in 2 Sam is in 18:21 with the framing verb הגיד.

[16]Munro (302–3) notes that in many languages the contrast between direct and indirect speech is not marked by overt subordination. She suggests that pronominal reference is a better test for distinguishing the two.

(19) ויען יונדב בן־שׁמעה אחי־דוד ויאמר אל־יאמר אדני את כל־הנערים בני־
המלך המיתו כי־אמנון לבדו מת

And Jonadab the son of Shimeah the brother of David answered and said, "Let not my lord say [that] they killed all the lads, the sons of the king, because Amnon alone is dead" (2 Sam 13:32).

In (20) the quotation is also reported from the perspective of the quoting speaker and so must be indirect speech, although it is without any explicit subordination:

(20) ויאמר מה־אתם אמרים אעשׂה לכם׃

And he said, "What are you_i saying [that] I should do for you_i?" (2 Sam 21:4).

In these examples, the framing clause is either a mitigated command (jussive) (19) or a question (20). From these limited examples it seems that an indirect quotation may be introduced without explicit subordination when the framing clause is not a declarative clause. That is, indirect speech usually exhibits syntactic subordination of the quotation to the frame. But when the framing clause is non-declarative, explicit syntactic subordination may be omitted. In such cases, the only mark of indirect quotation is transparent pronominal reference. We can also note that indirect speech without explicit subordination only occurs embedded within direct speech.

In summary, indirect speech is distinguished from direct speech by transparent pronominal reference. Within indirect speech, four types may be formally distinguished with respect to the degree to which the quotation is syntactically subordinated to the frame.[17]

2.2 The Form of the Quotative Frame

2.2.1 Quotative Frames of Indirect Speech

The quotative frames of indirect speech reflect a reduced inventory of speech verbs when compared to direct speech. Within 2 Samuel, only the following verbs are attested in quotative frames: שׁלח, שאל, אמר, צוה, הגיד, דבר. The use of these verbs shows a close

[17]In referring to the relative dependence of the quotation of indirect speech to the frame, Li prefers to speak of differences of "fusion" between the clause of the frame and the clause of the quotation (36–37). Coulmas refers to the same phenomenon as "grammatical integration" (1986:19–21). By both of their analyses, sentences of types three and four should be included in an analysis of indirect speech even though a high degree of "fusion" or "grammatical integration" has taken place.

correlation with the syntactic form of the quotative frame. The data are summarized in Table 1.

TABLE 1

THE SYNTACTIC FORMS OF INDIRECT SPEECH IN 2 SAMUEL

	Subordination	Clause Type of Quotation	Framing Verb	Context of Quotation Narrative	Direct Speech
(1)	כי "that"	independent	נגד "declare"	12:18[1]	7:11; 19:7
(2)	ל "to"	dependent	צוה "command"	17:14	
			אמר "say"	21:16	2:26
			שאל "ask"	11:7	
			שלח "send"	8:10	
(3)	את (אשר)	dependent	נגד "declare"	11:18;11:22; 21:11	
			דבר "tell"	3:19[1]	
(4)	Ø	independent	אמר "say"		13:32; 21:4

NOTES TO TABLE 1:

1 The framing verb is in a complement clause.

2.2.2 Quotative Frames of Direct Speech

The quotative frames of direct speech may be summarized in three categories.[18] In the first category, the quotative frame has one finite speech verb. In the second category, the quotative frame has more than one finite speech verb, and each verb agrees in verbal aspect, number and gender.[19] The third category involves quotative frames with one finite speech verb plus לאמר. The three categories are summarized in (21):

(21) category of frame	variable verb slot		form of אמר
single-verb	finite verb		
multiple-verb	finite verb	+	finite form
לאמר	finite verb	+	infinitive construct

Examples (22) through (24) illustrate these three categories:

(22) ויאמר המלך שלום לנער לאבשלום

And the king *said*, "Is the lad Absalom safe?" (2 Sam 18:29).

[18]Not discussed here are instances of two successive quotations by a single speaker, each with its own quotative frame (e.g., 15:3–4; 15:25–27; 16:10–11; 17:7–8) (see Conroy: 130; Bar-Efrat: 43).

[19]Usually there are two non-identical speech verbs, the second of which is אמר "to say," but this is not always the case. Occasionally three speech verbs may appear in the quotative frame (e.g., 2 Sam 11:5). Occasionally a verb other than אמר appears in second position (such as דבר "to speak"; see Josh 22:21). In rare cases, the verb אמר may appear twice in the same quotation formula (e.g., 2 Sam 24:17).

(23) ויען יואב ויאמר חלילה חלילה לי אם־אבלע ואם־אשחית׃

And Joab *answered* and *said*, "Far be it! Far be it from me either that I should swallow up or that I should destroy!" (2 Sam 20:20).

(24) ויצו המלך את־יואב ואת־אבישי ואת־אתי לאמר לאט־לי לנער לאבשלום

And the king *commanded* Joab and Abishai and Ittai *saying*, "Deal gently with the lad Absalom for me" (2 Sam 18:5).

In addition to the syntactic differences between the three categories, quotative frames differ with respect to the verbs which may fill the variable verb slot. Single-verb frames are the most common, but only when the variable verb is אמר, the generic verb of saying. Communication verbs other than אמר occasionally occur alone, but more commonly they are mediated by some form of אמר (O'Connor, 1980:410). Note also that the widest range of verbs, some of them not even speech verbs, occurs in frames with לאמר. The data for 2 Samuel are summarized in Table 2.

TABLE 2
QUOTATIVE FRAMES OF DIRECT SPEECH IN 2 SAMUEL[1]

		Single-verb	Multiple-verb[2]	לאמר
אמר	"to say"	[245 times]	24:17	3:18; 5:1; 5:6; 17:6; 20:18
דבר (D)	"to speak"	24:12	22:1–2	7:7; 19:12; 20:18
שׁלח	"to send"	11:6; 19:15	2:5; 10:5; 12:27	3:12; 3:14; 13:7; 14:32 (2x); 15:10; 19:12
נגד (H)	"to report"	19:2	17:21; 18:10; 24:13	2:4; 3:23 4:10; 6:12; 11:10; 15:31; 17:16; 19:9
ענה	"to answer"	19:43	4:9; 13:32; 14:18; 14:19; 15:21; 19:22; 19:44; 20:20	1:16
קרא	"to call"	20:16	1:15; 2:26; 9:9; 13:17; 15:2; 18:26; 18:28; 21:2	
זעק	"to cry out"	19:5		
ברך (D)	"to bless"		14:22	
קון (R)	"to lament"		3:33	
שׁמע	"to hear"			19:3
שׁאל	"to ask"			2:1; 3:13; 5:19
שׁבע (N)	"to swear"			3:35; 21:17
צוה	"to command"			11:19; 13:28; 18:5; 18:12
נדר	"to vow"			15:8
דין (N)	"to argue"			19:10
סות (H)	"to incite"			24:1
גלה	"to uncover"			7:27
שׂים	"to put"			13:33
היה	"to be"			3:17; 7:4; 24:11
גדל	"to become great"			7:26
בוא	"to come"[3]			13:30; 15:13
כתב	"to write"			11:15
[no verb]				3:12; 5:6

NOTES TO TABLE 2:

1 Underlined references occur embedded within direct speech; all other references occur in narrative.

2 Usually only two finite speech verbs appear in this frame. However, three verbs (שׁלח, נגד, אמר) ccur in the frame in 11:5. Two other quotative frames which possibly belong in this column are תקע + אמר in 20:1 and אוה + אמר in 23:15.

3 בוא occurs in the clause preceding אמר at 13:24; 16:16; 17:20; 18:31; 19:6 and 19:42. However, בוא in these instances is a part of the preceding narrative and not a part of the quotative frame.

2.2.3 *Quotative Frames with* לאמר

The infinitive construct לאמר has traditionally been understood as the marker which introduces direct speech (GKC: §114o; Joüon: 364). The syntax of this form in quotative frames has been explained in diverse ways.[20] Most modern grammarians, however, explain לאמר as an extension of the gerundive use of infinitives (Miller, 1970: 224; Seow: 190; Waltke and O'Connor: §36.2.3e). Thus, it is said to mean literally "by saying," i.e., "by virtue of the statement" (Williams: §195). Practically, students are urged not to translate it (Lambdin: 49). Stylistically, it is seen as tautological—either as a mark of rhetorical verbosity (Avishur: 11 n. 42) or as formal and prolix (GKC: 351 n. 1).

However, this description is clearly insufficient for a number of reasons. The simplistic generalization that לאמר introduces "direct speech" is misleading for two reasons. First, it ignores direct speech which is not so introduced. However, direct speech without לאמר is far more common than direct speech with לאמר. Within the corpus of 2 Samuel there are over 325 quotative frames, but only 46 occurrences of quotative frames introduced with לאמר; לאמר is clearly the marked case. Second, all of the examples of gerundive infinitives cited by the grammars are syntactically different from quotative frames with לאמר.[21] Gerundive infinitives may have objective suffixes, whereas לאמר never takes object suffixes. Gerundive infinitives may govern prepositional phrases or adverbial phrases; לאמר does not.[22] We must

---

[20]Rabbinic interpretation centered around the use of the infinitive to indicate an obligation (see Segal: §348). On the basis of this usage, לאמר was thought to mean "the speech introduced ought to be recited or to have been recited" (see Daube: 3–14).

A modern explanation relates לאמר to the Egyptian *rḏd* (*r*- preposition plus the infinitive of the verb *ḏd* "to say"). See, e.g., Boyd: 191–95 and Novetsky: 92–109. For a comprehensive survey of the Egyptian data, see Grapow: 4.88–89.

Labuschagne (279) explains the use of quotative frames in the Pentateuch as the result of numerological composition. He makes a connection between the ten references to divine speech introduced by לאמר and ten instances in which the phrase מתוך האש is used in connection with the people hearing God speak.

[21]Compare the following examples of gerundive infinitives cited in GKC: §114o: 1 Sam 20:36 (with object suffix), Gen 34:7 (followed by את and a noun phrase), 1 Sam 14:33 (with prepositional phrase following), 1 Sam 19:5 (followed by object and adverb), Gen 3:22 (functioning as the subject of the clause).

[22]In a few instances (e.g., Gen 23:5, 14) לאמר לו occurs, but each example has textual problems.

After the verb יסף, לאמר functions as an infinitival complement to the verb; see, e.g., 2 Sam 2:22: ויסף עוד אבנר לאמר אל־עשהאל סור לך מאחרי, "And Abner spoke

conclude that לאמר in these constructions is not a gerundive infinitive and seek an alternative explanation.[23]

The following discussion centers on the differences between the two mediated frames—multiple-verb frames, and frames with לאמר. Before examining the pertinent data, however, the prototypical features of reported speech will be presented as background information.

3.0 Prototypicality in Reported Speech

Prototypicality in reported speech relates to the extent to which the reported speech reflects a prototypical speech event. Any act of verbal communication minimally involves a message which is transferred between two participants, a speaker (or addresser) and an addressee. The message bears a relation to its referent(s) and is transmitted via a shared code by means of a channel (e.g., speech, writing, etc.; Silverstein, 1985:353–54).

A prototypical dialogue involves two participants who alternate speaking and listening in paired turns of talk, or adjacency pairs (Sacks, Schegloff, Jefferson). The dialogue occurs with the two participants speaking face-to-face and in the same location, not across a distance. In addition, the role of "speaker" in the dialogue is not distributed among more than one person. Goffman notes that the role of "speaker" may be decomposed into three diverse notions: "principal," "author," and "animator."[24] The principal is the person "whose position is established by the words that are spoken, someone whose beliefs have been told, someone who is committed to what the words say" (144). The author frames the speech act in language. The animator produces the speech act, whether in writing or orally. In a

---

again to Asahel, 'Turn aside from behind me.'" Note that although infinitives construct of speech verbs other than אמר do not appear in quotation frames with לאמר, other speech verbs may appear as an infinitival complement after יסף, e.g., ענה in 1 Sam 9:8: ויסף הנער לענות את־שאול ויאמר הנה נמצא ביד רבע שקל כסף, "And the lad *answered* Saul *again* (lit. he added to answer) *and he said*, 'Behold, I have in my possession a quarter of a shekel of silver. . . .'" The framing construction—finite verb + infinitive construct (לאמר) + finite verb (a composite of the second and third categories)—does not occur except when the first verb is יסף.

[23]For the syntactic arguments that לאמר is a complementizer, see my dissertation (n. 2 above).

[24]Levinson (184) prefers the terms "motivator," "composer," "transmitter" for these notions; his other modifications of Goffman's analysis do not concern us here.

prototypical speech event, a single individual performs all of these roles of speaker. It is possible, however, for the roles to be distributed among more than one individual. For example, when the president of the United States is scheduled to deliver an address, a speech writer may frame the speech in language (the author), a stand-in may deliver the speech (the animator), but the president is held responsible for the content therein (the principal). Similarly, when a message is sent, the persons enacting the various roles of speaker may not be the same. The principal commissions that the message be sent, the author composes the message, and the animators produce the speech act in the presence of the addressee(s).

Because a reported speech event necessarily analyzes as it reports, reported speech and reported dialogue may radically diverge from a mimetic representation of the supposed original speech situation. Prototypical reported speech and dialogue will, therefore, exhibit the following additional features. The reported speech event is a single event, not iterative (many similar speech events reported as one), nor is the speech retold from a previous conversation. The participants of the speech event are full characters in the narrative, not agents or props; nor are they groups represented as speaking chorally (Jakobson, 1960:353–59; 1980:81–87). A prototypical reported dialogue thus purports to mirror, as closely as possible, the supposed original speech situation which is itself prototypically dialogic.

4.0 Messages and Quotative Frames

Quotative frames with לאמר occur most commonly in 2 Samuel with verbs which indicate the receiving or sending of a message, namely, הגיד "to tell, report," and שׁלח "to send [a message/messenger(s)]." Therefore, quotative frames with these two verbs are examined in an attempt to isolate the differences among the three categories of direct quotative frames.

4.1 Quotative Frames with הגיד "to Tell"

The verb הגיד may introduce direct speech in all three types of quotative frames. When the verb stands alone in a quotative frame, the Hiphil is never used to introduce direct speech. Instead, the Hophal is used (as in [25]):

(25) ויגד ליואב הנה המלך בכה ויתאבל על־אבשלם:

And it was reported to Joab, "Behold the king is weeping and mourning over Absalom" (2 Sam 19:2).

הגיד may be followed by a finite form of אמר as in (26):

(26) וירא איש אחד ויגד ליואב ויאמר הנה ראיתי את־אבשלם תלוי באלה:

And a man saw [it] and *he reported* to Joab and *he said*, "Behold, I saw Absalom hanging in an oak tree" (2 Sam 18:10).

In each instance of הגיד in a multiple-verb frame, the subject of the verb (that is, the animator who relates the information) is the principal of the speech event. In the above example (26), although the man is not named, he is an eyewitness and thus both principal and animator of the information that he reports.

Most commonly, the verb הגיד appears in quotative frames with לאמר. In this construction, the verb may appear in the Hophal or Hiphil. In the Hophal, the speaker is always anonymous and simply the animator for an unspecified principal. In the Hiphil, two situations obtain with respect to the speaker of the quotation. With the Hiphil singular, the speaker is always a known character and the principal of the speech event. With the Hiphil plural, however, the speakers may be unknown, anonymous persons who are only the animators of the speech event. In these instances, the speech act is a way of introducing additional information into the narrative:

(27) ויגדו לדוד לאמר לא־ירד אוריה אל־ביתו

And *they (impersonal plural) reported* to David *saying*, "Uriah did not go to his house" (2 Sam 11:10).

From this sample, we may make the following observations. Direct speech framed by the verb הגיד is usually mediated by a form of the verb אמר. A finite form of אמר is used (as the second verb of a multiple-verb frame) when there is an explicit mention of the animator in the narrative. The infinitival form, לאמר, may be used when the principal is unknown and the animator is anonymous. Thus, only לאמר frames allow for the displacement of animator and principal—a nonprototypically dialogic feature of reported speech. Multiple-verb frames, by contrast, are used in more prototypically dialogic contexts, since the principal of the speech event is an explicit character in the narrative.

4.2 Quotative Frames with שלח "to Send [a Message/Messenger]"

The verb שלח is commonly used in the communicative sense of sending a message. It may frame both direct and indirect speech.

In direct speech, שלח occurs in a single-verb frame only two times in 2 Samuel. One instance (in 19:15) is textually disputed. The undisputed instance is (28):

(28) וישלח דוד אל־יואב שלח אלי את־אוריה החתי

And David *sent* [a message/messenger] to Joab, "Send to me Uriah the Hittite" (2 Sam 11:6).

The verb שלח occurs with two speech verbs (a multiple-verb frame) only three times in 2 Samuel (2:5; 10:5; 12:27). An example is given in (29):

(29) וישלח דוד מלאכים אל־אנשי יביש גלעד ויאמר אליהם ברכים אתם ליהוה

And David *sent* messengers to the men of Jabesh Gilead and he *said* to them, "May you be blessed by the LORD. . . ." (2 Sam 2:5).

It is important to note that both verbs agree in number with the principal (David), not the animators (the messengers). The personal pronouns within the quotation are also presented from the perspective of the principal and not the animators.

Frames with לאמר are the most common quotative frame for שלח (3:12; 3:14; 13:7; 14:32; 15:10; 19:12). An example is given in (30):

(30) וישלח דוד מלאכים אל־איש־בשת בן־שאול לאמר תנה את־אשתי את־מיכל

And David *sent* messengers to Ish-Bosheth the son of Saul *saying*, "Give my wife Michal. . ." (2 Sam 3:14).

Note again that personal pronouns within the quotation reflect the principal's perspective.

That quotations introduced by לאמר are reported from the perspective of the principal can be seen clearly in instances of embedded speech acts (31):

(31) ויאמר אבשלום אל־יואב
הנה שלחתי אליך לאמר
בא הנה ואשלחה אתך אל־המלך לאמר
למה באתי מגשור . . .

And Absalom$_i$ *said* to Joab,
"Behold I$_i$ *sent* to you *saying*,
'Come here so that I$_i$ may *send* you to the king *saying*,
"Why have I$_i$ come from Geshur? . . ."'" (2 Sam 14:32).

In this example there are three quotative frames and three quotations. In the first frame (introduced with ויאמר), Absalom is the speaker and Joab is the addressee. In the second frame (introduced with שׁלח לאמר), Absalom is the principal, an unnamed messenger is the animator, and Joab is the addressee. In the third frame (also introduced with שׁלח לאמר), Absalom is the principal, Joab is the animator, and the king is the addressee. Note that the most deeply embedded speech ("Why have *I* come from Geshur?") is still represented from the perspective of the principal.[25] In actually delivering Absalom's message to the king, Joab would have said, "Why has *Absalom* come from Geshur?"

The prevalence of לאמר frames with שׁלח is expected because the semantics of the verb allows for the displacement of principal and animator. שׁלח occurs much less frequently with multiple-verb frames which emphasize the prototypically dialogic nature of the speech event. Multiple-verb frames with שׁלח contrast with לאמר in that they always explicitly mention the messengers (or, animators) who convey the message, whereas the messengers need not be explicitly mentioned in לאמר frames, and usually are not. In addition, only quotations introduced with multiple-verb frames may begin with the phrase כה אמר; quotations introduced with לאמר frames never include this phrase. Thus, multiple-verb frames explicitly indicate the principal of the speech event, even when the message is animated by someone else.

We may summarize by saying that when a message is received or sent, quotative frames with לאמר are less than prototypically dialogic. They allow for the distribution of the role of speaker to more than one participant in the narrative. In multiple embeddings of quotations introduced by לאמר, each successively embedded quotation is still represented from the deictic perspective of the principal. When a message is received, quotative frames with לאמר emphasize the addressee's role in the speech situation. In such instances, the fact that information is conveyed is often more important than the principalship of the conveyor of the message; the speaker becomes merely an animator, often an anonymous animator, for introducing information into the narrative.

---

[25]A similar example of embedding occurs in Exod 31:3.

5.0 More Quotative Frames with לאמר

5.1 Transmitting and Receiving Messages

The previous analysis dealt with only two framing verbs, הגיד and שׁלח. However, other verbs may be used with לאמר in the transmitting or receiving of messages in the same way. Thus, we find אמר לאמר (as in 2 Sam 5:6) for sending an oral message and כתב לאמר (as in 2 Sam 11:15) for sending a written message.

In the receiving of messages, לאמר may be used with expressions which emphasize the reception of the message rather than its production. For example, in (32) we have no clue of the principals or animators of the speech, but only the fact that the people received it:

(32) ותהי התשׁעה ביום ההוא לאבל לכל־העם כי־שׁמע העם ביום ההוא לאמר
נעצב המלך על־בנו׃

Now on that day the victory was turned into mourning for all the people because they *heard* on that day (*saying*), "The king is grieving for his son" (2 Sam 19:3).

Similar examples occur in 13:30 and 15:13.

In communication between persons and God, speech is often represented with לאמר in much the same way. God's communication to the prophets is often represented in a roundabout fashion as "the word of the LORD was to PN לאמר" (24:11; 7:4) with the message to be transmitted introduced by כה אמר יהוה. The distribution of speaker role between principal (God) and animator (prophet) may be discerned from statements such as וידבר יהוה ביד־עבדיו הנביאים לאמר, "And the LORD spoke by the agency of his servants the prophets *saying*" (2 Kgs 21:10).

When people contact God, the communication is often represented by שׁאל ביהוה לאמר as in (33):

(33) וישׁאל דוד ביהוה לאמר האעלה באחת ערי יהודה ויאמר יהוה אליו עלה
ויאמר דוד אנה אעלה ויאמר חברנה

And David *inquired* of the LORD *saying*, "Shall I go up to one of the cities of Judah?" And the LORD *said* to him, "Go up." And David *said*, "Where shall I go up?" *And he said*, "To Hebron" (2 Sam 2:1).

After the initiating communication is introduced by לאמר, the stage for communication with the divine has been set. Turn-taking in the subsequent exchange is introduced simply by ויאמר.

5.2 Distribution of Speaker Roles

Quotative frames with לאמר may be used with verbs other than those for sending or receiving messages to indicate that the persons filling the roles of animator and principal are not the same. An instructive example occurs in 2 Sam 1:16 in the account of the Amalekite who reports to David that he has killed Saul. David questions him and then has him executed on the spot. He then stands over the corpse and pronounces the following statement (34):

(34) ויאמר אליו דוד דמיך (Q) על־ראשך כי פיך ענה בך לאמר אנכי מתתי את־משיח יהוה:

And David said to him, "Your blood be upon your head because your mouth testified against you *saying*, 'I killed the anointed of the LORD'" (2 Sam 1:16).

It is interesting to note that David attributes to the Amalekite a statement which the Amalekite does not utter in the preceding dialogue. David's addition of the charged phrase משיח יהוה, "the anointed of the LORD," to refer to the dead Israelite king appears to be his own paraphrase of the Amalekite's report, since it is questionable whether an Amalekite would have framed the statement in such terms. As Savran suggests, David is probably paraphrasing the quotation for covert purposes—to suppress rumors that he might have been involved in Saul's death (71–72). Our analysis of quotative frames with לאמר permits us to state the nature of the paraphrase more precisely. David has taken the report which the Amalekite (the principal) previously uttered and, as animator and author, has re-worded it for his own ends.[26]

A quotative frame with לאמר may introduce a proverbial statement in which the speaker's role is reduced to that of a mere animator (35):

(35) ותאמר לאמר דבר ידברו בראשנה לאמר שאל ישאלו באבל וכן התמו:

And she said (saying), "They (impersonal plural) certainly formerly said (*saying*), 'Ask indeed at Abel' and thus they settled [the matter]" (2 Sam 20:18).

The proverb has no principal, and its author is not known; only the animator, the wise old woman of Abel, is present.

---

[26]A use of לאמר which is similar (and related to the same incident) is found in 2 Sam 4:10.

5.3 Suppression of Speaker or Addressee

We observed above that quotative frames with לאמר often indicate a less than prototypically dialogic context. An extension of this analysis to other speech verbs in narrative reveals that quotative frames with לאמר are used in a number of related ways.

The dialogue is less than prototypical if the addressee makes no verbal response to the speech act in the narrative (36):

(36) ויצו המלך את־יואב ואת־אבישי ואת־אתי לאמר לאט־לי לנער לאבשלום

And the king *commanded* Joab and Abishai and Ittai *saying*, "Deal gently with the lad Absalom for me" (2 Sam 18:5).

In this example, the following narrative does not record the response of the three men to whom the command was addressed, but rather notes that it was overheard and noticed by the people. Other similar examples in which addressees make no verbal response in the narrative are found in 3:35; 13:28; 18:5; 21:17.

If the addressees are numerous and/or in diverse locations, their role in the narrative may not be emphasized. For example:

(37) ודבר־אבנר היה עם־זקני ישראל לאמר גם־תמול גם־שלשם הייתם מבקשים את־דוד למלך עליכם:

Now the word of Abner was with the elders of Israel *saying*, "Formerly you were seeking David as king over you. . ." (2 Sam 3:17).

Abner's reported statement presumably compresses many animations of similar speeches to the elders of Israel. The narrative presents the essential content of the various animations in one quotation. The addressees' response is not indicated in the narrative.

Finally, if the principals of a speech are numerous, a quotation which is attributed to the group gives the content of what were presumably numerous speech acts (38):

(38) ויהי כל־העם נדון בכל־שבטי ישראל לאמר המלך הצילנו מכף איבינו

Now throughout all the tribes of Israel the people *were arguing with one another saying*, "The king saved us from the hand of our enemies. . ." (2 Sam 19:10).

The quotation gives the salient points of the dispute without reproducing all of the speech acts that contributed to the dispute.

6.0 Summary and Conclusions

6.1 Direct Speech, Indirect Speech and לאמר

We are now able to summarize the differences between direct and indirect quotation and to describe how both types relate to quotations introduced with לאמר. Direct speech is syntactically independent of any introductory frame, as are quotations introduced by לאמר. Indirect speech is syntactically dependent.

The pronominal reference of direct speech is opaque and must be calculated on the basis of the frame; the pronominal reference of indirect quotation is transparent and remains the same throughout a sentence. Pronominal reference in quotations introduced by לאמר is identical to that of direct speech except in embedded quotations when principal and animator are not the same person. In such a quotation, the principal retains first person status.

Direct speech may contain exclamatives and expressives such as אוי "woe" and חלילה לי "far be it from me," which never occur in indirect speech or in quotations introduced by לאמר.[27] The frames of full direct speech may also contain the deictic כה "thus," which is coreferential with the quoted clause, whereas the frames of indirect speech may not.

Quotative frames with לאמר exhibit syntagmatic features of direct and indirect speech. They pattern with direct speech in their syntactic independence from the quoted clause and in pronominal reference. Like other frames of direct speech, they may introduce internal speech (see 1 Kgs 1:5) and semidirect speech (see 1 Kgs 2:30). Quotative frames with לאמר pattern with indirect speech with respect to exclamatives and expressives. However, the resemblance between indirect speech and quotative frames with לאמר is only a superficial one. Exclamatives and expressives do not occur in indirect speech because the deictic perspective of the quotation is that of the reporting speaker, not the reported speaker. In quotations framed with לאמר the speech is marked as non-dialogic. Exclamatives presuppose a dialogic context in which the speaker is both animator and principal and both speaker and addressee are present in the narrative.

[27]This observation holds for all of the Deuteronomistic History.

6.2 Discourse Functions of Frames with לאמר

All quotative frames function within discourse to signal the end of narration and the onset of reported speech and to track the participants who fill the roles of speaker and addressee (Rebera: 135). These features are universally recognized. However, the specific form of the quotative frame also contributes to the meaning of the discourse. The discourse functions of quotative frames with לאמר may now be specified on the basis of the preceding discussion.

Frames with לאמר are used to indicate that the reported speech event is less than prototypically dialogic. They are used to introduce information into the narrative without recourse to representation of the entire dialogic exchange. They are used to introduce speech acts of unknown or anonymous persons, that is, persons who are less than full characters in the narrative. Finally, they are used to relate a series of embedded quotations all of which are reported from the perspective of the principal.

The use of לאמר in quotative frames is not a mark of rhetorical verbosity or prolix style. Rather, quotative frames with לאמר function within the system of oppositions present in the language as a whole.

WORKS CONSULTED

Alter, Robert
1981 *The Art of Biblical Narrative.* New York: Basic.

Austin, J. L.
1962 *How to Do Things with Words.* 2nd ed. Ed. J. O. Urmson and Marina Sbisà. Cambridge, MA: Harvard University Press.

Avishur, Y.
1976 "Studies of Stylistic Features Common to the Phoenician Inscriptions and the Bible." *UF* 8:1–22.

Bandstra, Barry Louis
1982 "The Syntax of the Particle *ky* in Biblical Hebrew and Ugaritic." Ph.D. dissertation: Yale.

Banfield, Ann
1973 "Narrative Style and the Grammar of Direct and Indirect Speech." *Foundations of Language* 10:1–39.
1983 *Unspeakable Sentences.* London: Routledge Kegan Paul.

Bar-Efrat, Shimon
1989 *Narrative Art in the Bible.* Trans. Dorothea Shefer-Vanson. JSOTSup 70. Sheffield: Almond.

Berlin, Adele
1983 *Poetics and Interpretation of Biblical Narrative.* Sheffield: Almond.

Boyd, Jesse L.
1986 "An Example of the Influence of Egyptian on the Development of the Hebrew Language during the Second Millennium B.C." Pp. 191–95 in *A Tribute to Gleason Archer.* Ed. Walter C. Kaiser, Jr., and Ronald F. Youngblood. Chicago: Moody.

Brown, Gillian, and George Yule
1983 *Discourse Analysis.* Cambridge: Cambridge University Press.

Conroy, Charles
1978 *Absalom Absalom! Narrative and Language in 2 Samuel 13–20.* AnBib 81. Rome: Pontifical Biblical Institute.

Coulmas, Florian
1985 "Direct and Indirect Speech: General Problems and Problems of Japanese." *Journal of Pragmatics* 9:41–63.
1986 "Reported Speech: Some General Issues." Pp. 1–28 in *Direct and Indirect Speech.* Ed. Florian Coulmas. Trends in Linguistics, Studies and Monographs 31. Berlin, New York, Amsterdam: Mouton/W. de Gruyter.

Daube, D.
1977 "The Rabbinic Treatment of 'And He Said, Saying.'" Pp. 3–14 in *Hebraica*. Ed. O. Rössler. Marburger Studien zur Afrika- und Asienkunde, Series B. Asien 4. Berlin: D. Reimer.

Fox, A.
1983 "Topic Continuity in Biblical Hebrew Narrative." Pp. 215–54 in *Topic Continuity in Discourse: A Quantitative Cross-Language Study*. Ed. T. Givón. Amsterdam: John Benjamins.

Givón, T.
1974 "Verb Complements and Relative Clauses: A Diachronic Case Study in Biblical Hebrew." *AAL* 1:1–22.

Goffman, Erving
1981 *Forms of Talk*. Philadelphia: University of Pennsylvania Press.

Grapow, Hermann
1939–43 *Wie die alten Ägypter sich anredeten, wie sie sich grüssen und wie sie miteinander sprachen*. 4 vols. Abhandlungen der Preussischen Akademie der Wissenschaften 11. Berlin: Akademie der Wissenschaften.

Gumperz, John J.
1982 *Discourse Strategies*. Cambridge: Cambridge University Press.

Jakobson, Roman
1960 "Closing Statement: Linguistics and Poetics." Pp. 350–77 in *Style in Language*. Ed. Thomas A. Sebeok. Cambridge, MA: MIT Press.
1971 "Shifters, Verbal Categories, and the Russian Verb." Pp. 130–147 in *Selected Writings II, Word and Language*. Mouton: The Hague.
1990 "Metalanguage as a Linguistic Problem." Pp. 81–92 in *The Framework of Language*. Ed. Irwin R. Titunik. Michigan Studies in the Humanities, no. 1. Ann Arbor: University of Michigan Press, 1980.

Joüon, Paul
1923 *Grammaire de l'hébreu biblique*. Rome: Pontifical Biblical Institute.

Khan, G. A.
1984 "Object Markers and Agreement Pronouns in Semitic Languages." *BSOAS* 47:496–97.

Labov, William, and Joshua Waletzky
1967 "Narrative Analysis: Oral Versions of Personal Experience." Pp. 12–44 in *Essays on the Verbal and Visual Arts: Proceedings of the 1966 Annual Spring Meeting of the American Ethnological Society*. Ed. June Helm. Seattle and London: University of Washington Press.

Labuschagne, C. J.
1983 "The Pattern of the Divine Speech Formulas in the Pentateuch." *VT* 32:268–96

Lambdin, Thomas O.
1971 *Introduction to Biblical Hebrew*. New York: Charles Scribner's Sons.

Levinson, Stephen C.
1988 "Putting Linguistics on a Proper Footing: Explorations in Goffman's Concepts of Participation." Pp. 161–227 in *Erving Goffman: Exploring the Interaction Order.* Ed. Paul Drew and Anthony Wootton. Cambridge: Polity.

Li, Charles N.
1986 "Direct and Indirect Speech: A Functional Study." Pp. 29–45 in *Direct and Indirect Speech.* Ed. Florian Coulmas. Trends in Linguistics, Studies and Monographs 31. Berlin: Mouton/W. de Gruyter.

Longacre, Robert E.
1989 *Joseph: A Story of Divine Providence—A Text-Theoretical and Text-linguistic Analysis of Genesis 37 and 39–48.* Winona Lake, IN: Eisenbrauns.

Macdonald, J.
1975 "Some Distinctive Features of Israelite Spoken Hebrew." *BiOr* 3:162–75.

Meier, Samuel A.
1992 *Speaking of Speaking: Marking Direct Discourse in the Hebrew Bible.* VTSup 46. Leiden: E. J. Brill.

Miller, Charles H.
1970 "The Infinitive Construct in the Lawbooks of the Old Testament: A Statistical Study." *CBQ* 32:222–26.

Munro, Pamela
1982 "On the Transitivity of 'Say' Verbs." Pp. 301–18 in *Studies in Transitivity.* Ed. Paul J. Hopper and Sandra A. Thompson. Syntax and Semantics 15. New York: Academic.

Novetsky, Chaikie
1986 "Pseudo-Verbal Constructions in Biblical Hebrew." Ph.D. dissertation: New York University.

O'Connor, M.
1980 *Hebrew Verse Structure.* Winona Lake, IN: Eisenbrauns.
(forthcoming) "Quotation in Biblical Hebrew Verse." *Hebrew Studies.*

Rebera, Basil
1981 "The Book of Ruth: Dialogue and Narrative—The Function and Integration of the Two Modes in an Ancient Hebrew Story." Ph.D. dissertation: Macquarie University.

Sacks, Harvey, Emanuel A. Schegloff, and Gail Jefferson
1974 "A Simplest Systematics for the Organization of Turn-Taking for Conversation." *Language* 50:696–735.

Savran, George W.
1988 *Telling and Retelling: Quotation in Biblical Narrative.* Bloomington: Indiana University Press.

Schiffrin, Deborah
1987 *Discourse Markers*. Cambridge: Cambridge University Press.

Segal, M. H.
1927 *A Grammar of Mishnaic Hebrew*. Oxford: Clarendon.

Seow, C. L.
1987 *A Grammar for Biblical Hebrew*. Nashville: Abingdon.

Silverstein, Michael
1985 "The Culture of Language in Chinookan Narrative Texts; or, On Saying That . . . in Chinook." Pp. 132–71 in *Grammar Inside and Outside the Clause*. Ed. Johanna Nichols and Anthony C. Woodbury. Cambridge: Cambridge University Press.

Sternberg, Meir
1982a "Proteus in Quotation-Land: Mimesis and the Forms of Reported Discourse." *Poetics Today* 3:107–56.
1982b "Language, World, and Perspective in Biblical Art: Free Indirect Discourse and Modes of Covert Penetration." *Hasifrut* 32:88–131 [in Hebrew].
1985 *The Poetics of Biblical Narrative*. Bloomington: Indiana University Press.

Tannen, Deborah
1987 "Repetition in Conversation: Toward a Poetics of Talk." *Language* 63:574–605.

Trubetzkoy, N.
1958 *Grundzüge der Phonologie*. Reprinted. Göttingen: Vandenhoeck & Ruprecht.

Voloshinov, V. N.
1973 "Indirect Discourse, Direct Discourse, and Their Modifications." Pp. 125–59 in *Marxism and the Philosophy of Language*. Trans. Ladislav Martejika and I. R. Titanik. New York: Seminar.

Waltke, Bruce K., and M. O'Connor
1990 *An Introduction to Biblical Hebrew Syntax*. Winona Lake, IN: Eisenbrauns.

Williams, Ronald J.
1976 *Hebrew Syntax: An Outline*. 2nd ed. Toronto: University of Toronto Press.

7

PROGRESS AND COHESION IN BIBLICAL HEBREW NARRATIVE: THE FUNCTION OF kĕ–/bĕ– + THE INFINITIVE CONSTRUCT

Douglas M. Gropp

ABSTRACT

While the usual characterization of *kĕ-/bĕ-* + infinitive construct as temporal and subordinative constructions is true enough as far as it goes, the function of these constructions can only be more adequately described within a model of syntax that goes above or beyond the "sentence." In this light the primary function of these constructions, at least in the position before the main verb, is backreference to provide cohesion within a narrative. A variety of backreferencing techniques exploiting these infinitive constructions are classified. These two infinitival constructions may also introduce a grammatical pause in a narrative, breaking up the flow of the narrative into larger units.

Important formal and functional differences between *kĕ-* + infinitive construct and *bĕ-* + infinitive construct are often overlooked: Certain verbs only occur in one or the other construction because of their lexical aspect. *kĕ-* + the infinitive construct is almost always clause-initial, whereas *bĕ-* + the infinitive construct has a freer privilege of distribution. *kĕ-* + infinitive construct usually backreferences to the immediately preceding narrative event. *bĕ-* + infinitive construct may be used to resume a narrative strand that has been interrupted or to introduce a flashback or merely to provide a new setting. Of the two constructions, *kĕ-* + infinitive construct is more consistently followed by a *waw*-consecutive. The main verb to follow *kĕ-* + infinitive construct is nearly always in a relation of contingent succession to the latter, whereas the relation between *bĕ-* + infinitive construct to the main verb to follow is more diversified, often involving temporal overlap. From a derivational point of view *kĕ-* + infinitive construct could be considered an infinitival transformation of a narrative clause, while *bĕ-* + infinitive construct might be viewed as derived from a circumstantial clause.

1. Orientation

While the usual characterization of *kĕ-/bĕ-* + infinitive construct as temporal and subordinate constructions is true enough as far as it goes, the function of these constructions can only be more adequately described within a model of syntax that goes above or "beyond the sentence."[1] In this light the primary function of these constructions, at least when they precede the main clause, is backreference or recapitulation, to provide cohesion within a narrative.

According to Robert E. Longacre (1978), two parameters define the narrative genre of discourse: contingent temporal succession and agent orientation. Progress in narrative is achieved primarily by a succession of events. But often a succession of temporal horizons and/or geographical locations (as in a journey narrative) is superimposed on the main-event line. Nevertheless, progress in narrative can never be achieved at the expense of cohesion. Particularly because narrative is agent oriented, the hearer/reader must be able to track the participants through a narrative by such devices as anaphoric reference.

Similarly, the hearer/reader must be able to follow the main-event line through a narrative. In some languages specialized conjunctions aid in keeping the succession of events straight, but they are not enough. No language can continue to layer on new information endlessly without some backreference to older information.

In many languages adverbial clauses (or constructions) function as devices for backreferencing. For example: "John did X. Having done X, he did Y." The various strategies of backreferencing are language specific.

In some languages (e.g., of the Philippines and Papua New Guinea) every successive sentence in a narrative backreferences to the previous sentence (Longacre, 1968; 1972). English, on the other hand, backreferences more discriminatingly. In some languages backreferencing devices link sentences together within a larger unit, which we may loosely label a "paragraph,"[2] whereas in other languages similar devices link successive "paragraphs" together within a larger narrative.

---

[1]Cf. Pike: 129–35. For two more recent introductions to "discourse analysis" or "text linguistics," cf. de Beaugrande and Dressler; Brown and Yule.

[2]While using the term "paragraph" throughout this paper, I do not mean to commit myself at this point to the existence of a coded syntactic unit or to a clearly defined level of syntactic analysis beyond the clause. I would affirm only that the syntactic analysis of Classical Biblical Hebrew prose must reach beyond the level

Classical Biblical Hebrew prose carries the main-event line forward by means of a specialized verb form, *wayyiqtōl.* the *waw*-consecutive, which I will call the "narrative" tense. The narrative tense adds new information to the main-event line almost by definition.[3] I will call *narrative* clauses those which have a narrative tense-form as their nucleus. In general, narrative clauses chain together into clumps (which we may designate "paragraphs"). Cohesion through backreference is commonly achieved by *kĕ-/bĕ-* + the infinitive construct.[4] In Classical Biblical Hebrew narrative such backreferencing techniques appear not to link "sentences" within a "paragraph," but successive "paragraphs" within a larger narrative.[5]

Because of the enormity of the data, I will examine only the uses of the infinitive construct with *kĕ-* and *bĕ-*. Further, for easier access to the data, I am examining only those instances introduced by *wayhî.*[6] This sample, I think, is roughly representative for such constructions in the position before the main clause

The present study will first survey the variety of backreferencing techniques employing *kĕ-/bĕ-* + infinitive construct and then try to pinpoint the differences in function between *bĕ-* + infinitive construct and *kĕ-* + infinitive construct. Finally, I will suggest a way to understand the differences between *kĕ-* + infinitive construct and *bĕ-* + in-

---

of the clause to embrace inter-clausal relations, and even beyond the domain of inter-clausal relations to assess various devices for articulating larger segments of a text. Even "sentence" in Biblical Hebrew prose is extremely problematic if understood as a clearly definable syntactical level above the clause. I will avoid it, with reference to Biblical Hebrew.

[3]In my understanding of the general (i.e., paradigmatic) meaning of finite verb forms in Classical Biblical Hebrew, the narrative tense shares with the perfect tense (in opposition to the imperfect and converted perfect) the feature + ANTERIOR. But in opposition to the perfect the narrative tense has the additional feature + SEQUENCE. Cf. further, Gropp (1991).

[4]Or by *ʾaḥărê* + infinitive construct, *middê* + infinitive construct, *kaʾăšer* + perfect (before the main clause), *kî* + perfect (before the main clause), and others.

[5]The phrase (*wayhî*) *ʾaḥărê haddĕbārîm hāʾēlleh* links even larger units together (Gen 22:1, 20; 39:7; 40:1; 48:1; Josh 24:29; 1 Kgs 17:17; 21:1). Compare also *ʾaḥărê-kēn* (which occurs 14 times with *wayhî*).

[6]The *wayhî* seems to reinforce the "paragraph"-initial status of backreferencers. If one factors out the use of *wayhî* as a copula with predicate nouns and adjectives, in the large majority of remaining cases it appears to serve to introduce a new "paragraph," normally with a new time horizon, new set of participants and circumstances, and/or a backreference to previous events.

finitive construct in the context of the syntax of Classical Biblical Hebrew more broadly.

2. Survey of Backreferencing Techniques

Let the following contrived[7] narrative segment serve to illustrate the most common types of backreferencing techniques in Classical Biblical Hebrew narrative.

Sentence	Old Information	New Information
1		God told Abraham to go to Canaan.
2	And when Abraham heard these words,	he set off on his journey.
3	And having arrived,	he pitched his tent.
4	After he pitched it,	he ate some supper.
5	When he had finished eating,	he fell asleep.

The first base of sentence 4 recapitulates the action of the second base of 3 by simple repetition of the verb. This is a widespread form of backreference throughout the world. Closely related to backreference by lexical repetition is backreference by synonymy. For example, sentence 4 could have begun, "After he set it up. . . ." Sentence 2 illustrates backreference by means of the verb "to hear." Closely related is backreference by means of "seeing." The verb "to finish" also commonly serves as a summary backreference to a previous action. This method of backreferencing is often reinforced with lexical repetition as in sentence 5, with the verb "to eat." The backreferencing device in the first base of sentence 3 is a little more elusive. It exploits what Longacre calls an "expectancy chain," i.e., a stock sequence of events, the second of which is almost predictable given the preceding event.

> Around the world we find expectancy chains which involve actions which customarily occur in sequence such as: leave (some place) . . . go . . . arrive; search . . . find; waste away . . . die; fall down . . . smash; take out a corpse . . . bury; eat a quantity of food . . . be satisfied; get . . . bring/take . . . dispose of. Some expectancy chains are especially

[7]One would, of course, never find such a cluster of backreferencing devices together in a Biblical Hebrew narrative. I noted earlier that backreferencing techniques in Biblical Hebrew narrative tend not to link "sentences within" paragraphs as in this English illustration, but "paragraphs" within larger narratives. I have only contrived this example for purposes of illustration.

> conditioned by the particular culture area in which they are found. Thus from Papua New Guinea, Bougainville, New Hebrides, and aboriginal Australia, we find such expectancy chains as the following: see a pig . . . catch/kill it; kill . . . cook . . . eat; dig . . . cook . . . eat (referring to sweet potatoes); go with hooks . . . tie hooks . . . catch fish . . . bring fish . . . eat; cook in leaves . . . put into container . . . bring to the canoe . . . come down; tie up . . . put into canoe; climb a log . . . see at a distance. Expectancy chains may involve succession with different actors (reciprocity) as in the following: shoot . . . die; hit . . . die; call . . . answer; give (to someone) . . . appreciate; give (to someone) . . . cook (it) (Longacre, 1983:135–36).

An established inventory of expectancy chains specific to Biblical Hebrew would be helpful, especially in clarifying certain instances of back reference.[8]

Remarkably, out of 93 instances of *kĕ-* + infinitive construct (introduced by *wayhî*),[9] 65 of the constructions, or 70%, use the verbs *šāmaʿ* (34 times), *rāʾâ* (17 times), and *killâ* (14 times). This distribution supports my view that the chief (and almost sole) function for *kĕ-* + infinitive construct, at least, is backreference and indicates the kinds of backreferencing devices that predominate in Biblical Hebrew narrative.

The following set of categories of backreference describes the relation between the infinitive construct and the events it recapitulates.

1. Backreference by *lexical repetition* is easier to illustrate than to explain:

Se	Old Information	New Information
1	(Gen 19:16b–17)	*wayyōṣīʾūhû wayyannīḥūhû miḥûṣ lāʿîr*
2	*wayhî kĕhôṣîʾām ʾōtām haḥûṣâ*	*wayyōʾmer . . .*
1		They brought him out and set him down outside the city.
2	When they had brought them outside,	he said . . .

[8]Nevertheless, it is really impossible to "establish" with any confidence such a broad inventory for a dead language such as Biblical Hebrew. There has been some work done on "fixed sequences" of events in Hebrew and Ugaritic in the context of the study of formulaic composition of oral and written literature (e.g., Lichtenstein). I thank Edward L. Greenstein for alerting me to this study.

[9]I do not include in the total 93 four simple time references using this construction (1 Sam 9:26; 1 Kgs 18:29; 2 Kgs 3:20; Jonah 4:8). Similarly, with respect to the 44 instances of *wayhî* + *bĕ-* + infinitive construct I do not include 1 Kgs 18:36.

1	(Josh 10:23–24)	*wayyōṣîʾû ʾēlāyw ʾet-ḥămēšet hammĕlākîm hāʾēlleh min-hammĕʿārâ*
2	*wayhî kĕhôṣîʾām ʾet-hammĕlākîm hāʾēlleh ʾel-yĕhôšūaʿ*	*wayyiqrāʾ yĕhôšuāʿ ʾel-kol–ʾîš yiśrāʾēl . . .*
1		They brought brought these five kings out to him from the cave . . .
2	When they brought out these kings to Joshua,	Joshua summoned all the men of Israel . . .
1	(1 Kgs 15:28b–29)	*wayyimlōk taḥtāyw*
2	*wayhî kĕmolkô*	*hikkâ ʾet-kol bēt yārobʿām*
1		He became king in his place.
2	As soon as he became king,	he killed all the house of Jeroboam.
1	(2 Kgs 2:8b–9)	*wayyaʿabrû šĕnêhem beḥārābâ*
2	*wayhî kĕʿobrām*	*wĕʾēlîyāhû ʾāmar ʾel-ʾĕlîšāʿ . . .*
1		The two of them crossed on dry ground.
2	When they had crossed,	Elijah said to Elisha . . .
1	(Ruth 1:19)	*wattēlaknâ štêhem ʿad-bōʾānâh bêt lāḥem*
2	*wayhî kĕbōʾānâ bêt leḥem*	*wattēhōm kol-hāʿîr ʿălêhen . . .*
1		The two of them went on until they came to Bethlehem.
2	When they came to Bethlehem,	the whole city went into an uproar because of them . . .
1	(2 Sam 4:4)	*wattānōs*
2	*wayhî bĕḥopzāh lānûs*	*wayyippōl wayyippāsēaḥ . . .*
1		She fled.
2	As she was hastening to flee,	he fell and became lame . . .
1	(2 Chr 13:15)	*wayyārîʿû ʾîš yĕhûdâ*
2	*wayhî bĕhārîaʿ ʾîš yĕhûdâ*	*wĕhāʾĕlōhîm nāgap ʾet-yārobʿām . . .*
1		The men of Judah gave the battle cry.
2	As soon as the men of Judah gave the battle cry,	God struck Jeroboam . . .

These examples backreference to the previous clause or sequence of clauses. In other cases circumstantial clauses[10] may intervene (Jer

[10]By "circumstantial clause" I mean a clause type that encodes information off the main-event line, whose form involves the following structural features: (obligatory) *wĕ-*, the constituent order of subject followed by predicate (which may be verbal or nominal—including a participial predicate), and distribution either

36:23; 2 Sam 1:2b; cf. also Gen 38:28). Larger chunks may also intervene as in 2 Chr 12:1, which backreferences to 11:17 (11: 18–23 constitutes a digression).

In some instances the infinitive construct not only recapitulates an event, but also carries it forward. This is more often the case with *bĕ-* + infinitive construct.

Se	Old Information	New Information
1	(2 Kgs 4:40)	*wayyiṣqû la᾿ănāšîm le᾿ĕkôl*
2	*wayhî kĕ᾿oklām mēhannāzîd*	*wĕhēmmâ ṣā῾āqû . . .*
1		They poured out for the men to eat.
2	When they had eaten some of the stew,	they cried out . . .
1	(Gen 35:16b–17)	*wattĕqaš bĕlidtāh*
2	*wayhî bĕhaqšōtāh bĕlidtāh*	*wattō᾿mer lāh hamyalledet . . .*
1		She had hard labor.
2	While she was in her hard labor,	the midwife said to her . . .
1	(Dan 8:2)	*wā᾿er᾿eh bĕḥāzôn*
2	*wayhî bir᾿ōtî*	*wa᾿ănî bĕšûšan habbîrâ . . .*
1		I saw in the vision;
2	and at the time that I saw,	I was in Susa the capital . . .

2. Backreference by *synonymy* is the same in principle as backreference by lexical repetition, but uses synonyms to recapitulate an earlier event.

Se	Old Information	New Information
1	(Jer 41:6)	*wayyēṣē᾿ yišmā῾ē᾿l ben-nĕtanyâ liqrā᾿tām . . .*
2	*wayhî kipgōš ᾿ōtām*	*wayyō᾿mer ᾿ălêhem . . .*
1	Ishmael son of Nethaniah went out to meet them . . .	
2	When he came upon them,	he said to them . . .
1	(2 Chr 22:7b–8)	*. . . yēhû᾿ ben-nimšî ᾿ăšer mĕšāḥô YHWH lĕhakrît ᾿et-bêt ᾿aḥ᾿āb*
2	*wayhî kĕhiššāpēṭ yēhû᾿ ῾im-bêt ᾿aḥ᾿āb*	*wayyimṣā᾿ ᾿et-śārê yĕhûdâ . . .*
1		. . . Jehu son of Nimshi, whom the Lord had anointed to cut off the house of Ahab.

preceding or following the clause it gives support to. Further formal qualifications need to be made to further specify the circumstantial clause, but that would take us beyond our immediate purpose here.

2	When Jehu had executed judgment on the house of Ahab,	he came upon the princes of Judah . . .[11]
1	(Josh 10:10b–11)[12]	*wayyirdĕpēm derek maʿălēh bêt-hôrōn wayyakkēm ʿad-ʿăzēqâ wĕʿad-maqqēdâ*
2	*wayhî bĕnûsām mippĕnê yiśrāʾēl hēm bĕmôrad bêt hôrōn*	*waYHWH hišlîk ʿălêhem ʾăbānîm gĕdōlôt . . .*
1		They pursued them by way of the ascent of Beth-horon and struck them down as far as Azekah and Makkedah.
2	As they fled from Israel, while they were on the slope going down from Beth-horon,	the Lord threw down on them large stones . . .

Backreference by synonymy is less common than backreference by lexical repetition.[13]

A subcategory of backreference by synonymy might be called *speech attribution.* In these instances the infinitive construct is derived from a verb of speaking (*kĕdabbĕrāh* in Gen 39:10; *kĕdabbēr* in Judg 2:4; *kĕhazkîrô* in 1 Sam 4:18; *kĕhinnābĕʾî* in Ezek 11:13) that is not identical with the original quotation formula.

3. Most commonly the narrator uses the verb *šāmaʿ*, "hear" to recapitulate speech and events. Joseph E. Grimes (1975:320) calls verbs like "see," "hear," and "know" (over against "believe," for example) "referentially transparent" because they "reflect a state of affairs on which both speaker and hearer can agree." The referential transparency of these verbs makes them appropriate for backreferencing purposes.

We can divide the backreferencing techniques using the verb *šāmaʿ* into two basic categories: *hearing-speech* and *hearing-occurrence,* depending on whether the information recapitulated is speech or other events. This breakdown highlights the relatively high proportion of dialogue to third person narrative in Biblical Hebrew narrative.

[11]Cf 2 Kgs 10:11–14.

[12]In Josh 10:10b–11 *rādap* and *nûs* are in a reciprocal relation. But it is also possible to classify this infinitival phrase as backreference by expectancy chain. See below.

[13]Num 17:7 may be another example.

Hearing-Speech

Se	Old Information	New Information
1	(1 Kgs 5:16–21)	*wayyišlaḥ šĕlōmōh ʾel-ḥîrām lēʾmōr* + QUOTE
2	*wayhî kišmōaʿ ḥîrām ʾet-dibrê šĕlōmōh*	*wayyiśmaḥ mĕʾōd wayyōʾmer . . .*
1		Solomon sent word to Hiram saying . . .
2	When Hiram heard the words of Solomon,	he rejoiced greatly and said . . .
1	(1 Kgs 20:11–12)	*wayyaʿan melek yiśrāʾēl wayyōʾmer dabbĕrû ʾal-yithallēl ḥōgēr kimpattēh*
2	*wayhî kišmōaʿ ʾet-haddābār hazzeh wĕhûʾ šōteh hûʾ wĕhammĕlākîm bassukkôt*[14]	*wayyōʾmer ʾel-ʿabādāyw . . .*
1		The king of Israel answered and said, "Tell him: 'Let not him that girds on his armor brag like one who unbuckles it.'"
2	When he heard this message, as he and the kings were drinking in the pavilions,	he said to his servants . . .

Hearing-Occurrence

Se	Old Information	New Information
1	(Gen 39:14b–15)	*wāʾeqrāʾ bĕqôl gādôl*
2	*wayhî kĕšomʿô kî hărîmōtî qôlî wāʾeqraʾ*	*wayyaʿăzōb bigdô ʾeṣlî wayyānos . . .*
1		I cried out with a loud voice;
2	and when he heard me raise my voice and cry,	he left his garment by me and fled . . .
1	(2 Kgs 5:7–8)	*wayyiqraʿ bĕgādāyw wayyōʾmer* + QUOTE
2	*wayhî kišmōaʿ ʾĕlîšāʿ ʾîs-hāʾĕlōhîm kî-qāraʿ melek yiśrāʾēl ʾet-bĕgādāyw*	*wayyišlaḥ ʾel-hammelek lēʾmōr . . .*
1		He tore his clothes and said . . .
2	When Elisha the man of God heard that the king of Israel had torn his clothes,	he sent word to the king, saying . . .

[14]The string *wĕhûʾ . . . bassukkôt* is a circumstantial clause. While it communicates new information off the main-event line, it does not further the main-event line. Other examples of backreference by hearing-speech are 1 Kgs 13:4; 21:16, 27; 2 Kgs 6:30; Neh 1:4.

1	(2 Chr 10:1–2)	*wayyēlek rĕḥobʿām šĕkemâ kî šĕkem bāʾû kol-yiśrāʾēl lĕhamlîk ʾōtô*
2	*wayhî kišmōaʿ yārobʿām ben nĕbaṭ wĕhûʾ bĕmiṣrayim ʾăšer bāraḥ mipnê šĕlōmōh hammelek*	*wayyāšob yarobʿām mimmiṣrāyim*[15]
1		Rehoboam went to Shechem, because all Israel had come to Shechem to make him king.
2	When Jeroboam son of Nebat heard about it, being in Egypt at the time, where he had fled from the presence of Solomon the king,	Jeroboam returned from Egypt.

Note that in both varieties of backreference by hearing, the backreference may be reinforced. A noun or noun phrase may reinforce the backreference as direct object of the infinitive (e.g., Gen 29:13; Deut 5:23; Josh 6:20; Gen 24:30; 1 Kgs 15:21). Or an objective *kî* clause can accomplish the reinforcement as in two of the examples in the chart above (Gen 39:15; 2 Kgs 5:8).[16] Further, the direct object or object clause may contain lexical repetition, as in 2 Kings 5:8 above.[17] Frequently, though, the object is deleted as in 2 Chr 10:2 above.

Some instances of backreference by hearing seem to require an intermediate category, which we may call *hearing-report*. In these cases the narrator explicitly tells us of verbal communication between participants, but we are not let in on the direct discourse. Examples are: Gen 24:30; 29:13; 1 Kgs 21:15; 2 Kgs 19:1; Isa 37:1; Jer 36:16. We can also include in this category instances in which something is read without the disclosure of what is read, such as in 2 Kgs 22:11; Neh 13:3; 2 Chr 34:19.

[15]The treatment of this instance would be different if we were analyzing the Hebrew text underlying the Greek version. Cf. also the parallel passage in 1 Kgs 12:1–3 and the very different LXX version there.

[16]Cf. also Josh 10:1; 1 Kgs 12:20; 21:15, 16. In Josh 5:1 the infinitive takes as its object a clause introduced by *ʾēt ʾăšer*.

[17]Cf. also Josh 5:1; 1 Kgs 14:6; 21:15, 16.

Hearing-Report

Se	Old Information	New Information
1	(Gen 29:12b–13)	*wattāroṣ wattaggēd lĕʾābîhā*
2	*wayhî kišmōaʿ lābān ʾet-šēmaʿ yaʿăqōb ben-ʾăḥōtô*	*wayyāroṣ liqrāʾtô . . .*
1		She ran and told her father.
2	When Laban heard the news about Jacob, his sister's son,	he ran to meet him . . .
1	(2 Kgs 22:10b–11)	*wayyiqrāʾēhû šāpān lipnê hammelek*
2	*wayhî kišmōaʿ hammelek ʾet-dibrê sēper hattôrâ*	*wayyiqraʿ ʾet-bĕgādāyw . . .*
1		Shaphan read it before the king.
2	When the king heard the words of the book of the law,	he tore his clothes . . .

In summary, then, I found backreference by hearing-occurrence 16 times, by hearing-speech 7 times, and by hearing-report 9 times.

4. Backreference by *seeing-occurrence* is similar in principle to backreference by hearing. The verb *rāʾâ*, "see," is also referentially transparent. It, too, often takes a direct object or object clause that makes the backreference specific. Sometimes lexical repetition enhances the backreference (e.g., Gen 39:13; Esth 5:2), but more often the backreference by seeing-occurrence is not reinforced by lexical repetition.

Seeing-Occurrence

Se	Old Information	New Information
1	(Josh 8:13b–14)	*wayyālen (!) yĕhôšūaʿ ballaylâ hahûʾ bĕtôk hāʿēmeq*
2	*wayhî kirʾôt melek-hāʿay*	*waymahărû wayyaškîmû wayyēṣĕʾû . . .*
1		Joshua spent that night in the valley.
2	When the king of Ai saw this,	he hurried and went out early . . .
1	(Gen 39:12b–14)	*wayyaʿăzōb bigdô bĕyādāh wayyānos wayyēṣēʾ haḥûṣâ*
2	*wayhî kirʾôtāh kî ʿāzab bigdô bĕyādāh wayyānos haḥûṣâ*	*wattiqrāʾ lĕʾanšê bêtāh wattōʾmer . . .*
1		He left his garment in her hand and fled and went outside.

2	When she saw that he had left his garment in her hand and had fled outside,	she called to the men of her house and said . . .

Not all the occurrences of *kirʾôt* are best classified as backreference by *seeing-occurrence.* The constructions in 1 Kgs 18:17; 2 Kgs 4:25; 12:11, for example, are probably better described as backreferences by some form of *expectancy chain.* The distinction may not be a sharp one. See further below.

5. Perhaps, the primary function of the verb *killâ,* "finish," is backreference. As with the verb *šāmaʿ,* backreference using the verb *killâ* divides naturally into *finishing-speech,* which recapitulates speech, and *finishing-action,* which recapitulates events (all of which have an agent).

Finishing-speech often summarizes lengthy quotations. For example, 1 Sam 24:17 backreferences in this way to 24:10–16; 1 Kgs 8:54 backreferences to 8:23–53; Jer 26:8 backreferences to 26:2–6. Jer 43:1 is exceptionally elaborate: *wayhî kĕkallôt yirmĕyāhû lĕdabbēr ʾel-kol-hāʿām ʾet-kol-dibrê YHWH ʾĕlōhêhem ʾăšer šĕlāḥô YHWH ʾĕlōhêhem ʾălêhem ʾēt kol-haddĕbārîm hāʾēlleh,* "When Jeremiah finished telling all the people the words of the Lord their God, which the Lord had commissioned him to tell them. . . ." It backreferences to the whole section 42:9–22.

Because the verb *killâ* always takes a complementary infinitive, lexical repetition (or synonymy as in Josh 8:24 below) may reinforce the finishing-action backreferencing technique if the infinitive reinforces an earlier verb. In fact, this is more often the case than not.[18] Here are a few examples:

Finishing-Action

Se	Old Information	New Information
1	(1 Sam 13:9b–10)	*wayyaʿal hāʿōlâ*
2	*wayhî kĕkallōtô lĕhaʿălôt hāʿōlâ*	*wĕhinnēh šĕmûʾēl bāʾ . . .*
1		He offered the burnt offering.
2	As soon as he finished offering the burnt offering,	Samuel arrived . . .
1	(Josh 8:22, 24)	*wayyakkû ʾōtām ʿad-biltî hišʾîr-lô śārîd ûpālîṭ . . .*

[18]Cf. Deut 31:24; Josh 10:20; 1 Sam 13:10; and 2 Kgs 10:25 with Josh 8:24 and 1 Kgs 9:1.

2	*wayhî kĕkallôt yiśrāʾēl lahărōg ʾet-kol-yōšĕbê hāʿay baśśādeh . . .*	*wayyāšūbû kol-yiśrāʾēl hāʿay . . .*
1		They struck them down until no one survived or escaped.
2	When Israel finished killing all the inhabitants of Ai in the field . . .,	all Israel turned back to Ai . . .

Backreference by finishing-speech occurs 8 times, and by finishing-action 6 times (introduced by *wayhî*).

6. Backreference by *expectancy chain* is a subtler device. Which verbs tend to occur together in these expectancy chains is a matter of degree and also a matter in which we can only make outsiders' guesses. In general, the stronger the bond between two events in sequence, that is, the more predictable the event represented by the infinitive construct, given the occurrence of the first event, the greater will be the backreferencing potential of the infinitive construct. Conversely, the weaker the bond between the two events, the less the backreferencing potential.

In constructions introduced by *wayhî*, the verb *bāʾ*, "come," occurs 15 times with the infinitive construct governed by either *bĕ-* (7 times) or *kĕ-* (8 times). This verb is a good candidate to pattern as the second link of an expectancy chain. We might expect verbs like *wayyēlek*, "he went," *wayyišlaḥ*, "he sent," *wayyiqqaḥ*, "he took," *wayyēṣēʾ*, "he went out," *wayyissaʿ*, "he set out," to serve as the first verb in the sequence. In fact, *kĕbōʾ* or a similar construction appears in as many as 8 of the texts examined in which I suspect backreference by expectancy chain. Following is a display of backreference by the verb *bāʾ* patterning as the second element in apparently stock expectancy chains.[19] The verbs involved in the expectancy chain are underlined.

Backreference by Expectancy Chain

Se	Old Information	New Information
1	(1 Sam 4:4–5)	*wayyišlah hāʿām šīlōh wayyiśʾû miššām ʾet ʾărôn bĕrît-YHWH ṣĕbāʾôt . . .*

[19]It is impossible to be sure but *bĕbôʾāh* in Josh 15:18 (= Judg 1:14) may be a case of backreference by expectancy chain to *wayyitten-lô ʾet-ʿaksâ bittô lĕʾiššâ*, "he gave him Achsah his daughter as wife" (15:17b) if we presume that it exhibits a common pattern: a man gives a wife to someone and she comes to her husband for the first time.

2	*wayhî kĕbôʾ ʾărôn bĕrît-YHWH ʾel-hammaḥăneh*	*wayyārîʿû kol-yiśrāʾēl tĕrûʿâ gĕdôlâ*
1		The people *sent* to Shiloh and *brought* from there the ark of the covenant of the Lord of Hosts . . .
2	When the ark of the covenant of the Lord *came* into the camp,	all Israel gave a great shout.
1	(1 Sam 5:10)	*wayšallĕḥû ʾet-ʾărôn hāʾĕlōhîm ʿeqrôn*
2	*wayhî kĕbôʾ ʾărôn hāʾĕlōhîm ʿeqrôn*	*wayyizʿăqû hāʿeqrōnîm . . .*
1		They *sent* the ark of God to Ekron.
2	When the ark of God *came* to Ekron,	the Ekronites cried out . . .
1	(2 Kgs 6:19b–20)	*wayyōlek ʾōtām šōmĕrônâ*
2	*wayhî kĕbōʾām šōmĕrôn*	*wayyōʾmer ʾĕlîšāʿ . . .*
1		He *led* them to Samaria.
2	When they *came* to Samaria,	Elisha said . . .
1	(2 Kgs 10:6–7)	*wayyiktōb ʾălêhem sēper šēnît lēʾmōr . . .*
2	*wayhî kĕbōʾ hassēper ʾălêhem*	*wayyiqḥû ʾet-bĕnê hammelek wayyišḥăṭû šibʿîm ʾîš*
1		He *wrote* them a second letter, saying . . .
2	When the letter *came* to them,	they took the king's sons and slaughtered them, seventy persons.
1	(1 Sam 29:11–30:1)	*wayyaškēm dāwīd hûʾ waʾănāšāyw lāleket babbōqer lāšûb ʾel-ʾereṣ pĕlištîm . . .*
2	*wayhî bĕbōʾ dāwīd waʾănāšāyw ṣiqlag bayyôm haššĕlîšî*	*waʿămālēqî pāšĕṭû ʾel-negeb wĕʾel-ṣiqlag wayyakkû ʾet-ṣiqlag*
1		David got up, along with his men *to start off* early in the morning *to return* to the land of the Philistines . . .
2	When David and his men *came* to Ziklag on the third day,	The Amalekites had carried out raids on the Negeb and on Ziklag, and had attacked Ziklag.

Other seemingly stock sequences of events exploited for purposes of backreference are:

"was pouring . . . became filled" (2 Kgs 4:5b–6)
"gave spirit . . . spirit rested upon" (Num 11:25)
"went to meet . . . saw" (1 Kgs 18:16b–17)

"besieged a city . . . city was captured" (1 Kgs 16:17b–18).[20]

Very frequently in such cases of backreference by expectancy chain there is a reversal of roles associated with the events in sequence. In 13 of the 17 instances of infinitive constructs that I have classified loosely as exemplifying backreference by expectancy chain, a direct or indirect object of the first action becomes the subject of the infinitive. This process can be observed in the chart above. Note that in 1 Sam 4:4–5 and 5:10 *ʾărôn*, "ark," starts out as the direct object of the first verb in the expectancy chain and ends up as the subject of the infinitives. In 2 Kgs 10:6–7 *sēper* undergoes a similar shift. Sometimes the infinitive construct signals a shift in vantage point (as in Judg 3:27; 1 Kgs 4:25; Jer 41:13). In this light it is significant that the verb √*bwʾ*, "come," often implies motion toward the speaker. The infinitives *kirʾôt*, "when (he) saw," and *kišmōaʿ*, "when (he) heard," also often signal a shift in vantage point. The tendency to shift participant roles and vantage point in backreference by expectancy chain and in backreference by seeing and hearing supports the notion that backreference by the use of *kĕ-/bĕ-* + infinitive construct generally correlates with a "paragraph" break in Classical Biblical Hebrew prose.

Other combinations of events appear too weakly related to be called expectancy chains. The infinitive may record the result of a previous action, as in Gen 34:24–25: *wayyimmōlû kol-zākār . . . bihyôtām kōʾăbîm*, "every male was circumcised . . . when they were in pain.[21] Or the infinitive may record a reaction to a previous action, as in Gen 39:17b–18: *bāʾ ʾēlay hāʿebed hāʿibrî . . . lĕṣaḥeq bî . . . kahărîmî qôlî wāʾeqrāʾ*, "the Hebrew servant came to me . . . to make sport of me . . . when I raised my voice and cried out . . . (as any respectable woman would!).

7. We might call another technique backreference by *execution of proposal*. This technique takes advantage of a set of relations Longacre (1983:43–76) calls "repartee." The repartee calculus analyzes the relations between initiating and resolving utterances in dialogue by means of a set of binary relations such as question/answer, proposal/response, and remark/evaluation. Proposal/execution is a subvariety of proposal/response, in which a proposal (command, exhortation, or

---

[20]This last instance combines backreference by expectancy chain with seeing-occurrence.

[21]Other examples: Judg 13:20; 2 Kgs 12:11 = 2 Chr 24:11.

suggestion) finds a nonverbal resolution in a reported interaction.[22] In Biblical Hebrew narrative proposals in direct discourse are more often than not followed by a nonverbal response.

The bond between the proposal and its execution has affinities to the bond between events linked together in an expectancy chain. In fact, we could easily treat the technique of backreference by execution of proposal as a subvariety of backreference by expectancy chain. In Biblical Hebrew narrative when someone gives a command, especially the Lord, it is normally carried out. But I list it separately because of its own peculiar semantics and its use of direct discourse rather than actions reported by narrative verb forms. In the following examples I have underlined each proposal and its corresponding execution.

Execution of Proposal

Se	Old Information	New Information
1	(Exod 16:9–10)	*wayyōʾmer mōšeh ʾel-ʾahărōn ʾ<u>ĕmōr</u> ʾel-kol-ʿădat bĕnê yiśrāʾēl qirbû lipnê YHWH . . .*
2	*wayhî <u>kĕdabbēr</u> ʾahărōn ʾel-kol-ʿădat bĕnê yiśrāʾēl*	*wayyipnû ʾel-hammidbār wĕhinnēh kĕbôd YHWH nirʾâ beʿānān . . .*
1		Moses said to Aaron, "*Say* to the whole congregation of the Israelites, 'Come near before the Lord . . .'"
2	When Aaron *spoke* to the whole congregation of the Israelites,	they turned to face the desert and saw the glory of the Lord appearing in the cloud . . .
1	(Jer 41:6b–7)	*wayyōʾmer ʾălêhem <u>bōʾû</u> ʾel-gĕdalyāhû ben-ʾăḥîqām*
2	*wayhî <u>kĕbōʾām</u> ʾel-tôk hāʿîr*	*wayyišḥāṭēm yišmāʿʾēl ben-nĕtanyâ . . .*
1		He said to them, "*Come* to Gedaliah son of Ahikam.

[22]The sequence designated here as proposal/execution is basically the same as that called "command/fulfillment" or "command/performance" by others. However, the term "proposal" has broader application than "command." Cf. for example, the application of this term to the cohortative in Gen 4:8 cited in the category of backreference by execution of proposal.

2	When they *came* into the midst of the city,	Ishmael son of Nethaniah slaughtered them . . .
1	(Ezek 9:7–8)	*wayyōʾmer ʾălêhem ṭammĕʾû ʾet-habbayit ûmalʾû ʾet-haḥăṣērôt ḥălālîm ṣēʾû wĕyāṣĕʾû wĕhikkû bāʿîr*
2	*wayhî kĕhakkôtām*[23] *wĕnišʾār*[24] *ʾānî*	*wāʾeppĕlâ ʿal-pānay wāʾezʿaq . . .*
1		He said to them, "Defile the house, and fill the courts with the slain. Go out! So they they began to go out and kill in the city.
2	When they killed, and I was left alone,	I fell on my face and cried out . . .
1	(Gen 4:8)	*wayyōʾmer qayin ʾel-hebel ʾāḥîw* <*nēlĕkâ haśśādeh*>[25]
2	*wayhî bihyôtām baśśādeh*	*wayyāqom qayin ʾel-hebel ʾāḥîw wayyahargēhû*
1		Cain said to Abel his brother, <"Let's go to the field!">
2	While they were in the field,	Cain rose up against Abel his brother and killed him.
1	(1 Sam 16:5–6)[26]	*wayyōʾmer . . . hitqaddĕšû ûbāʾtem ʾittî bazzābaḥ . . .*
2	*wayhî bĕbôʾām*	*wayyarʾ ʾet-ĕlîʾāb wayyōʾmer . . .*
1		He said, ". . . consecrate yourselves and then come with me to the sacrifice . . ."
2	As they were coming,	he saw Eliab and said . . .

Note that the execution frequently copies a lexical item in the proposal, as in Jer 41:6b–7; Ezek 9:7–8; 1 Sam 16:5–6.[27]

---

[23]LXX ἐν τῷ κόπτειν αὐτούς "while they were killing" may reflect the reading *bĕhakkôtām,* which would be syntactically easier.

[24]MT וְנֵאשְׁאַר is a *forma mixta.* We, in fact, would have expected a circumstantial clause of the shape *waʾănî nišʾār.* LXX lacks the problematic clause. MT presents other syntactic problems if not emended.

[25]Whether or not we adopt—as I think we should—this restoration supported by many MSS, the Samaritan Pentateuch, LXX, and other versions, the underlying structure is the same.

[26]Alternatively, *bĕbôʾām* in 1 Sam 16:6 may be classified as a backreference by expectancy chain in relation to the immediately preceding narrative clause: *wayyiqrāʾ lāhem lazzābaḥ,* "he invited them to the sacrifice."

[27]The two infinitive constructs in Esth 2:8 recaptitulate by the execution-proposal technique proposals made in 1:19–22 and 2:1–4. But these infinitives also function as resumptive of the main-event line after the digression in 2:5–7, which

We may summarize this survey by providing an outline of the backreferencing techniques we have found in Biblical Hebrew employing *wayhî kĕ-/bĕ-* + infinitive construct:

1. Lexical repetition
2. Synonymy
   a. Synonymy of actions
   b. Synonymy of speech attribution
3. Hearing
   a. Hearing-occurrence
   b. Hearing-speech
4. Seeing-occurrence
5. Finishing
   a. Finishing-action
   b. Finishing-speech
6. Expectancy chain
7. Execution of proposal

8. Residue

Not all infinitive constructs governed by *kĕ-/bĕ-* backreference. An infinitive construct governed by *kĕ-/bĕ-* preceding the main clause that does not function clearly as a backreference, still maintains a certain function. It introduces a grammatical pause between "paragraphs" and also produces an effect that Grimes (1978:126–29) calls "staging." By "infinitivalizing" one event in a succession of events on a main-event line, the narrator puts it into lower relief than the following event represented by the next main verb.

In several cases the infinitive construct is resumptive. For example, 2 Kgs 3:5 echoes 1:1; 2 Chr 12:1 echoes 11:17; Exod 13:17 picks up on 12:31–42, 51; 2 Sam 11:16 resumes the plot from 11:1–2. Ezek 10:6 may be the same command as in 10:2.[28] Resumption is another way the infinitive construct achieves cohesion in narrative. When the infinitive construct is used resumptively, more often than not it is governed by *bĕ-*.

In 1 Kgs 11:14 and 18:4 the infinitive construct with *bĕ-* signals flashback. The flashbacks digress to contribute information supportive

---

introduces Esther and Mordecai as new participants essential to the resumed main-event line. *ûkĕbô*ʾ in Josh 3:15 records the fulfillment of an earlier prediction (cf. 3:8). The binary relationship between prediction (or promise) and fulfillment resembles the repartee structure of proposal and execution.

[28] 1 Sam 18:6 echoes 1 Sam 17:57, which in turn picks up from 1 Sam 17:54. 1 Sam 17:55–18:6aα inclusive of the infinitival phrase is lacking in Vaticanus which I presume to reflect the primitive Hebrew text here.

to the main-event line. In several other instances, the infinitive construct with *bĕ-* merely introduces a new setting (as an Josh 5:13; 1 Kgs 25:2; Jer 35:11).[29]

A few instances can be categorized as backreference by expectancy chain in the loosest sense. We may paraphrase the gist of 1 Kgs 22:31 as: "The chariot commanders were to look around for Ahab." The event narrated in the following infinitive construction flows naturally from this: "When the chariot commanders thought they saw Ahab." On the principle "what goes in must come out," Gen 35:18 and 1 Sam 25:37 can also be regarded as examples of backreference by expectancy chain in a loose sense. We may appeal to staging considerations to account for *binsōaʿ hāʿām*, "when (the people) set out," in Josh 3:14 or *bĕṣēʾt hakkōhănîm*, "when the priests came out," in 1 Kgs 8:10. The same might be said for Exod 34:29, but there the infinitive construct seems to carry on a trajectory of locations:

> *wayyaškēm mōšeh babbōqer wayyaʿal ʾel-har sînay* . . . (34:4) *wayhî-šām ʿim-YHWH ʾarbāʿîm yôm wĕʾarbāʿîm laylâ* . . . (34:28) *wayhî bĕredet mōšeh mēhar sînay* . . . (34:29).
>
> Moses rose early in the morning and went up Mount Sinai . . . (34:4), and he was there with the Lord forty days and forty nights . . . (34:28). When Moses came down from Mount Sinai . . . (34:29).

Gen 19:29 and 2 Kgs 2:1 may instance a striking phenomenon in Biblical Hebrew narrative. These clauses or clause-sequences can be described as "abstracts" or "epitomies" of a whole narrative. They give the kernel of a whole story in one clause or clause-sequence. These clauses or clause-sequences may be introduced by a narrative form (Gen 23:20) or a perfect (Gen 22:1), as well as by *bĕ-* + infinitive construct. They may come at the beginning of a narrative and almost look like a title sentence (as in 2 Kgs 2:1). They may come at the end of a narrative and summarize the whole narrative or make explicit its main issue. Or they may come at the climax of the narrative and contribute to the marking of the peak with a kind of rhetorical underscoring.[30] Gen 19:29 comes at the peak of the narrative of the

[29]Cf. also Gen 11:2.

[30]For an inventory of common devices for marking the peak of a narrative, see Longacre, 1983:25–38.

destruction of Sodom and Gomorrah and epitomizes that narrative (Gen 18–19) as a whole.[31]

The only apparent motivation for *bĕ-* + infinitive construct in Dan 8:15 and 2 Chr 25:16 is the authors' desire to break up a vision and a speech, respectively, into segments. That is, *bĕ-* + infinitive construct creates a grammatical pause. In Dan 8:15, the infinitive resonates with the identical construction in 8:2.

It is difficult to capture the force of *beʿzōr hāʾĕlōhîm* in 1 Chr 15:26 in terms of the preceding categories. It would seem to supply an attending circumstance, "with God helping," in contrast to God's earlier opposition, or is intended to be causal, "because God helped. . . . It would be difficult to classify this construction as temporal. On the other hand, it would be easy to turn this infinitive construction into a circumstantial clause with little change in narrative function: *wĕhāʾĕlōhîm ʿōzēr ʾet-halwīyîm nōśĕʾê ʾărôn bĕrît-YHWH,* "with God helping the Levites who were carrying the ark of the covenant of the Lord."

3. Differences between kĕ- + Infinitive Construct and bĕ- + Infinitive Construct

As I have already hinted, *kĕ-* + infintive construct functions more consistently as a backreferencing device. Though the narrator may use *bĕ-* + infinitive construct to achieve backreference, this construction is used for other specialized functions as well, such as resumption of a narrative after interruption, flashback to provide information supportive to the main narrative line, or merely the establishment of a new setting. In a number of cases *bĕ-* + infinitive construct (but not *kĕ-* + infinitive construct) narrates an action which globally characterizes a whole episode, in the compass of which a particular event narrated by the following main verb takes place (e.g., Exod 13:17).[32]

---

[31]Though I hasten to add that it was the Priestly writer who penned this verse as rhetorical underscoring to the Yahwist's narrative in front of him. Besides marking peak, the Priestly writer formulated the destruction in his own theological terms, and, perhaps, set up echoes with other key episodes in his work. Recognition of the role of Gen 19:29 within Genesis 18–19 as a whole provides empirical support for the thesis of Frank M. Cross (293–325) that the Priestly stratum is largely the result of redaction rather than an independent narrative source.

[32]Cf. also, e.g., Gen 35:7, 9a, where *bĕ-* + infinitive construct is subordinated to a main verb that precedes.

The construction *wayhî kĕ-/bĕ-* + infinitive construct syntactically requires a main verb to follow. We must examine more closely the next main verb to follow the infinitive. The analytical decision as to which following verb form constitutes the main verb involves semantic intuition, though intuition of the simplest kind. To which verb is the infinitive construct subordinated? That is generally an easy question to answer.

By far the most regular finite verb form to serve as the first main verb following *kĕ-/bĕ-* + infinitive construct is the narrative form. Of the 93 examples of *wayhî kĕ-* + infinitive construct, 73 of them, or 78%, are followed by the narrative tense. The narrative form clearly predominates also after *wayhî bĕ-* + infinitive construct, though a little less consistently—29 out of 44 examples (66%). The perfect in clause-initial position serves as first main verb after *kĕ-* + infinitive construct 7 times, but never after *bĕ-* + infinitive construct. It is difficult to tell whether this is significant or not. It seems that in such instances of verb-initial asyndetic clauses the perfect like the narrative form normally narrates events on the main-event line.

A *wĕhinnēh* clause[33] fills the place of the first main verb after *wayhî kĕ-* + infinitive construct in two clear cases (1 Sam 13:10; 2 Sam 13:36), and once after *wayhî bĕ-* + infinitive construct (Dan 8:15). The verb of 2 Sam 13:36 is a perfect, and the verb of 1 Sam 13:10 may also be one. These cases would suggest that *wĕhinnēh* clauses may expound the first of a series of events on the main-event line.

The perfect with subject in clause-initial position may serve as the first main verb following *kĕ-/bĕ-* + infinitive construct. In all, there are 13 instances of this clause type. Generally, this clause type does not, I think, encode an event on the main-event line. It may encode simultaneity with either the preceding infinitive (Josh 10:11;[34] 1 Sam 23:6;[35]

[33]The *wĕhinnēh* clause has structural affinities to the circumstantial clause, but nevertheless seems to be raised to the level of the main-event line.

[34]Josh 10:11 as a whole might be viewed as a digression. The infinitival phrase is followed by an asyndetic circumstantial clause bound in a construction with a following syndetic circumstantial clause. Such combinations of asyndetic circumstantial clause and syndetic circumstantial clause belong to a regular pattern in which two (or three) events or circumstances may be depicted as simultaneous (while not necessarily being mutually conditioned). For other examples of this construction, which I will call the "compound circumstantial clause," cf. Gen 19:23–24; 29:9; 38:25; 44:3, 4; [possibly 50:24]; Exod 10:14b; [possibly, Num 11:33]; Josh 10:11; Judg 15:14; 18:3; 19:11; 1 Sam 9:5, 11, 27; 20:36b; 2 Sam 20:8; 1 Kgs 14:17b; 2 Kgs 4:5b; 9:25b (slightly emended); 10:12b–13a; Job 1:14b. Compare

2 Chr 13:15) or with the following narrative verb (1 Sam 18:1). Other examples of this clause type either are not on the main-event line at all or do not begin a chain of narrative clauses on the main-event line (Josh 6:8;[36] 2 Sam 17:27;[37] 2 Kgs 2:9[38]).

Apparent exceptions are 2 Kgs 4:40 and 1 Kgs 22:32 (= 2 Chr 18:31). In 2 Kgs 4:40 Vaticanus and Alexandrinus read καὶ ἰδοὺ ἀνεβόησαν where the MT has *wĕhēmmâ ṣāʿāqû*. In the context, *hēmmâ* is redundant. It does not seem to contrast with anything. The word *hinnēh* would fit the emotional tone of the passage as well as resolve the difficulty of the subject-predicate sequence on what appears to be the main-event line. It is possible that the particle *hēmmâ* is not the third person independent pronoun but a deictic particle equivalent to *hinnēh* in force.[39] If this solution be adopted, then perhaps the same option should be appealed to for *wĕhēmmâ ʾāmĕrû* (where the putative third person plural independent pronoun is also redundant) in 1 Kgs 22:32 (= 2 Chr 18:31), which directly follows the infinitive *kirʾōt*.[40] Other-

---

also instances of the same structure but with the whole introduced by *wayhî*: Gen 15:12a, 17a; Josh 2:5a; 1 Sam 7:10; 2 Sam 13:20; 1 Kgs 20:39; 2 Kgs 6:26; 19:37 (= Isa 37:38); 20:4 (≠ Isa 38:4); 1 Chr 15:29 (cf. 2 Sam 6:16). There are further variations on the same basic structure, but we need not exhaust the subject here. Cf. Driver (§§ 165–69).

[35]1 Sam 23:6 also constitutes a digression. The main clause to follow is evidently an asyndetic circumstantial clause where we might have expected a syndetic circumstantial clause. In any case I believe the writer could have structured the same segment alternatively as, *wayhî ʾebyātār ben ʾăḥîmelek bāraḥ ʾel-dāwīd qĕʿîlâ wĕʾēpôd yārad bĕyādô*, "when Abiathar son of Ahimelech fled to David at Keilah, he brought down an ephod with him," i.e., as a compound circumstantial clause introduced by *wayhî*.

[36]LXX lacks the infinitival phrase.

[37]I would have expected *bĕbôʾ*! Alternatively, *wayyipqōd*, "(David) mustered . . .," in 18:1 could be taken as the first main verb following the infinitive in 17:27.

[38]LXX has ἐν τῷ διαβῆναι αὐτούς for MT *kĕʿobrām*.

[39]Compare the Ugaritic deictic/conditional particle *hm*. Cf. in Biblical Hebrew, possibly Deut 33:17 (so Cross and Freedman, 207, n. 62); Moran (1961:61). For a comparable use of *šumma* in the El-Amarna letters, cf. Moran (1953). De Moor (201–2) claims that Ugaritic *hm* never means "behold," and Greenstein (161, n. 29) questions virtually every alleged instance of it in Biblical Hebrew. Even if it were true that Ugaritic *hm* never has deictic force, the presumption would not be changed that this deictic function lay at the origin of its conditional use (cf. Speiser) and may have survived with this more primitive function in various Northwest Semitic contexts.

[40]LXX has καὶ αὐτοὶ εἶπον. Note that *hinnēh* comes before the verb *ʾāmartî* in 2 Kgs 5:11. This putative deictic particle *hmh* may have been changed to *hinnēh* wherever

wise, it is difficult to explain the subject-predicate constituent order in these two passages.[41]

A perfect with a preposed *wĕlōʾ* occurs as the first main verb after the infinitive construct in Gen 39:10 and Esth 3:4 in past iterative contexts, and in Exod 13:17. In Exod 13:17 it is better to see the infinitive construct as modifying the two parallel clauses together:

wayhî bĕšallaḥ parʿōh ʾet-hāʿām
wĕlōʾ-nāḥām ʾĕlōhîm derek ʾereṣ pĕlištîm . . .
wayyāsseb ʾĕlōhîm ʾet-hāʿām derek hammidbar yam-sûp

When Pharaoh let the people go,
God did not lead them by way of the land of the Philistines . . .
But God made the people go around by way of the desert of the Red Sea.

After *kĕ-* + infinitive construct, there is one instance of a clause-initial imperfect (Jer 36:23), and one of a converted perfect (2 Chr 24:11). Both come in past iterative contexts. A verbless circumstantial clause follows *birʾotî* in Dan 8:2. There are several cases of anacoluthon initiated by *bĕ-* + infinitive construct (1 Sam 25:2; 30:1; 2 Chr 5:11). In two cases *bĕ-* + infinitive construct combines with *kĕ-* + infinitive construct (Josh 3:14–15; 1 Kgs 16:11; cf. also 2 Chr 5:11–13) In these instances, we should regard the main verb as more closely tied to the second infinitive construct governed by *kĕ-*.

The most significant difference between *kĕ-* + infinitive construct and *bĕ-* + infinitive construct emerges when we examine the temporal relations encoded between the event narrated by the infinitive and the event narrated by the first main verb to follow. Longacre (1983:95–100) provides us with a "statement calculus" for describing the "deep structure" of temporal relations between clauses. The basic distinction is between temporal succession and temporal overlap. Or we might state the opposition as that between succession and nonsuc-

---

it could not be reinterpreted by scribes as the 3 m. pl. independent pronoun.

[41]Note, however, that LXX has ἐν τῷ ἐσθίειν αὐτούς for preceding infinitive in 2 Kgs 4:40, where the MT has *kĕʾoklām*, evidently reflecting the reading *bĕʾoklām*. If this reading be original, then, the syntactic string *wayhî bĕʾoklām mēhannāzîd wĕhēmmâ ṣāʿāqû* could be regarded as being in a derivative relation to the compound circumstantial clause of the shape (*wahyî*) *hēmmâ ʾōkĕlîm mēhannāzîd wĕhēmmâ ṣāʿāqû*, both translatable as "while they were eating from the stew, they cried out." In that case, *hēmmâ* would be the 3 m. pl. independent pronoun as required by the structure of the circumstantial clause. This analysis, however, would not work in 1 Kgs 22:32 (= 2 Chr 18:31).

cession. Four varieties of temporal overlap are conceivable: continuous–continuous, continuous–punctiliar, punctiliar–continuous, and punctiliar–punctiliar. Of these, punctiliar-continuous is of no significance to our study. There are also four varieties of temporal succession: span–span, event–span, span–event, and event–event. In the case of temporal succession, these four subdivisions are of negligible importance for analyzing the relationship between the infinitive construct and the first main verb to follow.

The largely intuitive judgment as to whether the relationship between the event narrated by the infinitive construct and the event narrated by the following verb form is one of succession or nonsuccession is difficult to make in many cases. Temporal succession should be defined more precisely as contingent temporal succession. This makes the analysis a little easier. For example, in 1 Kgs 5:21 we read: *kišmōaʿ ḥîrām ʾet-dibrê šĕlōmōh wayyiśmaḥ mĕʾōd* . . ., "When Hiram heard the words of Solomon he rejoiced greatly. . . ." We cannot necessarily say that any time has elapsed between Hiram's hearing and his rejoicing. Nevertheless, his rejoicing follows contingently upon his hearing. Further, two totally unrelated events, though in strict chronological succession, are not here regarded as successive.

The infinitive construct governed by *kĕ-* is very consistent in implying that the following main verb will be in contingent succession to the event narrated by the infinitive. Out of 93 examples, 88 fairly clearly involve some form of succession. Of the remaining five examples, one involves textual difficulties (1 Kgs 12:2). The other four (2 Kgs 2:9; Ezek 9:8; 11:13; 2 Chr 22:8) appear to involve temporal overlap of the continuous-punctiliar variety. 2 Kgs 2:9, *kĕʿobrām* . . . *wĕʾēlîyāhû ʾāmar ʾel-ʾĕlîšāʿ*, "when they crossed . . . Elijah said to Elisha," could conceivably be handled as contingent succession, but with less probability.[42] Note the durative aspect of the clause that follows the dialogue between Elijah and Elisha (2:11a), *wayhî hēmmâ hōlĕkîm hālôk wĕdabbēr* . . ., "as they continued walking and talking. . . ." In the two passages in Ezekiel, the Greek translates the infinitives *kĕhakkōtām* and *kĕhinnābĕʾî*[43] by present infinitives ἐν τῷ κόπτειν αὐτούς and ἐν τῷ προφητεύειν με where we might have expected aorists. Did the translator follow the obvious sense of the passage, or could he have

[42]Some MSS read *bĕʿobrām*, a reading supported also by LXX and some MSS of *Tg. Neb.*

[43]A few MSS have *bĕhinnābĕʾî*, which is also supported by a few MSS of *Tg. Neb.*

been following a *Vorlage* which had *bĕ-* instead of *kĕ-*? In view of the fairly rigid consistency in the kinds of temporal relations signaled by *kĕ-* + infinitive construct, and the possibility for confusion between *bet* and *kap* in the Hasmonean and Herodian periods, we may justifiably suspect the text of this handful of examples which seem to imply temporal overlap.

When we come to *bĕ-* + infinitive construct, the picture is more complex because the data is more diversified. For example, in two cases *bĕ-* + infinitive construct is conjoined to *kĕ-* + infinitive construct and therefore has no main verb of its own (Josh 3:14; 1 Kgs 16:11; cf. 2 Chr 5:11). There are several possible anacoluthons for which a main verb never completes the pattern (1 Sam 25:2; 30:1; 2 Chr 5:11).[44]

Clear temporal overlap occurs in 17 cases. As we might expect in narrative, the continuous-punctiliar variety predominates (11 examples). Examples of continuous-continuous overlap are Josh 10:11; Judg 13:20; 2 Sam 3:6; Dan 8:2, 15. The lone clear example of punctiliar-punctiliar overlap is 2 Chr 13:15.

The data require us to posit a further category of temporal overlap to account for passages like the following:

wayhî bĕšaḥēt ʾĕlohîm ʾet-ʿārê hakkikkār wayyizkōr ʾĕlōhîm ʾet-ʾabrāhām wayšallaḥ ʾet-lôt . . .

When God destroyed the cities of the plain, God remembered Abraham and sent forth Lot . . . (Gen 19:29).

wayhî bĕšallaḥ parʿōh ʾet-hāʿām wĕlōʾ-nāḥām ʾĕlōhîm derek ʾereṣ pĕlištîm . . .

When Pharaoh let the people go, God did not lead them by way of the desert of the Philistines (Exod 13: 17).

In these two examples, God's destroying and Pharaoh's expelling do not merely designate single actions, but globally represent whole episodes. The events recorded in the following main verbs, then, are specific aspects of those episodes. For this reason, the relation between the whole episode recalled by the infinitive construct and the following event narrated by the main verb I will call *rubric-specific.* A number of other cases of *bĕ-* + infinitive construct can best be handled as encoding a rubric-specific relationship with the following main verb (1 Kgs 11:15; 18:4; 2 Kgs 2:1; Jer 35:11; 1 Sam 23:6). I have not found any

---

[44]In 1 Kgs 8:10–11, the parallel to 2 Chr 5:11, the syntax is easier. The thread of the narrative initiated in the infinitive in 1 Sam 30:1 is picked up in 30:3 by repeating the same verb in its narrative form.

clear instances of this relation in connection with *kĕ-* + infinitive construct.

Past iterative narrative was handled somewhat inconsistently by the Hebrew narrator. Observe, for instance, the past iterative narrative in 2 Kgs 12:10–17. Here we find a motley collection of verb forms: *bĕbôʾ . . . wĕnātĕnû . . . wayhî kirʾôtām . . . wayyaʿal . . . wayyāṣūrû wayyimnû . . . wĕnātĕnû . . . wayyôṣîūhû . . . yēṣēʾ . . . yēʿāśeh . . . yittĕnūhû,* etc. Compare the parallel passage in 2 Chr 24:11–13 where the narrator expresses the iterative aspect by a different set of verb forms. Past iterative narrative, then, represents a shadowy area where *kĕ-* + infinitive construct and *bĕ-* + infinitive construct seem to be used interchangeably. All these instances of infinitive constructs in iterative contexts involve contingent succession, but this abstract sequence is repeated over and over. So we find *kĕ-* + infinitive construct in past iterative contexts four times (Gen 39:10; 2 Kgs 12:11; Jer 36:23; 2 Chr 24:11) and *bĕ-* + infinitive construct three times (Num 10:35; 1 Sam 18:6; Esth 3:4). It seems likely to me that in this past iterative context *kĕ-* + infinitive construct signals succession, but not iterativity, while *bĕ-* + infinitive construct signals iterativity, but not succession. But this is not an empirical finding.

Five separate instances of *bĕ-* + infinitive construct outside of past iterative narrative do seem clearly to exhibit contingent succession with the following main verb (Josh 15:18 = Judg 1:14; 3:27; 1 Sam 16:6; 2 Sam 1:2b; 1 Kgs 8:10). I am not willing to treat all these examples as textual problems. In three cases, LXX translates the infinitive construct by a present infinitive. In Josh 15:18 the MT reads *bĕbôʾāh,* and LXX reads ἐν τῷ εἰσπορεύεσθαι αὐτήν. In Judg 1:14, where the MT reads *bĕbôʾāh,* Alexandrinus has ἐν τῷ εἰσπορεύεσθαι αὐτήν, while Vaticanus has ἐν τῇ εἰσόδῳ αὐτῆς. In 1 Sam 16:6 the MT reads *bĕbōʾām,* while LXX has ἐν τῷ αὐτοὺς εἰσιέναι. Are the Greek translators rendering these passages literalistically, or do they understand some durative aspect in the Hebrew infinitive that I cannot find? Perhaps, the narrator may choose *bĕ-* + infinitive construct to express contingent succession of a rather close kind. Judg 3:27 seems to fit this characterization: *wayhî bĕbôʾô wayyitqaʿ baššôpār . . . ,* "just as soon as Ehud returned, he sounded the horn" (LXX^{AB}: καὶ ἐγένετο ἡνίκα ἦλθεν . . . καὶ ἐσάλπισεν . . .). In 2 Sam 1:2b and 1 Kgs 8:10, LXX translates *bĕ-* + infinitive construct with aorist verb forms. Again, are the Greek translators following a clear sense of the passage, or do they read *kĕ-* instead of *bĕ-*? The relation between the infinitive construct and the first main verb in Num 17:7 and 1 Sam 25:37 also seems to be one of succession, but the relationship between the two events in each case may not be a succession on a main event line. Instead, the event represented by the infinitive may provide a circumstantial context for the main event to follow.

So, apart from the shadowy area of past iterative narrative, while *kĕ-* + infinitive construct nearly always implies contingent temporal succession with the following main verb, *bĕ-* + infinitive construct normally (though not exclusively) involves temporal overlap of some kind. We might argue that while *kĕ-* + infinitive construct is marked for succession, *bĕ-* + infinitive construct is merely unmarked for succession, and takes on the implicature of simultaneity only through context.

Lexically, the verbs *šāmaᶜ*, "hear," and *killâ*, "finish," occur frequently with *wayhî kĕ-* + infinitive construct, but never with *wayhî bĕ-* + infinitive construct.[45] The verb *rāʾâ* is commonly governed by *kĕ-*, but virtually never does it occur with *bĕ-*.[46] Lambdin (129) explains in his introductory Hebrew grammar: "There are reasons, founded in the aspectual nature of these verbs, which govern this choice." Conversely, the verb *hāyâ* occurs with *bĕ-*, but never with *kĕ-*.[47]

It is very interesting to observe that though *kĕ-* + infinitive construct as a temporal construction virtually always precedes the main clause, *bĕ-* + infinitive construct has a freer privilege of distribution. It may either precede or follow the main verb it is subordinated to.[48]

---

[45]Apart from those infinitives introduced by *wayhî*, *bĕ-* + the infinitive construct of *šāmaᶜ* occurs in Exod 16:7; Deut 29:18; Josh 6:5K (but read Q); 1 Sam 11:6K; 2 Sam 5:24K (Q = 1 Chr 14:15); 2 Kgs 22:19 = 2 Chr 34:27; Ps 106:44; 2 Chr 20:29. Note also *bĕkallôtî* in Ezek 5:13; *bĕkallôtĕkā* in Ezek 43:23.

[46]With *wayhî* it occurs in Dan 8:2, 15. Without *wayhî*, *birʾôt* occurs in 1 Chr 21:28; 2 Chr 12:7; 15:9; 26:5 (but text?); Exod 13:17; 1 Sam 17:24; 2 Sam 24:17; 2 Kgs 23:29 (several MSS); Isa 29:23.

[47]Similarly, we find the infinitive construct of *šākan/šākēn* once with *bĕ-* (Gen 35:22). We would not expect to find it with *kĕ-*, since the verb is lexically stative.

[48]This observation takes us beyond the instances of *kĕ-/bĕ-* + infinitive construct introduced by *wayhî*. I believe that if all occurrences of the infinitive construct with *kĕ-* and *bĕ-*, in all positions, were studied, the proportion of *bĕ-* + infinitive construct would increase significantly. This in itself would be very revealing for the difference in function between the two constructions. As a matter of fact, *kĕ-* + infinitive construct not preceding the main clause is quite rare. I am aware of *kĕṣēʾt* in Exod 21 :7; *kĕbôʾ haššemeš* in Deut 16:6; 24: 13; 1 Kgs 22:36 (in contrast to initial position in Deut 23:12; Josh 8:29); *kaᶜălôt haššaḥar* in Josh 6:15; Judg 19:25Q (in contrast to *wayhî kaᶜălôt haššaḥar* in initial position in 1 Sam 9:26; and *ûkĕmô haššaḥar*

In a somewhat simplistic generative formulation we could say that the infinitival phrase headed by *kĕ-* is a transformation of a narrative clause. It is as if the narrator takes the chain of narrative verb forms which carries forward the progress of the narrative on the main-event line and twists or turns the chain back on itself in order to insure greater cohesion and periodicity in the narrative. The narrator achieves this cohesion through backreference which he builds into his narrative by "infinitivalizing" a narrative clause.[49] The event narrated by *kĕ-* + infinitive construct is still on the main-event line, but it is subordinated to the following event encoded in the next main verb.

If we also observe that *bĕ-* + infinitive construct in distinction from *kĕ-* + infinitive construct often initiates material that we would have to say is off the main-event line, then from this and the preceding observations, it is natural to suggest that there may also be a special relationship between the infinitival phrase headed by *bĕ-* and the circumstantial clause. We could consider *bĕ-* + infinitive construct to be in a derivational relationship with the circumstantial clause.[50] Note that the predicate of a circumstantial clause may be either verbal or non-verbal—hence the naturalness of *bihyôt*! I also suspect that there is a systematic relationship between the free distribution of the circum-

ʿālâ in Gen 19:15; contrast also *baʿălôt haššaḥar* after the main verb in Jonah 4:7); *kirʾōt* in Gen 33:10; *kĕkallôtô* in Exod 31:18 (between a verb and its direct object!); *kinṭôt* in Josh 8:19 (some MSS have *binṭôt*); *kĕšassaʿ* in Judg 14:6; *kĕbaššēl* in 1 Sam 2:13; *kišmōaʿ* in 1 Sam 15:22; *kirʾōtô* in 2 Kgs 6:21; *kirʾōtô* in 2 Kgs 23:29 (but several MSS have *birʾōtô*; cf. LXX ἐν τῷ ἰδεῖν αὐτόν); *kĕbôʾ* in Ezek 23:44; *kĕʾahăbat* in Hos 3:1; *kĕhāmēr* in Zech 12:10; *kiṣrōp* and *kibḥōn* in Zech 13:9; *kĕšomʿām* in Neh 8:9. *kĕšomʿām* in Gen 34:7 should be taken with the clause that follows rather than with the clause that precedes contrary to the Masoretic accentuation. Aside from the stereotyped *kĕbôʾ haššemeš* (and the similar *kaʿălôt haššaḥar*) the other instances of *kĕ-* + infinitive construct are correlative/comparative rather than temporal constructions—with the exception of Exod 31:18; Josh 8:19 (read *binṭôt*?); 1 Sam 2:13; 2 Kgs 6:21; 23:29 (read *birʾōtô*?); Neh 8:9. I doubt this is a coincidence. (*keʾĕsōp* in Isa 10:14 and *kirʾôt* in Job 10:5 are correlative/comparative, even though they precede the main verb.) A similar correlation between function and syntactic distribution can be found for clauses headed by *kaʾăšer* and *kî*. For *kî* clauses, cf. Aejmelaeus. The same correlation may hold also for the rarer construction *kĕmô* + perfect in Gen 19:15; Zech 10:8 (cf. also Prov 23:7 in which *kēn* crossreferences to the preceding *kĕmô*).

[49]It is next to impossible to prove such an inference in a dead language like Biblical Hebrew. There are plenty of examples of a sequence of narrative clauses beginning with the verbs *wayyišmaʿ* and *wayyarʾ*, where the narrator presumably would have had the option of infinitivalizing the first narrative clause.

[50]Cf. n. 10 above for a basic formal/functional definition of the circumstantial clause.

stantial clause and the free distribution of the infinitival phrase headed by *bĕ-*. Conversely, the more fixed distribution of the *kĕ-* + infinitive construct (with temporal force) preceding the main verb is consonant with the fixed distribution of the narrative clause.

Even if we work within a non-transformational framework, say that of Jakobsonian stucturalism, we should still view the relationship between *kĕ-* + infinitive construct and the narrative clause, on the one hand, and the relationship between *bĕ-* + infinitive construct and the circumstantial clause, on the other, as two systematic correspondences between coded constructions.[51] In any case, a syntactic framework that goes beyond the sentence is desiderated to describe even the most basic functioning of *kĕ-/bĕ-* + infinitive construct.

WORKS CONSULTED

Aejmelaeus, Anneli
1986 "Function and Interpretation of כי in Biblical Hebrew." *JBL* 105:193–209.

Beaugrande, Robert de, and Wolfgang U. Dressler
1981 *Introduction to Text Linguistics*. New York: Longman.

Brown, Gillian, and George Yule
1983 *Discourse Analysis*. Cambridge Textbooks in Linguistics. Cambridge: Cambridge University Press.

Cross, Frank M.
1973 *Canaanite Myth and Hebrew Epic*. Cambridge, MA: Harvard University Press.

Cross, Frank M., and David Noel Freedman
1948 "The Blessing of Moses." *JBL* 67:191–210.

Driver Samuel R.
1892 *A Treatise on the Use of the Tenses in Hebrew*. 3rd ed. Oxford: Clarendon.

Greenstein, Edward L.
1973 "Another Attestation of Initial *h* > ʾ in West Semitic." *JANES* 5:157–64.

[51]The suggestion of a systematic relationship between these temporal infinitival phrases and specific clause types presupposes a system of clause types in Classical Biblical Hebrew prose that would include as distinctive members what I have labeled the "narrative clause," the "circumstantial clause," the "*wĕhinnēh* clause," and others not defined in this paper. It would go far beyond the scope of this paper to outline in detail the system of clause types in Classical Biblical Hebrew.

Grimes, Joseph E.
1975 *The Thread of Discourse.* The Hague: Mouton.
1978 "Narrative Studies in Oral Texts." Pp. 121–32 in Wolfgang U. Dressler, ed., *Current Trends in Textlinguistics.* New York: W. de Gruyter.

Gropp, Douglas M.
1991 "The Function of the Finite Verb in Classical Biblical Hebrew." *HAR* 13:45–62.

Lambdin, Thomas O.
1971 *Introduction to Biblical Hebrew.* New York: Scribner's.

Lichtenstein, Murray H.
1968 "The Banquet Motif in Keret and in Proverbs 9." *JANES* 1:19–31.

Longacre, Robert E.
1968 *Philippine Languages: Discourse, Paragraph and Sentence Structure.* Santa Ana, CA: Summer Institute of Linguistics.
1972 *Hierarchy and Universality of Discourse Constituents in New Guinea Languages: Discussion.* Washington, DC: Georgetown University Press.
1978 "Discourse Genre." Pp. 551–54 in *Proceedings of the Twelfth International Congress of Linguistics.* Ed. Wolfgang U. Dressler and Wolfgang Meid. Innsbruck: Institut für Sprachwissenschaft der Universität Innsbruck.
1983 *The Grammar of Discourse.* New York: Plenum.

Moor, Johannes C. de
1969 "Ugaritic *hm*—Never 'Behold.'" *UF* 1:201–202.

Moran, William L.
1953 "Amarna *šumma* in Main Clauses." *JCS* 7:78–80.
1961 "The Hebrew Language in its Northwest Semitic Background." Pp. 54–72 in *The Bible and the Ancient Near East: Essays in Honor of William Foxwell Albright.* Ed. G. E. Wright. Garden City, NY: Doubleday.

Pike, Kenneth L.
1964 "Beyond the Sentence." *Journal of the Conference on College Composition and Communication* 15:129–135.

Speiser, E. A.
1947 "A Note on the Derivation of *šumma.*" *JCS* 1:321–28.

A CLASSIFIED DISCOURSE ANALYSIS BIBLIOGRAPHY

Kirk E. Lowery

ABSTRACT

This bibliography presents the reader with a doorway into the rapidly growing literature on discourse analysis. It is ordered on the basis of the classification system offered in the companion article in this volume by the same author. In addition, it attempts to provide some coverage of current work in the analysis of biblical discourse.

INTRODUCTION

Discourse analysis is nothing if not multidisciplinary. The discourse level of language touches every aspect of human experience and behavior, and so nearly every social science has an interest in discourse. Each discipline brings its own perspective, questions, goals, and methodology, creating problems for the taxonomist who would attempt to classify trends in research. Researchers are uninhibited in crossing disciplinary lines, borrowing concepts, procedures, vocabulary, and results from each other, making nice, neat categories difficult to define. Nevertheless, there are clear trends in the literature, and there are recognizable centers around which research will orbit.[1]

[1] Grateful acknowledgement is due Sarah Lind and Harold Scanlin of the United Bible Societies for permission to use Ms. Lind's excellent unpublished discourse bibliography covering the years 1983–1987.

The purpose of this bibliography is to guide the reader to the type of research that is of interest. The clearest distinctions in discourse analysis are not methodology or theory, but rather the type of question the researcher is trying to answer.

The broadest distinction the discourse researcher brings to the task is the object of research. Is the goal in studying discourse to increase our knowledge of human experience and behavior (human behavior orientation)? Or is the aim to understand the nature of language and how it functions at the text level of language (language orientation)?

I have grouped the most important entries on theory and methodology together, regardless of approach, for the user's convenience. Although "Syntax and Semantics" is not strictly discourse analysis, it is intimately related to discourse. No other level of language influences discourse so strongly. Significant works which have influenced discourse analysts are included here. The "Sociological Orientation" section is subdivided, not because this is the full spectrum of possible subtopics, but because there is an identifiable body of literature which coheres together, i.e., "Speech Act Theory," "Conversation/Dialogue Analysis," and "Pragmatics." This is true of all subclasses.

The final section, "Biblical Discourse" is subdivided into three parts: general works, Biblical Hebrew, and Biblical Greek text analysis. I have included only those works which avowedly apply some discourse theory or methodology. They are examples of how biblical researchers are using discourse analysis. I have excluded those works which have some other goal than discourse as their primary purpose. Even at this the listing is by no means comprehensive, but it will provide an entry into the literature.

Entries marked with an asterisk are especially rich with bibliography or are significant for theory and method.

CONTENTS

GENERAL

Theory and Methodology

Admoni, V. G.
1985 "Grammatika i tekat [Grammar and Text]." *Voprosy vazykoznaniya* 34:63–69.

Alcaraz Varo, Enrique
1983 "De la Linguistica Oracional a la Supraoracional." *Estudios de Linguistica* 1:7–24.

Ballmer, Thomas, ed.
1985 *Linguistic Dynamics: Discourses Procedures and Evolution.* Berlin: W. de Gruyter.

Bar-Lev, Zev
1984 "Towards Superlogic." *ITL, Review of Applied Linguistics* 64:23–55.

Beaugrande, Robert-Alain de
*1980 *Text, Discourse, and Process: Toward a Multidisciplinary Science of Texts.* Norwood, NJ: Ablex.
1984 *Text Production: Toward a Science of Composition.* Norwood, NJ: Ablex.

Beaugrande, Robert-Alain de, and Wolfgang U. Dressler
*1981 *Introduction to Text Linguistics.* London: Longman.

Benson, James D., and William S. Greaves, eds.
1985 *Systemic Perspectives on Discourse.* 2 vols. Norwood, NJ: Academic.
1987 *Functional Perspectives on Discourse.* Norwood, NJ: Ablex.

Brede, Ruediger
1985 *Aussage und Discours. Untersuchungen zur Discours-Theorie bei Michel Foucault.* Frankfurt: Lang.

Brown, Gillian, and George Yule
*1983 *Discourse Analysis.* New York: Cambridge University Press.

Cicourel, Aaron V.
1985 "Text and Discourse." *Annual Review of Anthropology* 14:159–85.

Cortès, Jacques
1985 "La Grande Traque des Valeurs Textuelles: Quelques Principes Liminaires pour Comprendre la GT." *Le Français dans le Monde* 24/192:28–40.

Coulthard, Richard Malcolm
1977 *An Introduction to Discourse Analysis.* Harlow: Longman.

Dijk, Teun A. van, ed.
*1985a *Disciplines of Discourse Analysis.* New York: Academic.
*1985b *Dimensions of Discourse Analysis.* New York: Academic.
*1985c *Discourse and Dialogue Analysis.* New York: Academic.
*1985d *Discourse Analysis in Society.* New York: Academic.

Dressler, Wolfgang U.
1972 *Einführung in die Textlinguistik.* Tübingen: Niemeyer.

Dressler, Wolfgang U., ed.
1978 *Current Trends in Textlinguistics.* Berlin: W. de Gruyter.

Eikmeyer, Hans-Jürgen
1983 "Procedural Analysis of Discourse." *Text* 3:11–37.

Ellis, Donald G., and William A. Donohue
1986 *Contemporary Issues in Language and Discourse Processes.* Norwood, NJ: Ablex.

Enkvist, Nils-Erik
1973 *Linguistic Stylistics.* The Hague: Mouton.

Facci, Paolo
1983 "Il Problema del Ritmo nel Pensiero e nel Discorso." *Nominazione* 4:no page number.

Fairclough, Norman L.
1985 "Critical and Descriptive Goals in Discourse Analysis." *JP* 9:739–63.

Fleming, Bruce E.
1984 "Rational Discourse and Poetic Communication: Methods of Linguistic, Literary, and Philosophical Analysis." *Kodikas* 7:1–2, 161–73.

Frawley, William J.
1987 "Review Article: van Dijk (ed.): Handbook of Discourse Analysis, I-IV." *Language* 63:361–97.

Fuchs, Catherine
1983 "Variations Discursives." *Languages* 18/70:15–33.

Garnham, Alan
1983 "What's Wrong with Story Grammars." *Cognition* 15:145–54.

Gibbard, Allan
1986 "An Expressivistic Theory of Normative Discourse." *Ethics* 96:472–85.

Givón, Talmy
1979 *On Understanding Grammar.* New York: Academic.

Goga, Ecaterina
1983 "Un Mundo—un Texto." *Revue Roumaine de Linguistique* 28:223–26.

Graustein, Gottfried, and Wolfgang Thiele
1986 "Zur Einführung in die Textlinguistik." *Frendsprachenunterricht* 30:125–33.

Grimaud, Michel
1983 "Mindful and Mind-free Rhetorics: Method and Metatheory in Discourse Analysis." *Semiotica* 45:115–79.

Grimes, Joseph E.
1976 *The Thread of Discourse.* The Hague: Mouton.

Guilhaumou, Jacques, and Denise Maldidier
1986 "Effets de l'Archive; l'Analyse de Discours du Coté de l'Histoire." *Langages* 21/81:43–56.

Hartmann, R. R. K.
1980 *Contrastive Textology.* Heidelberg: Groos.
1985 "Contrastive Textology—Towards a Dynamic Paradigm for Interlingual Lexical Studies?" *Language and Communication* 5:107–10.

Hasan, Ruqaiya
1985 "Discourse on Discourse: Introduction." *Occasional Papers—Applied Linguistics Association of Australia* 7:5–14.

Hatim, Basil
1984 "Discourse/Text Linguistics in the Training of Interpreters." Pp. 298–317 in *Die Theorie des Übersetzens und ihr Aufschlusswert für die Übersetzungs- und Dolmetschdidaktik.* Eds. Wolfram Wilss and Gisela Thome. Tübingen: Gunter Narr.

House, Juliane
1984 "Some Methodological Problems and Perspectives in Contrastive Discourse." *Applied Linguistics* 5:245–54.
1985 "Contrastive Discourse Analysis and Universals in Language Usage." *Papers and Studies in Contrastive Linguistics* 20:5–14.

Hwang, Shin Ja Joo
1984 "A Cognitive Basis for Discourse Grammar." *Southwest Journal of Linguistics* 7:133–56.

Hymes, Dell H.
1986 "Discourse: Scope without Depth." *IJSL* 57:49–89.

Ingberg, Alfhild
1987 *The Enigma of the Translator: A Poststructuralist Reading of Theories of Translation.* Ph.D. dissertation. Purdue University Press.

Kedar, Leah, ed.
1987 *Power Through Discourse.* Norwood, NJ: Ablex.

Khrapchenko, M. B.
1985 "Tekst i ego svoystva [Text and Its Properties]." *Voprosy Yazykoznaniya* 34:3–9.

Lamy, Marie Noëlle
1984 "In Defence of A. J. Greimas' Theory of Discourse." *JLS* 13:205–25.

Lee, Seunghwan
1984 "A Review of Story Grammars." *Ohak Yonku/Language Research* 20:275–98.

Leech, G. N., and M. H. Short
1981 *Style in Fiction: A Linguistic Introduction to English Fictional Prose.* London: Longman.

Leongómez, Jaime Bernal
1985 "En Torno a la Lingüística Textual." *Thesaurus* 40:390–95.

Levy, Elena
1987 "A Vygotskian Perspective on Discourse: From Complex to Concept." *The Quarterly Newsletter of the Laboratory of Comparative Human Cognition* 9:100–105.

Lier, Leo A. W. van
1984 "Discourse Analysis and Classroom Research: A Methodological Perspective." *IJSL* 49:111–33.

Linde, Charlotte
1983 "A Framework for Formal Models of Discourse: What Can We Model and Why." *Text* 3:271–76.

Lindemann, Bernhard F.
1983 "Text as Process: An Integrated View of a Science of Texts." *JLS* 12:5–41.

Longacre, Robert E.
*1976 *An Anatomy of Speech Notions.* Atlantic Highlands, NJ: Humanities.
*1983 *The Grammar of Discourse.* New York: Plenum.
1984 "Reshaping Linguistics: Context and Content." Pp. 79–95 in *New Directions in Linguistics and Semiotics.* Ed. J. Copeland. Amsterdam: John Benjamins.

Longacre, Robert E., ed.
1984 *Theory and Application in Processing Texts in Non-Indoeuropean Languages.* Hamburg: Helmut Buske.

Longacre, Robert E., and Stephen Levinsohn
1978 "Field Analysis of Discourse." Pp. 103–22 in *Current Trends in Textlinguistics.* Ed. Wolfgang U. Dressler. Berlin: W. de Gruyter.

Matsuhashi, Ann, and Karen Quinn
1984 "Cognitive Questions from Discourse Analysis: A Review and Study." *Written Communication* 1:307–39.

Neild, Elizabeth
1986 "Kenneth Burke, Discourse Analysis and Translation." *Meta* 31:253–57.

Oltean, Stefan
1985 "Reflections on the Concept of Text." *Revue Roumaine de Linguistique* 30:321–26.

Orlandi, Eni Pulcinelli
1986 "A Analise de Discurso: Algumas Observacoes." *Revista de Documentacao de Estudos em Linguistica Teorica e Aplicada (D.E.L.T.A.)* 2:105–26.

Orletti, Franca
1984 "Some Methodological Problems in Data Gathering for Discourse Analysis." *JP* 8:559–67.

Petöfi, János S., ed.
1987 *Text and Discourse Constitution: Empirical Aspects Theoretical Approaches.* Berlin: W. de Gruyter.

Pickering, Wilbur
1980 *A Framework for Discourse Analysis.* Dallas, TX: Summer Institute of Linguistics and University of Texas at Austin Press.

Pike, Kenneth L.
*1967 *Language in Relation to a Unified Theory of the Structure of Human Behavior.* 2nd ed. The Hague: Mouton.
1976 "Toward the Development of Tagmemic Postulates." Pp. 91-127 in *Tagmemics. Volume 2: Theoretical Discussion.* Ed. Ruth M. Brend and Kenneth L. Pike. The Hague: Mouton.
1981 *Tagmemics, Discourse, and Verbal Art.* Ann Arbor, MI: Michigan Studies in the Humanities.

1982 *Linguistic Concepts: An Introduction to Tagmemics.* Lincoln, NE: University of Nebraska Press.

Ringbom, Håkan, ed.
1975 *Style and Text. Studies Presented to Nils Erik Enkvist.* Stockholm: Språkförlaget Skriptor.

Robin, Régine
1986 "Postface; l'Analyse du Discours Entre la Linguistique et les Sciences Humaines: l'Éternal Malentendu." *Langages* 21:121–28.

Rude, Noel Emerson
1985 *Studies in Nez Perce Grammar and Discourse.* Ph.D. dissertation. University of Oregon Press.

Sherzer, Joel
1987 "A Discourse-Centered Approach to Language and Culture." *American Anthropologist* 89:295–309.

Sherzer, Joel, and Anthony C. Woodbury, eds.
1987 *Native American Discourse.* New York: Cambridge University Press.

Steele, Ross, and Terry Threadgold, eds.
1987 *Language Topics: Essays in Honour of Michael Halliday.* Amsterdam: John Benjamins.

Tchekhoff, Claude, and R. David Zorc
1983 "Discourse and Djambarrpuynu: Three Features." *Linguistics* 21:849–78.

Todd, Alexandra Dundas and Sue Fisher, eds.
1988 *Gender and Discourse: The Power of Talk.* Norwood, NJ: Ablex.

Torsueva, I. G.
1986 "Determinirovannost' Vyskazyvaniya Parametrami Teksta [Determination of the Utterance by Textual Parameters]." *Voprosy Yazykoznaniya* 35:65–74.

Syntax and Semantics

Anderson, John M.
1971 *The Grammar of Case: Towards a Localistic Theory.* Cambridge: Cambridge University Press.

Chafe, Wallace L.
1970 *Meaning and the Structure of Language.* Chicago: The University of Chicago Press.

Chomsky, Noam
1965 *Aspects of the Theory of Syntax.* Cambridge, MA: MIT Press.

Cook, Walter A.
1979 *Case Grammar: Development of the Matrix Model (1970-1978).* Washington, DC: Georgetown University Press.

Dik, Simon C.
1981 *Functional Grammar.* 3rd rev. ed. Dordrecht, Holland: Foris Publications.

Fillmore, Charles J.
*1968 "The Case for Case." Pp 1–88 in *Universals in Linguistic Theory.* Eds. Emmon Bach and Robert T. Harms. New York: Holt, Rinehart & Winston.

Givón, Talmy
1984 *Syntax: A Functional-Typological Introduction,* vol. 1. Amsterdam: John Benjamins.
1990 *Syntax: A Functional-Typological Introduction,* vol. 2. Amsterdam: John Benjamins.

Givón, Talmy, ed.
*1979 *Discourse and Syntax.* New York: Academic.

Gülich, Elisabeth, and Wolfgang Raible
1977 *Linguistische Textmodelle.* Munich: Fink.

Halliday, M. A. K.
1966 "Notes on Transitivity and Theme in English. Part 1. *JL* 3:37–81.
1967 "Notes on Transitivity and Theme in English. Part 2." *JL* 3: 199–244.
1968 "Notes on Transitivity and Theme in English. Part 3." *JL* 4:179–308.

Petöfi, János S.
1979 *Text vs. Sentence: Basic Questions of Text Linguistics.* 2 vols. Hamburg: Helmut Buske.

Stubbs, Michael
1983 *Discourse Analysis.* Chicago: University of Chicago Press.

Wirth, Jessica R., ed.
1983 *Beyond the Sentence: Discourse and Sentential Form.* Ann Arbor, MI: Karoma.

Bibliographies

Bennett, J. R.
*1986 *Bibliography of Stylistics and Related Criticism. 1967–83.* New York: Modern Language Association of America.

Dressler, Wolfgang U., and S. J. Schmidt, eds.
*1973 *Textlinguistik: Kommentierte Bibliographie.* Munich: Fink.

Jelitte, Herbert
*1973 "Kommentierte Bibliographie zur Sowjetrussischen Textlinguistik, Teil 1." *LBer* 28:83–100.
*1974 "Kommentierte Bibliographie zur Sowjetrussischen Textlinguistik, Teil 2." *LB* 29:74–92.
*1976 Sowjetrussische *Textlinguistik.* Bern: Lang.

Lind, Sarah
*1989 "A Bibliography on Discourse Analysis, 1983-1987." Unpublished. New York: United Bible Societies.

Preuss, Horst Dietrich
*1982 "Linguistik—Literaturwissenschaft—Altes Testament." *Verkundigung und Forschung* 27.2:2–28.

Verschueren, J.
*1978 *Pragmatics: An Annotated Bibliography with Particular Reference to Speech Act Theory.* Amsterdam: John Benjamins.

HUMAN BEHAVIOR ORIENTED

Psychologically Oriented

Bateson, G.
1972 *Steps to an Ecology of Mind.* New York: Ballantine.

Carroll, J. B., and Roy O. Freedle, eds.
1972 *Language Comprehension and the Acquisition of Knowledge.* Washington, DC: Winston.

Dijk, Teun A. van, and Walter Kintsch
1983 *Strategies of Discourse Comprehension.* New York: Academic.

Dijk, Teun A. van, ed.
1980 *Poetics 9: Story Comprehension.* Nos. 1-3. Amsterdam: North-Holland.

Goffman, E.
1974 *Frame Analysis: An Essay on the Organization of Experience.* New York: Harper & Row.

Joshi, A. K., B. L. Webber, and I. A. Sag, eds.
1981 *Elements of Discourse Understanding.* London: Cambridge University Press.

Just, M. A., and P. Carpenter, eds.
1977 *Cognitive Processes in Comprehension.* New York: Wiley.

Kintsch, Walter
1977 "On Comprehending Stories." Pp. 33–62 in *Cognitive Processes in Comprehension.* Eds. M. A. Just and P. Carpenter. New York: Wiley.
1979 "On Modeling Comprehension." *Educational Psychologist* 14:3–14.

Kintsch, Walter, and J. M. Keenan
1973 "Reading Rate and Retention as a Function of the Number of Propositions in the Base Structure of Sentences." *Cognitive Psychology* 5:257–74.

Kintsch, Walter, and Teun A. van Dijk
1978 "Toward a Model of Text Comprehension and Production." *Psychological Review* 85:363–94.

Laberge, D. L. and S. J. Samuels, eds.
1977 *Basic Processes in Reading: Perception and Comprehension.* Hillsdale, NJ: Erlbaum.

Labov, William, and D. Fanshel
1977 *Therapeutic Discourse: Psychotherapy as Conversation.* New York: Academic.

Meyer, B.
1975 *The Organization of Prose and its Effects on Memory.* Amsterdam: North-Holland.

Sanford, Anthony J., and Simon C. Garrod
1981 *Understanding Written Language: Explorations of Comprehension Beyond the Sentence.* Chichester, England: John Wiley & Sons.

Stein, N. L. and T. Nezworski
1978 "The Effects of Organization and Instructional Set on Story Memory." *Discourse Processes* 1:177–94.

Tulving, E.
1983 *Elements of Episodic Memory.* New York: Clarendon.

Sociologically Oriented

Fisher, Sue, and Alexandra Dundas Todd, eds.
1983 *The Social Organization of Doctor-Patient Communication.* Washington, DC: Center for Applied Linguistics.

Freedle, Roy O., ed.
1977 *Discourse Production and Comprehension.* Norwood, NJ: Ablex.
1979 *New Directions in Discourse Processing.* Norwood, NJ: Ablex.

Giglioli, P. P., ed.
1972 *Language and Social Context.* Harmondsworth: Penguin.

Gregory, M., and S. Carroll
1978 *Language and Situation: Language Varieties and Their Scoial Contexts.* London: Routledge & Kegan Paul.

Gumperz, John J.
1982 *Discourse Strategies.* Cambridge: Cambridge University Press.

Gumperz, John J., and Deborah Tannen
*1979 "Individual and Social Differences in Language Use." Pp. 305–25 in *Individual Differences in Language Ability and Language Behavior.* Eds. Charles J. Fillmore, D. Kempler, and W. Wang. New York: Academic.

Halliday, M. A. K.
*1978 *Language as Social Semiotic: the Social Interpretation of Language and Meaning.* London: Arnold.

Liebes-Plesner, T.
1984 "Rhetoric in the Service of Justice: The Sociolinguistic Construction of Stereotypes in an Israeli Trial." *Text* 4:373–92.

Ochs, Elinor
1979a "Planned and Unplanned Discourse." Pp. 51–80 in *Discourse and Syntax.* Ed. Talmy Givón. New York: Academic.
*1979b "Social Foundations of Language." Pp. 207–21 in *New Directions in Discourse Processing.* Ed. Roy O. Freedle. Norwood, NJ: Ablex.

Sinclair, J. M., and Richard Malcolm Coulthard
1975 *Towards an Analysis of Discourse: The English used by Teachers and Pupils.* London: Oxford University Press.

Tannen, Deborah, ed.
1982a *Analyzing Discourse: Text and Talk.* Washington, DC: Georgetown University Press.
1982b *Spoken and Written Language: Exploring Orality and Literacy.* Washington, DC: Georgetown University Press.

Tsuda, A.
1984 *Sales Talk in Japan and the United States: An Ethnographic Analysis of Contrastive Speech Events.* Washington, DC: Georgetown University Press.

Speech Act Theory

Austin, J. L.
1962 *How to Do Things with Words.* Cambridge, MA: Harvard University Press.

Bach, K., and R. M. Harnish
1979 *Linguistic Communication and Speech Acts.* Cambridge, MA: MIT Press.

Beauvais, Paul Jude
1986 *A Speech Act Theory of Metadiscourse.* Ph.D. dissertation. Michigan State University.

Cole, Pete, and Jerry Morgan, eds.
1975 *Speech Acts.* York: Academic.

Drogas, Elena
1985 "Relations between Discourse Units and Speech Acts." *Revue Roumaine de Linguistique* 30:421–26.

Hutchison, Chris
1984 "The Act of Narration: A Critical Survey of Some Speech-Act Theories of Narrative Discourse." *JLS* 13:3–34.

Pratt, Mary Louise
1977 *Toward a Speech Act Theory of Literary Discourse.* Bloomington: Indiana University Press.

Searle, John R.
1970 *Speech Acts: An Essay in the Philosophy of Language.* Cambridge: Cambridge University Press.
1979 *Expression and Meaning: Studies in the Theory of Speech Acts.* Cambridge: Cambridge University Press.

Verschueren, J.
1980 *On Speech Act Verbs.* Amsterdam: John Benjamins.

Conversation/Dialogue Analysis

Burton, Deirdre
1980 *Dialogue and Discourse: A Sociolinguistic Approach to Modern Drama Dialogue and Naturally Occurring Conversation.* London: Routledge & Kegan Paul.

Edmondson, W.
1981 *Spoken Discourse: A Model for Analysis.* London: Longman.

Levinson, Stephen C.
1981 "Some Pre-Observations on the Modelling of Dialogue." *Discourse Processes* 4:93–116.

Miller, Cynthia L.
1992 *Reported Speech in Biblical and Epigraphic Hebrew: A Linguistic Analysis.* Ph.D. dissertation. University of Chicago.

Sacks, Harvey, Emanuel A. Schegloff, and Gail Jefferson
1974 "A Simplest Systematics for the Organization of Turn-taking for Conversation." *Language* 50:696–735.

Schenkein, J., ed.
1978 *Studies in the Organization of Conversational Interaction.* New York: Academic.

Tannen, Deborah
1984 *Conversational Style: Analyzing Talk Among Friends.* Norwood, NJ: Ablex.

Pragmatics

Adams, Jon K.
1987 "Pragmatics and Fiction." *Pragmatics and Beyond* 6:1–79.

Berthoud, Anne Claude
1986 "Ambiguité, Malentendu et Activité Paradiscursive." *Travaux Neuchatelois de Linguistiaue (TRANEL)* 11:109–17.

Biber, Douglas
1984 "Pragmatic Roles in Central Somali Narrative Discourse." *Studies in African Linguistics* 15:1–26.

Borutti, Silvana
1984 "Pragmatics and its Discontents." *JP* 8:437–47.

Burton-Roberts, Noel
1985 "Utterance, Relevance and Problems with Text Grammar." *Australian Journal of Linguistics* 5:285–96.

Castagnino, Lucrecia Escudero
1983 "Remarques pour une Pragmatique du Discours Politique." Pp. 477–83 in *Semiotics Unfolding*. Vol. 1. Ed. Tasso Borbe. Berlin: Mouton.

Choul, Jean-Claude
1982 "Les Operateurs sémiotiques en Discours." *Recherches Sémiotiques* 2:150–65.

Cole, Peter
*1978 *Pragmatics*. New York: Academic.

Coupland, Nikolas
1983 "Patterns of Encounter Management: Further Arguments for Discourse Variables." *Language in Society* 12:459–76.

Dijk, Teun A. van, ed.
1985 *Discourse and Communication*. Berlin: W. de Gruyter.

DuBois, John W.
1987 "The Discourse Basis of Ergativity." *Language* 63:805–55.

Ensink, T.
1987 "Interpretative Processes in Discourse: The Approach by John Gumperz." *JP* 11:517–32.

Flower, Linda
1987 "Interpretive Acts: Cognition and the Construction of Discourse." *Poetics* 16:109–30.

Frake, Charles O.
1983 "Notes toward a Cultural Analysis of Formal Language." *Text* 3:299–304.

Givón, Talmy
1984 "Prolegomena to Discourse-Pragmatics." *JP* 8:489-516.

Glauner, Jeffry Lane
1984 *Written Discourse: A Model for Pragmatic Analysis*. Ph.D. dissertation. University of Kansas.

Guilhaumou, Jacques, and Denise Maldidier
1986 "De l'Énonciation à l'Évenement Discursif en Analyse de Discours." *Histoire Epistemologie Langage* 8:233–42.

Gumperz, John J.
1984 "Communicative Competence Revisited." Pp. 278–89 in *Georgetown University Round Table on Languages and Linguistics*. Washington, DC: Georgetown University Press.

Gunji, Takao
1981 *Toward a Computational Theory of Pragmatics—Discourse, Presupposition, and Implicature*. Ph.D. dissertation. Ohio State University.

Harder, Bernhard D.
1984 "Cultural Attitudes in Discourse Analysis." *Canadian Journal of Linguistics/La Revue Canadienne de Linguistique* 29:115–30.

Helbig, Gerhard
1985 "Valenz und Kommunikation." *Deutsch als Fremdsprache* 22:153–56.

Hickmann, M., ed.
1987 *Social and Functional Approaches to Language and Thought.* Orlando: Academic.

Hidi, Suzanne E., and William Baird
1986 "Interestingness—A Neglected Variable in Discourse Processing." *Cognitive Science* 10:179–94.

Jacques, Francis
1983 "La Mise en Communauté de l'Énonciation." *Langages* 18/70:47–71.

Knapp, Karlfried, Werner Enninger, and Annelie Knapp-Potthoff
1987 *Analyzing Intercultural Communication.* Berlin: W. de Gruyter.

Koch, Ingedore Grünfeld Villaça
1985 "A Situacionalidade como Elemento de Textualidade." *Letras de Hoje* 18:21–28.

Levinson, Stephen C.
1983 *Pragmatics.* London: Cambridge University Press.

Lüger, Heinz-Helmut
1983 "Some Aspects of Ritual Communication." *JP* 7:695–711.

Maranhao, Tullio
1984 "The Force of Reportive Narratives." *Papers in Linguistics* 17:235–65.

Mayordomo, Tomás Albaladejo
1983 "Componente Pragmático, Componente de Representación y Modelo Lingüistico-textual." *Lingua e Stile* 18:3–46.

Miller, Bowman H.
1987 "Terrorism and Language: A Text-Based Analysis of the German Case." *Terrorism* 9:373–407.

Net, Mariana
1985 "Metatext and Metalanguage within Poetic Discourse." *Semiotische Berichte* 9:242–51.

Nystrand, Martin, and Margaret Himley
1984 "Written Text as Social Interaction." *Theory into Practice* 23:198–207.

Ochs, Elinor, and B. B. Shieffelin, eds.
1979 *Developmental Pragmatics.* New York: Academic.

Oliva, Joseph
1983 "Rhythmicity and Iconicity in Signed Discourse." Pp. 579–85 in *Semiotics Unfolding.* Vol. 1. Ed. Tasso Borbe. Berlin: Mouton.

Posner, Roland
1983 "L'Analyse Pragmatique des Enoncés Dialogués." *Degrés* 11/33:e1–e24.

Poyatos, Fernando
1984 "The Multichannel Reality of Discourse: Language-Para-language-Kinesics and the Totality of Communicative Systems." *Language Sciences* 6:307–37.

Richards, Christine
1985 "Inferential Pragmatics and the Literary Text." *JP* 9:261–85.

Rosenblum, Karen E.
1987 "When is a Question an Accusation?" *Semiotica* 65:143–56.

Roulet, Eddy
1984 "Speech Acts, Discourse Structure and Pragmatic Connectives." *JP* 8:31–47.

Sánchez, Rosaura
1983 *Chicano Discourse: Socio-Historic Perspectives.* Rowley, MA: Newbury House.

Wright, S. and Talmy Givón
1987 "The Pragmatics of Indefinite Reference: Quantified Text-based Studies." *Studies in Language* 11:1–34.

Anthropologically Oriented

Agar, M., and J. Hobbs
1982 "Interpreting Discourse: Coherence and the Analysis of Ethnographic Interviews." *Discourse Processes* 5:1–32.

Bauman, R., and Joel Sherzer
*1974 *Explorations in the Ethnography of Speaking.* London: Cambridge University Press.

Chafe, Wallace L., ed.
*1980 *The Pear Stories: Cognitive, Cultural and Linguistic Aspects of Narrative Production.* Norwood, NJ: Ablex.

Cicourel, Aaron V.
1978 "Language and Society: Cognitive, Cultural and Linguistic Aspects of Language Use." *Sozialwissenschaftliche Annalen* 2:B25–B28.

Dijk, Teun A. van
1984 *Prejudice in Discourse.* Amsterdam: John Benjamins.

Gumperz, John J., and Dell H. Hymes, eds.
1972 *Directions in Sociolinguistics: The Ethnography of Communication.* New York: Holt, Rinehart and Winston.

Hendricks, William O.
1970 "Folklore and the Structural Analysis of Literary Texts." *Language and Style* 3:83–121.

Linde, Charlotte
1984 *The Creation of Coherence in Life Stories.* Norwood, NJ: Ablex.

Polanyi, Livia
1984 *Telling the American Story: From the Structure of Linguistic Texts to the Grammar of a Culture.* Norwood, NJ: Ablex.

Propp, Vladimir
1968 *The Morphology of the Folktale.* 2nd ed. Ed. Louis A. Wagner. Trans. Laurence Scott from Russian (1928). Austin: The University of Texas Press.

Saville-Troike, M.
1982 *The Ethnography of Communication: An Introduction.* Oxford: Blackwell.

Tannen, Deborah
1979 "What's in a Frame? Surface Evidence for Underlying Expectations." Pp 137–81 in *New Directions in Discourse Processing.* Ed. Roy O. Freedle. Norwood, NJ: Ablex.

Ulin, Robert C.
1986 "Peasant Politics and Secret Societies: The Discourse of Secrecy." *Anthropological Quarterly* 59:28–39.

Woods, Fran
1980 *The Interrelationship of Cultural Information, Linguistic Structure, and Symbolic Representatives in a Halbi Myth.* Ph.D. dissertation. University of Texas, Arlington.

Wyman, June R.
1985 "Linguistic Methods in Cultural Analysis: A Reconsideration." *Semiotics* 57:51–71.

LANGUAGE ORIENTED

Semantics of Discourse

Andor, J.
1985 *Frame Semantics and the Typology of Actions.* Amsterdam: John Benjamins.

Ariel, Mira
1985 "The Discourse Functions of Given Information." *Theoretical Linguistics* 12:99–113.

Austin, Timothy R.
1986 "(In)transitives: Some Thoughts on Ambiguity in Poetic Texts." *JLS* 15:23–38.

Ballard, D. Lee, Robert J. Conrad, and Robert E. Longacre
1971a "The Deep and Surface Grammar of Interclausal Relations." *Foundations of Language* 7:70–118.

1971b *More on the Deep and Surface Structure of Interclausal Relations.* Language Data, Asian-Pacific Series 1. Ukarumpa, Papua New Guinea: Summer Institute of Linguistics.

Blejer, Hatte Anne Rubenstein
1986 *Discourse Markers in Early Semitic, and Their Reanalyses in Subsequent Dialects.* Ph.D. dissertation. University of Texas, Austin.

Chafe, Wallace L.
1976 "Givenness, Contrastiveness, Definiteness, Subjects, Topics, and Point of View." Pp. 27–55 in *Subject and Topic.* Ed. Charles N. Li. New York: Academic.

Clancy, Patricia M.
1980 "Referential Choice in English and Japanese Narrative Discourse." Pp. 127–202 in *The Pear Stories: Cognitive, Cultural, and Linguistic Aspects of Narrative Production.* Ed. Wallace L. Chafe. Norwood, NJ: Ablex.

Daneš, František, ed.
1974 *Papers on Functional Sentence Perspective.* The Hague: Mouton.

Dijk, Teun A. van
*1972 *Some Aspects of Text Grammars.* The Hague: Mouton.
1977 *Text and Context. Explorations in the Semantics and Pragmatics of Discourse.* London: Longman.
1979 *Macrostructures: An Interdisciplinary Study of Global Structure in Discourse, Interaction and Cognition.* Hillsdale, NJ: Erlbaum.

DuBois, John W.
1980 "Beyond Definiteness: The Trace of Identity in Discourse." Pp. 203–74 in *The Pear Stories: Cognitive, Cultural, and Linguistic Aspects of Narrative Production.* Ed. Wallace L. Chafe. Norwood, NJ: Ablex.

Ehrlich, Susan
1987 "Aspect, Foregrounding and Point of View." *Text* 7:363–76.

Fagerberg, Sonja
1983 "Discourse Strategies in Pulsar: The Use of Focus." *Studies in African Linguistics* 14: 141–57.

Firbas, Jan
1966 "On Defining the Theme in Functional Sentence Perspective." Pp. 267–80 in *Travaux du Cercle linguistiques de Prague,* vol. 1. Prague: Academia.

Fronek, J.
1983 "Some Criticisms of Halliday's 'Information Systems.'" *Lingua* 60: 311–29.

Fuhrman, Ellsworth R., and Kay Oehler
1986 "Discourse Analysis and Reflexivity." *Social Studies of Science* 16: 293–307.

Fuller, Judith Wheaton
1985 *Topic and Comment in Hmong.* Ph.D. dissertation. University of Minnesota.

Gardner, Roderick
1987 "The Identification and Role of Topic in Spoken Interaction." *Semiotica* 65:129–41.

Givón, Talmy, ed.
1983 *Topic Continuity in Discourse: A Quantitative Cross-Language Study.* Amsterdam: John Benjamins.

Greenberg, Joseph H.
1985 "Some Iconic Relationships among Place, Time, and Discourse Deixis." Pp. 271–89 in *Iconicity in Syntax.* Ed. John Haiman. Amsterdam: John Benjamins.

Groenendijk, Jeroem, and Martin Stokhof, eds.
1986 *Studies in Discourse Representation Theory and the Theory of Generalized Quantifiers.* Dordrecht: Foris.

Hatav, Galia
1985 "Criteria for Identifying the Foreground." *Theoretical Linguistics* 12:265–73.

Hinds, John V.
1984 "Topic Maintenance in Japanese Narratives and Japanese Conversational Interaction." *Discourse Processes* 7:465–82.

Jones, Linda K.
1977 *Theme in English Expository Discourse.* Lakebluff, IL: Jupiter.

Jones, Larry B., and Linda K. Jones
1979a "Levels of Significant Information in Discourse." Pp. 307–16 in *Papers of the 1978 Mid-America Linguistics Conference at Oklahoma.* Eds. R. Cooley et al. Norman, OK: University of Oklahoma Press.

1979b "Multiple Levels of Information Relevance in Discourse." Pp. 3–28 in *Discourse Studies in Mesoamerican Languages,* 1. Eds. Linda K. Jones and Robert E. Longacre. Dallas: Summer Institute of Linguistics and University of Texas at Arlington Press.

Li, Charles N., ed.
1976 *Subject and Topic.* New York: Academic.

Linde, Charlotte, and William Labov
1975 "Spatial Networks as the Site for the Study of Language and Thought." *Language* 51:924–39.

Longacre, Robert E.
1981 "A Spectrum and Profile Approach to Discourse Analysis." *Text* 1:337–59.

1985 "Discourse Peak as Zone of Turbulence." Pp. 81–92 in *Beyond the Sentence.* Ed. Jessica R. Wirth. Ann Arbor, MI: Karoma.

Lumsden, Michael
1985 "The Definiteness Effect and Predication." *The Nottingham Linguistic Circular* 14:41–52.

Mann, William, and Sandra A. Thompson
1986 "Relational Propositions in Discourse." *Discourse Processes* 9:57–90.

Metzing, D., ed.
1980 *Frame Conceptions and Text Understanding.* New York: W. de Gruyter.

Neubauer, Fritz, ed.
1983 *Coherence in Natural-Language Texts.* Hamburg: Helmut Buske.

Ochs, Elinor, and Tina Bennett, eds.
1977 *Discourse Across Time and Space.* Los Angeles: Department of Linguistics, University of Southern California.

Okolo, Bertram Agodichukwu
1984 *Semantics and Pragmatics of Discourse. Narrative Fiction: An Igbo Example.* Ph.D. dissertation. University of Kansas.

Payne, Thomas Edward
1986 *Participant Coding in Yagua Discourse.* Ph.D. dissertation. University of California, Los Angeles.

Petöfi, János S., and Emel Sözer, eds.
1983 *Micro and Macro Connectivity of Texts.* Hamburg: Helmut Buske.

Rumelhart, D. E.
1975 "Notes on a Schema for Stories." Pp. 211–36 in *Representation and Understanding.* Eds. D. Bobrow and A. Collins. New York: Academic.

Schank, Roger, and Robert P. Abelson
1977 *Scripts, Plans, Goals and Understanding: An Inquiry into Human Knowledge Structures.* Hillsdale, NJ: Erlbaum.

Schiffrin, Deborah
1984 "How a Story Says What It Means and Does." *Text* 4:313–46.
1987 *Discourse Markers.* New York: Cambridge University Press.

Schwitalla, Johannes
1985 "Verbvalenz und Text." *Deutsch als Fremdsprache* 22/5:266–70.

Seuren, Peter A. M.
1985 *Discourse Semantics.* Cambridge: Cambridge University Press.

Spencer-Smith, Richard
1987 "Semantics and Discourse Representation." *Mind and Language* 2:1–26.

Stennes, Leslie H.
1987 "Foregrounding and Backgrounding of Participants in Fulfulde." *UBS Bulletin* 148/9:81–95.

Tomlin, Russell S.
1985 "Foreground-background Information and the Syntax of Subordination." *Text* 5:85–122.

Wahab, Abdul
1986 *Javanese Metaphors in Discourse Analysis.* Ph.D. dissertation. University of Illinois, Urbana-Champaign.

Ward, Gregory Louis
1986 *The Semantics and Pragmatics of Preposing.* Ph.D. dissertation. University of Pennsylvania.

Winograd, T.
1983 *Language as a Cognitive Process.* Reading, MA: Addison-Wesley.

Winter, E. O.
1982 *Towards a Contextual Grammar of English: The Clause and its Place in the Definition of the Sentence.* London: Allen & Unwin.

Coherence

Altenberg, Bengt
1984 "Causal Linking in Spoken and Written English." *Studia Linguistica* 38:20–69.

Brill, Gabriele
1983 "Zum Problem der Topikketten und ihrer Verflechtung als Mittel der Textkohärenz." *Wissenschaftliche Zeitschrift der Pädagogischen Hochschule Karl Liebknecht* 27/5:925–32.

Charolles, M.
1983 "Coherence as a Principle in the Interpretation of Discourse." *Text* 3:71–97.

Combettes, Bernard
1985 "Cohérence Textuelle et Pragmatiques." *Cahiers de l'Institut de Linguistique de Louvain* 10/4:39–59.

Conte, Maria-Elisaabeth, János S. Petöfi and Emel Sözer, eds.
1988 *Text and Discourse Connectedness: Proceedings of the Conference on Connexity and Coherence Urbino, July 16-21, 1984.* Amsterdam: John Benjamins.

Ellis, Donald G., Mark Hamilton, and Lynn Aho
1983 "Some Issues in Conversation Coherence." *Human Communication Research* 9:267–82.

Enkvist, Nils-Erik, ed.
1985 *Coherence and Composition: A Symposium.* Åbo, Finland: Research Institute of the Åbo Akademi Foundation.

Heydrich, W., Fritz Neubauer, János S. Petöfi, and Emel Sözer, eds.
1987 *Connexity and Coherence: Analysis of Text and Discourse.* Berlin: W. de Gruyter.

Khlebnikova, I. B.
1983 "K Probleme Aredstv Avyazi Mezhdu Predlozheniyami v Tekate [On the Means of Connecting Sentences in a Text]." *Inostrannye Yazyki v Shkole* 50:6–11.

Lébre-Peytard, Monique
1984 "Constructions Segmentées, Cohérence et 'Non -dit' des Discours Oraux." *Le Français dans le Monde* 24/188:105–108.

Neubauer, Fritz, ed.
1983 *Coherence in Natural-Language Texts.* Hamburg: Helmut Buske.

Newman, Jean E.
1985 "Processing Spoken Discourse: Effects of Position and Emphasis on Judgments of Textual Coherence." *Discourse Processes* 8:205–27.

Polanyi, Livia
1985 "A Theory of Discourse Structure and Discourse Coherence." *Papers from the Regional Meetings, Chicago Linguistic Society* 21:306–22.

Ross, Garry
1987 *Coherence Theory: An Interdisciplinary Study.* Ph.D. dissertation. Texas A & M University.

Schiffrin, Deborah
1985 "Conversational Coherence: The Role of 'Well.'" *Language* 61:640–67.

Tannen, Deborah, ed.
1984 *Coherence in Spoken and Written Discourse.* Norwood, NJ: Ablex.

Tomlin, Russell S., ed.
1987 *Grounding and Coherence in Discourse: Papers from a Symposium on Discourse, Cognition and Syntax held at the University of Oregon, June 1984.* Amsterdam: John Benjamins.

Vogeleer, Svetlana
1986 "Mécanismes de la Cohérence Textuele." *Le Langage et l'Homme* 21:57–63.

Werth, Paul
1984 *Focus, Coherence, and Emphasis.* London: Croon Helm.

Forms of Discourse

Bamroongraks, Cholticha
1987 *Sukhothai Thai as a Discourse-Oriented Language: Evidence from Zero Noun Phrases.* Ph.D. dissertation. University of Wisconsin, Madison.

Bashir, Elena
1986 "Beyond Split-Ergativity: Subject Marking in Wakhi." *Papers from the Regional Meetings.* Chicago Linguistic Society 22:14–35.

Beavon, Keith H.
1985 "Two Relativization Strategies in Koozime Discourse." *The Journal of West African Languages* 15:31–56.

Bresnan, Joan, and Sam Mchombo
1987 "Topic, Pronoun, and Agreement in Chichewa." *Language* 63:741–82.

Bronzwaer, M. M.
1975 "A Hypothesis concerning Deictic Time Adverbs in Narrative Structure." *JLS* 4:53–72.

Chen, Ping
1986 "Discourse and Particle Movement in English." *Studies in Language* 10:79–95.

Dijk, Teun A. van, and János S. Petöfi, eds.
1977 *Grammars and Descriptions.* Berlin: W. de Gruyter.

Dougherty, Ray
1969 "An Interpretive Theory of Pronominal Reference." *Foundations of Language* 5:488–519.
1970 "A Grammar of Coordinate Conjoined Structures [Part 1]." *Language* 46:850–98.
1971 "A Grammar of Coordinate Conjoined Structures [Part 2]." *Language* 47:298–339.

Ehrich, Veronika, and Charlotte Koster
1983 "Discourse Organization and Sentence Form: The Structure of Room Descriptions in Dutch." *Discourse Processes* 6:169–95.

Enkvist, Nils-Erik and V. Kohonen, eds.
1982 *Approaches to Word-Order: Reports on Text Linguistics.* 2nd ed. Åbo, Finland: Åbo Akademi.

Fox, Barbara A.
1985 "Word-order Inversion and Discourse Continuity in Tagalog." *Text* 5:39–54.
1986 "On the Creation of Discourse by Grammar." Pp. 97–107 in *Proceedings of the First Annual Meeting of the Pacific Linguistics Conference, October 1985, University of Oregon.* Eds. S. DeLancy and Russell S. Tomlin. Eugene, OR: Department of Linguistics, University of Oregon.

Gambhir, Vijay
1981 *Syntactic Restrictions and Discourse Functions of Word Order in Standard Hindi.* Ph.D. dissertation. University of Pennsylvania.

Gibbon, Dafydd, and Helmut Richter, eds.
1984 *Intonation, Accent, and Rhythm: Studies in Discourse Phonology.* New York: W. de Gruyter.

Grimes, Joseph E., ed.
1978 *Papers on Discourse.* Dallas: Summer Institute of Linguistics and University of Texas at Austin Press.

Haiman, John, and Sandra A. Thompson, eds.
1988 *Clause Combining in Grammar and Discourse.* Amsterdam: John Benjamins.

Hartzler, Margaret
1983 "Mode, Aspect, and Foregrounding in Sentani." *Language and Linguistics in Melanesia* 14:175–94.

Hopper, Paul J.
*1979a "Aspect and Foregrounding in Discourse." Pp. 213–42 in *Discourse and Syntax.* Ed. Talmy Givón. New York: Academic.
1979b "Some Observations on the Typology of Focus and Aspect in Narrative Language." *Studies in Language* 3:37–64.

Hopper, Paul J., and Sandra A. Thompson
*1980 "Transitivity in Grammar and Discourse." *Language* 56:251–99.

Hopper, Paul J., ed.
1982 *Tense-Aspect: Between Semantics and Pragmatics.* Amsterdam: John Benjamins.

Hwang, Shin Ja Joo
1987 *Discourse Features of Korean Narration.* Dallas: Summer Institute of Linguistics and University of Texas at Arlington Press.

Iida, Masayo, Stephen Wechaler, and Draga Zec, eds.
1987 *Working Papers in Grammatical Theory and Discourse Structure: Interactions of Morphology, Syntax, and Discourse.* Chicago: University of Chicago Press.

Inoue, Kazuko
1983 "Some Discourse Principles and Lengthy Sentences in Japanese." *Papers in Linguistics* 16:57–87.

Jones, Linda K., and Robert E. Longacre, eds.
1979 *Discourse Studies in Mesoamerican Languages.* 2 vols. Dallas: Summer Institute of Linguistics and University of Texas at Austin Press.

Klein-Andreu, Flora, ed.
1983 *Discourse: Perspectives on Syntax.* New York: Academic.

Kramsch, Claire J.
1983 "Discourse Function of Grammar Rules: Topic Construction in German." *Modern Language Journal* 67:13–22.

Kuerschner, Winfried and Ruediger Vogt, eds.
1985 *Grammatik, Semantik Textlinguistik. Akten des 19. Linguistischen Kolloquiums, Vechta 1984.* Tübingen: Niemeyer.

Levin, Nancy S., and Ellen F. Prince
1986 "Gapping and Causal Implicature." *Papers in Linguistics* 19:351–64.

Levy, Elena
1982 "Towards an Objective Definition of 'Discourse Topic.'" Pp. 295–304 in *Papers from the Eighteenth Regional Meeting. Chicago Linguistic Society.* Eds. K. Tuite et al. Chicago: Chicago Linguistic Society.

Longacre, Robert E.
1968 *Discourse, Paragraph, and Sentence Structure in Selected Philippine Languages.* 2 vols. Summer Institute of Linguistics.

1976a "Discourse." Pp. 1–44 in *Tagmemics. Volume 1. Aspects of the Field.* Eds. Ruth M. Brend and Kenneth L. Pike. The Hague: Mouton.

1976b "'Mystery' Particles and Affixes." Pp. 468-75 in *Papers Presented at the Twelfth Regional Meeting. Chicago Linguistic Society.* Eds. S. Mufwene et al. Chicago: Chicago Linguistic Society.

Longacre, Robert E., ed.
1971 *Philippine Discourse and Paragraph Studies in Memory of Betty McLachlin.* Canberra: The Australian National University Press.

Longacre, Robert E., and Fran Woods, eds.
1976-7 *Discourse Grammar: Studies in Indigenous Languages of Columbia, Panama, and Ecuador. Parts 1-3.* Dallas: Summer Institute of Linguistics and University of Texas at Austin Press.

Loriot, James, and Barbara Hollenbach
1970 "Shipibo Paragraph Structure." *Foundations of Language* 6:43–66.

Mohamed, Mohamed Abdulla
1986 *Ellipsis: A Contrastive Study of Swahili and English Discourse.* Ph.D. dissertation. Columbia University Teachers College.

Moshi, Lioba Priva
1985 *Grammatical Relations in Swahili Discourse.* Ph.D. dissertation. University of California, Los Angeles.

Motsch, Wolfgang
1983 "Satz und Sprachhandlung als Grundbegriffe der Textanalyse." *Neuphilologische Mitteilungen* 84:94–101.

Nichols, Johanna, and Anthony C. Woodbury, eds.
1985 *Grammar Inside and Outside the Clause.* New York: Cambridge University Press.

Noro, Ken
1986 "Ratio Analysis of Discourse." *Sophia Linguistica* 20:41–49.

Oestman, Jan-ola
1982 *'You Know:' A Discourse-Functional Study.* Amsterdam: John Benjamins.

Oishi, Toshio
1985 *A Description of Jasanese Final Particles in Context.* Ph.D. dissertation. University of Michigan.

Okamato, Shigeko
1985 *Ellipsis in Japanese Discourse.* Ph.D. dissertation. University of California, Berkeley.

Pike, Kenneth L., and Evelyn G. Pike
1983 *Text and Tagmeme.* Norwood, NJ: Ablex.

Polanyi, Livia, and R. J. H. Scha
1983 "The Syntax of Discourse." *Text* 3:261–70.

Sankoff, Fillian, and Penelope Brown
1976 "The Origins of Syntax in Discourse: A Case Study of Tok Pisin Relatives." *Language* 52:631–66.

Walrod, Michael R.
1979 *Discourse Grammar in Ga'dang.* Dallas: Summer Institute of Linguistics and University of Texas at Austin Press.

Wise, Mary Ruth
1971 *Identification of Participants in Discourse: A Study of Form and Meaning in Nomatsiguenga.* Santa Ana, CA: Summer Institute of Linguistics.

Yusuf, Ore
1987 *Verb Phrase Serialization in Yoruba in Discourse Perspective.* Ph.D. dissertation. University of California, Los Angeles.

Anaphora

Asher, Nicholas
1987 "A Typology for Attitude Verbs and their Anaphoric Properties." *Linguistics and Philosophy* 10:125–97.

Bosch, Peter
1983 *Agreement and Anaphora. A Study of the Roles of Pronouns in Syntax and Discourse.* London: Academic.

Colosimo, Wanda D'Addio
1984 "I Nominali Incapaulatori Anaforici: Un Aspetto della Coesione Lessicale." *Rassegna Italiana di Linguistica Applicata* 16:35–43.

Duranti, Alessandro
1984 "The Social Meaning of Subject Pronouns in Italian Conversation." *Text* 4:277–311.

Fox, Barbara A.
1984 *Discourse Structure and Anaphora in Written and Conversational English.* Ph.D. dissertation. University of California, Los Angeles.
1987 *Discourse Structure and Anaphora.* New York: Cambridge University Press.

Hinds, John V. ed.
1978 *Anaphora in Discourse.* Edmonton, Alberta: Linguistic Research.

Hinrichs, Erhard
1986 "Temporal Anaphora in Discourses of English." *Linguistics and Philosophy* 9:63–82.

Horvath, Julia, and Michael Rochemont
1986 "Pronouns in Discourse and Sentence Grammar." *Linguistic Inquiry* 17:759-66.

Kadmon, Nirit
1986 "Maximal Collections, Specificity, and Discourse Anaphora." *Papers from the Regional Meetings. Chicago Linguistic Society* 22:264–77.

Kameyama, Megumi
1985 *Zero Anaphora: The Case of Japanese.* Ph.D. dissertation. Stanford University.

King, Jeffrey
1985 *A Formal Semantics for Some Discourse Anaphora.* Ph.D. dissertation. University of California, San Diego.
1987 "Pronouns, Descriptions, and the Semantics of Discourse." *Philosophical Studies* 51:341–63.

Kuno, Susumu
1986 *Functional Syntax: Anaphora, Discourse, and Empathy.* Chicago: University of Chicago Press.

Macleod, Norman
1984 "More on Backward Anaphora and Discourse Structure." *JP* 8:321–27.

Malt, Barbara C.
1985 "The Role of Discourse Structure in Understanding Anaphora." *Journal of Memory and Language* 24:271–89.

Murphy, Gregory L.
1985 "Psychological Explanations of Deep and Surface Anaphora." *JP* 9:785–813.

Ng, En Tzu Mary
1984 *The Pronoun and the Topic of Discourse: A Functional Perspective on Text.* Ph.D. dissertation. University of Wisconsin, Madison.

Oehrle, Richard T.
1981 "Common Problems in the Theory of Anaphora and the Theory of Discourse." Pp. 509–31 in *Exigences et Perspectives de la Sémiotique.* Eds. H. Parret and H.-G. Ruprecht. Amsterdam: John Benjamins.

Payne, Thomas Edward
1987 "Pronouns in Yagua Discourse." *International Journal of American Linguistics* 53:1–20.

Prasse, Michael John
1987 *The Model of Anaphoric Reference.* Ph.D. dissertation. Ohio State University.

Root, Rebecca
1986 *The Semantics of Anaphora in Discourse.* Ph.D. dissertation. University of Texas, Austin.

Westergaard, Marit
1986 *Definite NP Anaphora: A Pragmatic Approach.* Oslo: Norwegian University Press.

Cohesion

Bear, Jean Munro
1987 *Development Segments in Discourse: The Interaction of Topic and Cohesion with Implications for Native and Non-native Speakers of English.* Ph.D. dissertation. University of Texas, Austin.

Couper-Kuhlen, Elizabeth
1983 "Intonatorische Kohäsion. Eine Makroprosodische Untersuchung." *LiLi, Zeitschrift für Literaturwissenschaft und Linguistik* 13/49:74–100.

Crewe, William J., Christine L. Wright, and Matthew Leun Wing Kwong
1985 "Connectives: On the Other Hand, Who Needs Them Though?" *Working Papers in Linguistics and Language Teaching* 8:61–75.

Do Amaral, Marisa Porto
1985 "As Categorias de Coesao Textual e a Complexidade do Texto." *Letras de Hoje* 18:29–40.

Fries, Peter H.
1986 "Language Features, Textual Cohesion and Reading." *Word* 37:13–29.

Giora, Rachel
1983 "Segmentation and Segment Cohesion: On the Thematic Organization of the Text." *Text* 3:155–81.

Gutwinski, W.
1976 *Cohesion in Literary Texts: A Study of Some Grammatical and Lexical Features of Discourse.* The Hague: Mouton.

Halliday, M. A. K., and Ruqaiya Hasan
*1976 *Cohesion in English.* London: Longman.

List, Kathleen Louise
1984 *Coherence and Cohesion: Contextualization of Oswald Ducrot's General Theory of Linguistic Semantics.* Ph.D. dissertation. University of Michigan.

Mario Tani, Rubén
1983 "Lingüistica Textual: Tres Aspectos de la Cohesión." *Lectura y Vida* 4:28–30.

Mattingly, Joseph Sherril
1987 *Lexical Cohesion and Text-as-Percept.* Ph.D. dissertation. University of Michigan.

Okurowski, Mary Ellen
1987 *Textual Cohesion in Modern Standard Chinese.* Ph.D. dissertation. Georgetown University.

Potechin, Gail Carol
1987 *The Relationship between the Cohesive Structure of Spoken and Written Language in School Age Children.* Ph.D. dissertation. University of Minnesota.

Scott, Graham
1983 "Discourse Cohesion in a Highland Language of PNG." *Language and Linguistics in Melanesia* 14:150–74.

Singh, Rejendra, and Balkrishan Kachroo
1987 "Textual Cohesion in Hindi: A Comparative Study." *ITL, Review of Applied Linguistics* 76:1–24.

Smith, Raoul N., and William J. Frawley
1983 "Conjunctive Cohesion in Four English Genres." *Text* 3:347–73.

Stoddard, Sara E.
1984 *Texture Pattern, and Cohesion in Written Texts: A Study with a Graphic Perspective.* Ph.D. dissertation. University of Nebraska.

Ter-Arakelyan, R. A.
1986 "Svyaz' Predlozheniy v Tekhate [The Connection of Sentences in a Text]." *Russkii Yazyk v Armyanskoi shkole* 1:36–41.

Types of Discourse

Adam, Jean-Michel
1985 "Quels Types de Textes?" *Le Français dans le Monde* 24/192:39–43.

Berrendonner, Alain
1986 "Discours Normatif vs. Discours Didactique." *Etudes de Linguistique Appliquée* 61:9–17.

Bruce, Bertram
1983 "Plans and Discourse." *Text* 3:253–59.

Chodchoey, Supa W.
1987 *Strategies in Thai Oral Discourse.* Ph.D. dissertation. Pennsylvania State University.

Dijk, Teun A. van, ed.
1985 *Discourse and Literature. New Approaches to the Analysis of Literary Genres.* Amsterdam: John Benjamins.

Ferguson, Charles A.
1985 "The Study of Religious Discourse." Pp. 205–13 in *Georgetown University Round Table on Languages and Linguistics.* Washington, DC: Georgetown University Press.

Ferrar, Madeleine
1984 "Linguistics and the Literary Text." *The Use of English* 35:33–39.

Grabe, William
1984 "Written Discourse Analysis." *Annual Review of Applied Linguistics* 5:101–23.

Grésillon, Almuthy, and Dominique Maingueneau
1984 "Polyphonie, Proverbe et Détournement, ou un Proverbe Peut en Cacher un Autre." *Langages* 19/73:112–25.

Hidi, Suzanne E., and Angela Hildyard
1983 "The Comparisons of Oral and Written Productions in Two Discourse Types." *Discourse Processes* 6:91–105.

Kelertas, Violeta
1984 *Oral and Written Narrative: Discourse Types and Functions.* Ph.D. dissertation. University of Wisconsin, Madison.

Larson, Mildred L.
1978 *The Functions of Reported Speech in Discourse.* Dallas: Summer Institute of Linguistics and University of Texas at Austin Press.

Smith, Edward L., Jr.
1985 "Text Type and Discourse Framework." *Text* 5:229–47.

Werlich, Egon
1983 *A Text Grammar of English.* 2nd ed. Heidelberg: Quelle & Meyer.

Discourse Structure

Abadi, Adina
1984 "Graphic Description of Discourse Structure." *Hebrew Computational Linguistics* 21:49–80.

Brody, Jill
1984 "Cleft in Tojolabal Maya: Structure and Discourse Function." *Journal of Mayan Linguistics* 4:65–90.

Cascio, Vincenzo Lo, and Co Vet, eds.
1986 *Temporal Structure in Sentence and Discourse.* Dordrecht: Foris.

Cheung, Evelyn Gaik Hoon
1986 "Structure in Written Text." *Working Papers in Linguistics and Language Teaching* 9:33–43.

Cho, Euiyon
1984 "Discourse Organization and Information Structure: Analysis of a Hortatory Text." *Ohak Yonku/Language Research* 20:453–64.

Colarusso, John
1983 "Fast vs. Slow Languages: Comments on the Structure of Discourse and the Evolution of Language." *Papiere zur Linguistik* 1(28):27–51.

Comrie, Bernard
1986 "Tense and Time Reference: From Meaning to Interpretation in the Chronological Structure of a Text." *JLS* 15:12–22.

Dijk, Teun A. van
1983 "Discourse Analysis: Its Development and Application to the Structure of News." *Journal of Communication* 33:20–43.

Frow, John
1980 "Discourse Genres." *JLS* 9:73–81.

Giarelli, Andrew L.
1984 *The Temporal Structure of Cheyenne Narrative.* Ph.D. dissertation. State University of New York, Buffalo.

Graesser, Arthur C. and Leslie F. Clark
1985 *Structures and Procedures of Implicit Knowledge.* Norwood, NJ: Ablex.

Graustein, Gottfried, and Wolfgang Thiele
1983 "Detailing Elements of Textual Structure." *Zeitschrift für Anglistik und Amerikanistik* 31:149–59.

Grimes, Joseph E.
1972 "Outlines and Overlays." *Language* 48:513–24.

Grosz, Barbara J., and Candace L. Sidner
1986 "Attention, Intentions, and the Structure of Discourse." *Computational Linguistics* 12:175–204.

Hinds, John V.
1976 *Aspects of Japanese Discourse Structure.* Tokyo: Kaitakusha.

Kadmon, Nirit, and Craige Roberts
1986 "Prosody and Scope: The Role of Discourse Structure." *Papers from the Regional Meetings, Chicago Linguistic Society* 22:16–28.

Longacre, Robert E.
1972 *Hierarchy and Universality of Discourse Constituents in New Guinea Languages.* 2 vols. Washington, DC: Georgetown University Press.

Miller, Percy Wilson
1987 *The Paragraph: Its Structure and Characteristic Features as Relates to Discourse Aim.* Ph.D. dissertation. Vanderbilt University.

Nakamura, Momoko
1985 "Structural Levels of Ethical Tales." *Sophia Linguistica* 18:144–52.

Payne, Doris L.
1987 "Information Structuring in Papago Narrative Discourse." *Language* 63:783–804.

Poythress, Vern S.
1982a "A Framework for Discourse Analysis: The Components of a Discourse, from a Tagmemic Viewpoint." *Semiotica* 38:277–98.

1982b "Hierarchy in Discourse Analysis: A Revision of Tagmemics." *Semiotica* 40:107–37.

Ryan, Marie-Laure
1987 "On the Window Structure of Narrative Discourse." *Semiotica* 64:59–81.

Scancarelli, Janine
1985 "Referential Strategies in Chamorro Narratives: Preferred Clause Structure and Ergativity." *Studies in Language* 9:335–62.

Schiffrin, Deborah
1985 "Multiple Constraints on Discourse Options: A Quantitative Analysis of Causal Sequences." *Discourse Processes* 8:281–303.

Schourup, Lawrence C.
1985 *Common Discourse Particles in English Conversation.* London: Garland.

Steward, Ann Harleman
1987 "Models of Narrative Structure." *Semiotica* 64:83–97.

Tatsuki, Masaaki
1984 "Thematic Structure of Japanese." *Doshisha Literature* 31:152–70.

Taylor, Talbot J.
1984 "Editing Rules and Understanding: The Case against Sentence-based Syntax." *Language and Communication* 4:105–27.

Tomlin, Russell S.
1986 *Basic Word Order. Functional Principles.* London: Croon Helm.

Turenius, Kimmo K.
1986 *On the Relationship Between Text and Linguistic Structure.* Ph.D. dissertation. State University of New York, Buffalo.

Ventola, Eija M.
1983 "Contrasting Schematic Structures in Service Encounters." *Applied Linguistics* 4:242–58.

Watanabe, Yasuko
1986 "Two Kinds of Ellipsis in Japanese Discourse: A Quantitative Text Study." *Studies in Language* 10:337–51.

Waugh, Linda R., and Monique Monville-Burston
1986 "Aspect and Discourse Function: The French Simple Past in Newspaper Usage." *Language* 62:846–77.

Wilka, Yorick
1983 "Text Structures and Knowledge Structures." *University of Essex Language Centre Occasional Papers* 27:311–23.

Young, Lynne
1986 "Static and Dynamic Discourse Structure: An Analysis within the Framework of Communication Linguistics." *ITL, Review of Applied Linguistics* 72:27–51.

Narrative

Abu-Ghazaleh, Ilham Nayef
1983 *Theme and the Function of the Verb in Palestinian Arabic Narrative Discourse.* Ph.D. dissertation. University of Florida.

Bartelt, H. Guillermo
1983 "Mode and Aspect Transfer in Navajo and Western Apache English Narrative Technique." *International Review of Applied Linguistics in Language Teaching* 21:105–24.

Burusphat, Somsonge
1987 *The Structure of Thai Narrative Discourse.* Ph.D. dissertation. University of Texas, Arlington.

Cazacu, B.
1984 "La Description Linguistique des Modalités Narratives." *Revue Roumaine de Linguistique* 29:9–16.

Cooreman, Anne M.
1986 *Transitivity and Discourse Continuity in Chamorro Narratives.* Ph.D. dissertation. University of Oregon, Eugene.

Crewe, William J.
1986 "Subject and Topic in Four Narratives." *Working Papers in Linguistics and Language Teaching* 9:14–32.

Crofts, Majorie
1984 "Ideofonos na Narracao Munduruku." *Serie Linguistica* 11:207–18.

Delormes, Jean
1985 "Mise en Discours et Structures Narratives ou la Dynamique du Récit." Pp. 709–19 in *Exigences et Perspectives de la Sèmiotique.* Eds. H. Parret and H.-G. Ruprecht. Amsterdam: John Benjamins.

Dyer, Michael G.
1983 "The Role of Affect in Narratives." *Cognitive Science* 7:211–42.

Fleischman, Suzanne
1985 "Discourse Functions of Tense-Aspect Oppositions in Narrative: Toward a Theory of Grounding." *Linguistics* 23:851–82.

Forster, Jannette
1983 "Use of Dialogue in a Dibabawon Narrative Discourse." *Philippine Journal of Linguistics* 14:45–60.

Francik, Ellen Palmer
1985 *Referential Choice and Focus of Attention in Narratives.* Ph.D. dissertation. Stanford University.

Franke, Wilhelm
1983 "Erzählen, Skizze zur Beschreibung einer Monologischen Kommunikationsform." *Deutsche Sprache* 3:235–49.

Geisler, Cheryl
1987 *Factors Affecting Precision: Discourse Constraints on Linguistic Choice in Narratives.* Ph.D. dissertation. Carnegie-Mellon University.

Gugelchuk, Gary Michael
1985 *A Generative-Transformational Analysis of the Plots of Limba (West Africa) Dilemma Tales.* Ph.D. dissertation. Ohio State University.

Jaggar, Philip John
1985 *Factors Governing the Morphological Coding of Referents in Hausa Narrative Discourse.* Ph.D. dissertation. University of California, Los Angeles.

Klammer, Thomas P.
1971 *The Structure of Dialogue Paragraphs in Written Dramatic and Narrative Discourse.* Ph.D. dissertation. University of Michigan, Ann Arbor.

Koontz, C.
1977 "Features of Dialogue within Narrative Discourse in Teribe." Pp. 111–32 in *Discourse Grammar: Studies in Indigenous Languages of Columbia, Panama and Ecuador, vol. 3.* Dallas: Summer Institute of Linguistics and University of Texas at Austin Press.

Margolin, Uri
1984 "Narrative and Indexicality: A Tentative Framework." *JLS* 13:181–204.

Momouchi, Yoshio
1987 "Constructing the Frame of Direct Speech in Japanese Narrative Text." *Keiryo Kokugo Gakkai/Mathematical Linguistics* 16:1–15.

Rauh, Gisa
1985 "Tempus und Erzähltheorie." *Anglistik und Englischunterricht* 27:63–81.

Reinhart, Tanya
1984 "Principles of Gestalt Perception in the Temporal Organization of Narrative Texts." *Linguistics* 22:779–809.

Thogmartin, Clyde
1984 "Tense, Aspect, and Context in French Narrative." *The French Review* 57:344–49.

Wise, Mary Ruth
1985 "Universales y Tecnicas de Organization de la Narrativa en Algunas Lenguas Vernaculas Latinoamericanas." *RLA, Revista de Linguistica Teorica y Aplicada* 23:33–43.

BIBLICAL DISCOURSE

General

Bergen, Robert Dale
1987 "Text as a Guide to Authorial Intention: An Introduction to Discourse Criticism." *JETS* 30 : 327–36.

Callow, Kathleen
1974 *Discourse Considerations in Translating the Word of God.* Grand Rapids, MI: Zondervan.

Dye, T. Wayne
1987 "Hermeneutics and the SMR Model of Communication." *OPTAT: Occasional Papers in Translation and Textlinguistics* 1:37–65.

Fuchs, Ottmar
1986 "Textanalyse im Horizont kommunikativer Praxis." *BN* 35:37–49.

Gill, Wayne
1985 "Further Considerations for the Presentation of New Material." *BT* 36:134–35.

Giroud, J.-C., and L. Panier
1987 *Sémiotique. Une pratique de Lecture et d'Analyse des Textes Bibliques.* Paris: Cerf.

Hollander, H. W., M. de Jonge, and E. W. Tuinstra
1984 "A New Type of Help for Translators." *BT* 35:341–46.

Lategan, B. C., and W. S. Vorster
1985 *Text and Reality. Aspects of Reference in Biblical Texts.* Atlanta: Scholars Press.

Longacre, Robert E.
1985 "Interpreting Biblical Stories." Pp. 169–85 in *Discourse and Literature.* Ed. Teun A. van Dijk. Amsterdam: John Benjamins.

Louw, Johannes P.
1985 "A Semiotic Approach to Discourse Analysis with Reference to Translation Theory." *BT* 36:101–107.

Newman, B. M.
1976 "Discourse Structure." Pp. 237–41 in *The Interpreter's Dictionary of the Bible. Supplementary Volume.* Nashville: Abingdon.

Olsson, Birger
*1985 "A Decade of Text-lingustic Analyses of Biblical Texts at Uppsala." *ST* 39:106–26.

Schmitz, Kenneth L.
1984 "World and Word in Theophany." *Faith and Philosophy* 1:50–70.

Schweizer, Harald
1986 *Biblische Texte Verstehen. Arbeitsbuch zur Hermeneutik un Methodik der Bibelinterpretation.* Stuttgart: Kohlhammer.

Smalley, William A.
1980 "Discourse Analysis and Bible Translation." *BT* 31:119–25.

Tuggy, Bruce Edward
1987 "Social Act Translation." *OPTAT* 1:66–82.

Wendland, Ernst R.
1987 "A Communications Model for the Measurement of Fidelity and Naturalness in Bible Translation." *OPTAT* 1:1–36.

Wolde, E. J. van
1989 "Trendy Intertextuality?" Pp. 43–49 in *Intertextuality in Biblical Writings. Essays in Honour of Bas van Iersel.* Ed. S. Draisma. Kampen, The Netherlands: Uitgeversmaatschappij J. H. Kok.

Biblical Hebrew and Texts

Andersen, Francis I.

1970 *The Hebrew Verbless Clause in the Pentateuch.* JBL Monograph Series, 14. Nashville: Abingdon.

*1974 *The Sentence in Biblical Hebrew.* The Hague: Mouton.

Baker, David W.

1979 "Division Markers and the Structure of Leviticus 1–7." Pp. 9–15 in *Studia Biblica 1978. Papers on Old Testament and Related Themes.* Ed. Elizabeth E. Livingston. Sheffield: University of Sheffield Press.

Bandstra, Barry L.

1982 *The Syntax of Particle /ky/ in Biblical Hebrew and Ugaritic.* Ph.D. dissertation. Yale University.

Bartelmus, Rüdiger

1982 *HYH. Bedeutung und Funktion eines hebräischen "Allerwortes"—zugleich ein Beitrag zur Frage des hebräischen Tempussystems.* St. Ottilien: EOS.

Boer, P. A. H. de

1974 "The Perfect with <waw> in II Samuel 6:16." Pp. 43–52 in *On Language, Culture, and Religion; in Honor of Eugene A. Nida.* Eds. M. Black and William A. Smalley. The Hague: Mouton.

Buth, Randall

1975 *An Introductory Study of the Paragraph in Biblical Hebrew Narrative.* M.A. thesis. Hebrew University, Jerusalem.

1987a "Word Order in the Aramaic of Daniel." *OPTAT* 1:78–86.

1987b *Word Order in Aramaic from the Perspectives of Functional Grammar and Discourse Analysis.* Ph.D. dissertation. University of California, Los Angeles.

Claassen, W. T.

1983 "Speaker-oriented Functions of /ki/ in Biblical Hebrew." *Journal of Northwest Semitic Languages* 11:29–46.

Clark, David J.

1985 "Discourse Structure in Zechariah 7:1–8:23." *BT* 36:328–35.

Clendenen, E. Ray

1987 "Discourse Strategies in Jeremiah 10:1–16." *JBL* 106:401–408.

Dempster, S. G.

1985 *Linguistic Features of Hebrew Narrative: A Discourse Analysis of Narrative from the Classical Period.* Ph.D. dissertation. University of Toronto.

Dorn, Louis

1978 "Chronological Sequences in Two Hebrew Narratives." *BT* 29:316–22.

Ehlich, Konrad

*1979 *Verwendungen der Deixis beim sprachlichen Handeln. Linguistisch-philologische Untersuchungen zum hebräischen deiktischen System.* 2 vols. Frankfurt am Main: Lang.

1983 "Deixis und Anapher." Pp. 79–97 in *Essays on Deixis.* Ed. Gisa Rauh. Tübingen: Gunter Narr.

Floss, J. P.

1977 "Die Wortstellung-des Konjugationsystems in Jes 24; ein Beitrag zur Forzkritik poetischer Texte im AT." Pp. 227–44 in *Festgabe für G Johannes Botterweck zum 60. Geburtstag dargebracht von seinen Schülern.* Ed. Heinz-Josef Fabry. Köln: Hanstein.

Fox, Andrew

1983 "Topic Continuity in Biblical Hebrew Narrative." Pp. 215–54 in *Topic Continuity in Discourse: A Quantitative Cross-Language Study.* Ed. Talmy Givón. Amsterdam: John Benjamins.

Givón, Talmy

1977 "The Drift from VSO to SVO in Biblical Hebrew: The Pragmatics of Tense-Aspect." Pp. 181–254 in *Mechanisms of Syntactic Change.* Ed. Charles N. Li. Austin: University of Texas Press.

Gross, Walter

1976 *Verbform + Funktion. Wayyiqtol für die Gegenwart. Ein Beitrag zur Syntax poetischer althebräischer Text.* St. Ottilien: EOS.

1980 "Syntaktische Erscheinungen am Anfang althebräischer Erzählungen: Hintergrund und Vordergrund." Pp. 131–45 in *Congress Volume, Vienna, 1980.* VTSup 32. Ed. James A. Emerton. Leiden: E. J. Brill.

Hardmeier, Christof

*1978 *Texttheorie und biblische Exegese. Zur rhetorischen Funktion der Trauermetaphorik in der Prophetie.* München: Kaiser.

*1990 *Prophetie im Streit vor dem Untergang Judas. Erzählkommunikative Studien zur Entstehungssituation der Jesaia-und Jeremiaerzählungen in II Reg 18–20 und Jer 37–40.* BZAW 187. Berlin: W. de Gruyter.

Jensen, H. J. L.

1981 "Reden, Zeit und Raum in Genesis 28:10–15. Textlinguistische und textsemiotische Exegese eines Fragments." *Linguistica Biblica* 49:54–70.

Lode, Lars

1984 "Postverbal Word Order in Biblical Hebrew: Structure and Function." *Semitics* 9:113–64.

Longacre, Robert E.

1979 "The Discourse Structure of the Flood Narrative." *JAAR* 47 (Sup. B): 89–133.

1981 "A Spectrum and Profile Approach to Discourse Analysis." *Text* 1:337–59.

*1989 *Joseph: A Story of Divine Providence. A Text Theoretical and Textlinguistic Analysis of Genesis 37 and 39–48.* Winona Lake, IN: Eisenbrauns.

Lowery, Kirk E.
1985 *Toward a Discourse Grammar of Biblical Hebrew.* Ph.D. dissertation. University of California, Los Angeles.

Muraoka, Takamitsu
1985 *Emphatic Words and Structures in Biblical Hebrew.* Jerusalem: Magnes.

Parunak, Henry Van Dyke
1978 *Structural Studies in Ezekiel.* Ph.D. dissertation. Harvard University.
1981 "Oral Typesetting: Some Uses of Biblical Structure." *Biblica* 62:153–68.
1983 "Transitional Techniques in the Bible." *JBL* 102:525–48.

Postma, Ferenc, Eep Talstra and Marc Vervenne
1983 *Exodus: Materials in Automatic Text Processing Part I. Morphological Syntactical and Literary Case Studies.* Amsterdam: VU Boekhandel/ Uitgeveerij.

Rabin, Chaim
1982 "Discourse Analysis and the Dating of Deuteronomy." Pp. 171–77 in *Interpreting the Hebrew Bible.* Eds. John A. Emerton and Stefan Reif. Cambridge: Cambridge University Press.

Rebera, Basil A.
1982 "Identifying Participants in Old Testament Dialogue." *BT* 33:201–207.
1987 "Lexical Cohesion in Ruth: A Sample." Pp. 123–49 in *Perspectives on Language and Text: Essays and Poems in Honor of Francis I. Andersen's Sixtieth Birthday, July 28, 1985.* Eds. Edgar W. Conrad and Edward G. Newing. Winona Lake, IN: Eisenbrauns.

Schicklberger, Franz
1974 "Jonatans Heldentat. Textlinguistische Beobachtungen zu 1 Sam. xiv 1-23a." *VT* 24:324–33.
1978 "Biblisch Literarkritik und linguistische Texttheorie. Bemerkungen zu einer Textsyntax von hebräischen Erzähltexten." *TZ* 32:65–81.

Schweizer, Harald
1979 "Texttheorie und Beelzebul. Die Impulse Christof Hardmeiers für die Methodik der Exegese." *BN* 9:26–44.
*1981a *Metaphorische Grammatik: Wege zur Integration von Grammatik und Textinterpretation in der Exegese.* St. Ottilien: EOS.
1981b "Prädikationen und Leerstellen im 1. Gottesknechtslied (Jes 42,1–4)." *BZ* 26:251–58.
1983 "Determination, Textdeixis—Erläutert an Genesis xviii 23–33." *VT* 31:113–18.

Segert, Stanislav

1980 "Syntax and Style in the Book of Jonah: Six Simple Approaches. Pp 121–30 in *Prophecy: Essays Presented to Georg Fohrer on his Sixty-fifth Birthday, 6 September 1980.* BZAW 150. Ed. John A. Emerton. Berlin: W. de Gruyter.

Talmon, Shemaryahu

1978 "The Presentation of Synchroneity and Simultaneity in Biblical Narrative." Pp. 9–26 in *Studies in Hebrew Narrative Art throughout the Ages.* Scripta Hierosolymitana, 27. Eds. J. Heinemann and S. Werses. Jerusalem: Magnes.

Talstra, Eep

1978 "Text Grammar and Hebrew Bible. I. Elements of a Theory" [Review of Wolfgang Schneider, *Grammatik des biblischen Hebräisch* (1974)]. *BiOr* 35:169–74.

1980 "Exegesis and the Computer Science: Questions for the Text and Questions for the Computer." *BiOr* 37:121–28.

1981 "The Use of /ken/ in Biblical Hebrew." *OTS* 21:228–39.

1982 "Text Grammar and Hebrew Bible. II. Syntax and Semantics." *BiOr* 39:26–38.

1983 *II Kön. 3: Etüden zur Textgrammatik.* Amsterdam: VU Boekhandel/ Uitgeverij.

Vanoni, Gottfried

1982 "Ist die Fügung HYY + Circumstant der Zeit im Althebräische ein Satz?" *BN* 17:73–86.

1986 "Volkssprichwort und YHWH-Ethos: Beobachtungen zu Spr 15:16." *BN* 35:73–108.

Vetter, D., and J. Walter

1971 "Sprachtheorie und Sprachvermittlung: Erwägungen zur Situation des hebräischen Sprachstudiums." *ZAW* 83:73–96.

Waard, Jan de

1979 "Vers une Identification des Participants dans le Livre de Michée." *Revue d'Histoire et de Philosophie Religieuses* 59:509–16.

Wehrle, Josef

1987 *Prophetie und Textanalyse. Die Komposition Obadja 1-21 Interpretiert auf der Basis Textlinguistischer und semiotischer Konzeptionen.* St. Ottilien: EOS.

Wiklander, Bertil

1984 *Prophecy as Literature: a Text-linguistic and Rhetorical approach to Isaiah 2–4.* Uppsala: CWK Gleerup.

Wolde, E. J. van

*1989 A *Semiotic Analysis of Genesis 2–3. A Semiotic Theory and Method of Analysis Applied to the Story of the Garden of Eden.* Assen: Van Gorcum.

Biblical Greek and Texts

Akin, Daniel L.
1987 "A Discourse Analysis of the Temptation." *OPTAT* 1:78–86.

Catchpole, David R.
1986 "Jesus and the Community of Israel: The Inaugural Discourse in Q." *BJRL* 68:296–316.

Combrink, H. J. Bernard
1983 "The Structure of the Gospel of Matthew as Narrative (Tyndale New Testament Lecture, 1982)." *Tyndale Bulletin* 34:61–90.

Cook, John Granger
1985 *A Text Linguistic Approach to the Gospel of Mark.* Ph.D. dissertation. Emory University.

Crossan, John D.
1983 "It is Written: A Structuralist Analysis of John 6." *Semeia* 26:3–21.

Du Toit, H. C.
1984 "Presuppositions of Source and Receptor." *Neotestamentica* 18:52–65.

Egger, W.
1987 *Methodenlehre zum Neuen Testament. Einführung in linguistische und historischkritische Methoden.* Freiburg: Herder.

Harm, Harry
1987 "Logic Line in Jude." *OPTAT* 1:147–72.

Hellholm, David
1986-7 "Une Construction de 'Grammaire du Texte' dans l'Évangile de Matthieu." *AES* 51–52:80–89.

Johanson, B. C.
1987 *To All the Brethren. A Text-linguistic and Rhetorical Approach to 1 Thessalonians.* Stockholm: Almqvist & Wiksell International.

Keller, Joseph
1985 "The Coherence of Religious Discourse." *Anglican Theological Review* 67:349–60.

1986 "Jesus and the Critics: A Logico-critical Analysis of the Marcan Confrontation (Mk 2.6-12)." *Interpretation* 40:29–38.

Levisohn, Stephen H.
1987 *Textual Connections in Acts.* Atlanta: Scholars Press.

Lode, Lars
1983 "Narrative Paragraphs in the Gospels and Acts." *BT* 34:322–35.

Malbon, Elizabeth Struthers
1983 "'No Need to have Anyone Write': A Structural Exegesis of 1 Thessalonians." *Semeia* 26:57–53.

Neeley, Linda Lloyd
1987 "A Discourse Analysis of Hebrews." *OPTAT* 1:1–146.

Nida, Eugene A., J. P. Louw, A. H. Snyman, and J. v W. Cronje
1983 *Style and Discourse. With Special Reference to the Text of the Greek New Testament.* New York: United Bible Societies.

Panier, Louis
1985 "Sémiotique du Discours Biblique et Questions Christologiques." *Laval Théologiques et Philosophique* 41:289–303.

Patte, Daniel
1983 "Method for a Structural Exegesis of Didactic Discourses: Analysis of 1 Thessalonians." *Semeia* 26:85–129.

Phillips, Gary A.
1983a "History and Text: The Reader in Context in Matthew's Parables Discourse." *SBLSP* 22:415–37.

1983b "'This is a Hard Saying, Who Can Be Listener to It?': Creating a Reader in John 6." *Semeia* 26:23–56.

Poythress, Vern S.
1984a "The Use of the Intersentence Conjunctions *de, oun, kai,* and Asyndeton in the Gospel of John." *Novum Testamentum* 26:312–40.

1984b "Testing for Johannine Authorship by Examining the Use of Conjunctions *de, kai, oun.*" *Westminster Theological Journal* 46:350–69.

Robbins, Vernon K.
1984 "A Rhetorical Typology for Classifying and Analyzing Pronouncement Stories." *SBLSP* 23:93–122.

Wallis, Ethel E.
1986 "Four Gospels, Four Discourse Genres." *Evangelical Journal* 1:78–91.

AUTHOR INDEX